The Career Atlas

By
Gail Kuenstler

D1608133

CAREER PRESS
3 Tice Road
P.O. Box 687
Franklin Lakes, NJ 07417
1-800-CAREER-1
201-848-0310 (NJ and outside U.S.)
FAX: 201-848-1727

MAI 350 8019

Copyright © 1996 by Gail Kuenstler

THE CAREER ATLAS
ISBN 1-56414-225-6, $12.99
Cover design by Foster & Foster
Cover photo by Digital Stock Corp.
Printed in the U.S.A. by Book-mart Press

To order this title by mail, please include price as noted above, $2.50 handling per order, and $1.00 for each book ordered. Send to: Career Press, Inc., 3 Tice Road, P.O. Box 687, Franklin Lakes, NJ 07417.

Or call toll-free 1-800-CAREER-1 (NJ and Canada: 201-848-0310) to order using VISA or MasterCard, or for further information on books from Career Press.

Library of Congress Cataloging-in-Publication Data

Kuenstler, Gail Baugher.
    The career atlas / by Gail Kuenstler.
      p.   cm.
    Includes index.
    ISBN 1-56414-225-6 (pbk.)
    1. Vocational guidance. 2. Vocational interests. I. Title.
HF5381.K754 1996
331.7'02--dc20   95-50920
                                                      CIP

This book is dedicated to all those hard-working American families who are struggling to pay for their children's education. May this book help them maximize their educational dollar and help the graduates, and their parents, find sustaining work.

First, I wish to thank The Danforth Foundation for sending me to graduate school. As a student I had the opportunity to work at City University of New York's Office of Academic Affairs, where I gained the bulk of my knowledge about degrees and the labor market. From this experience I wrote a book, *The Desk Guide to Training and Work Advisement*, published by Charles Thomas, in which I developed the various "paths" to occupations.

I also wish to thank all of my students, clients and participants in workshops who generously shared and helped to educate me. Thanks to all those who allowed me to interview them for this book. Without their help, this book would not have been possible. Thanks to Current Biography Yearbook and Vocational Biographies for the use of their materials. Thanks to Diana Lies-Delker, Director of the Rensselaer Polytechnic Institute Cooperative Education Program. Thanks to Carole Hyatt who was willing to advise a stranger on publishing trade practices. Judy Kelso encouraged me to write the proposal; without her interest, this book wouldn't have been written. Emily Kuenstler, my daughter, made several key suggestions and sat with me for many days helping me get organized. Simms Taback, my husband, read parts of the book and always supported and encouraged me. Datha Brack, Ph.D., gave me hours and hours of her time; her diligent friendship was a source of such joy and comfort to me as I labored to finish this project.

Contents

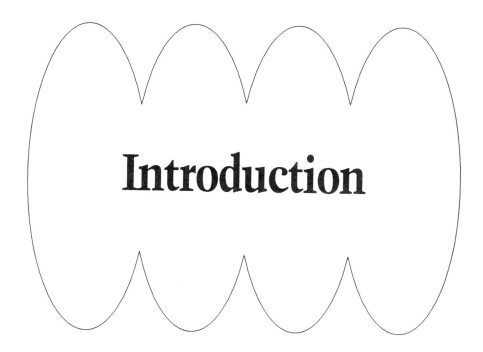

Introduction

This information has been compiled for you, the reader, so that you will not waste valuable time earning the wrong degree or use precious energy trying to get a job for which you don't have the proper credentials.

My work experience at the Office of Academic Affairs in a major university system showed me that not all degrees lead to employment. My work as a career counselor has shown me that work experience can often be substituted for degrees. Determination is the most powerful degree you can have. My clients have shown me over and over again that getting focused on a career goal leads to success.

Getting a marketable skill through short-term training after high school or emerging from college with work experience and valuable skills will protect you in the worst job market. Despite the fact that one third of college graduates take jobs that don't require college degrees, a degree will increase your earnings in the long run. My ideal goals for you are that you will: 1) have a skill to offer and know where to offer it, and 2) get paid for work that you would be willing to do for free. Self-understanding and hard work will make this possible.

In this book, occupations are placed in their context. For example, marketing can be considered in the context of its neighbors, advertising and sales. You need to consider all three to make an informed choice. You can enter a job through a variety of paths; these are described in the body of the book. Paths can be training programs, work experience or college degrees. After considering all paths, you may find you have the training or experience you need to enter a new field. Seeing connections will help you understand how preparing for one job may help you get a better job later on.

This book has been written to help you make the wisest possible career choice, whether it's your first time or your fifth. It is all about occupations—descriptions, methods of gaining experience, how to best prepare yourself educationally and how to get the job. Reading this book will help you calm your fears and see the possibilities; if you have formed some notions about particular fields, this is a chance to see if your ideas are accurate. In reading, you will realize what fields offer you the best chances for career success, what fields require your skills and interests, what fields are expanding and which academic programs will best prepare you for your field or fields of interest.

If you are a career-changer, now is the time to look at jobs you may have ruled out when you were younger. Consider everything that your self-assessment suggests, even if it surprises you. Instead of allowing prejudices to deter you from following your interests, try to understand where the prejudices stem from (i.e., the messages you get from your parents, your spouse and your children), and re-evaluate them in terms of the information you find here.

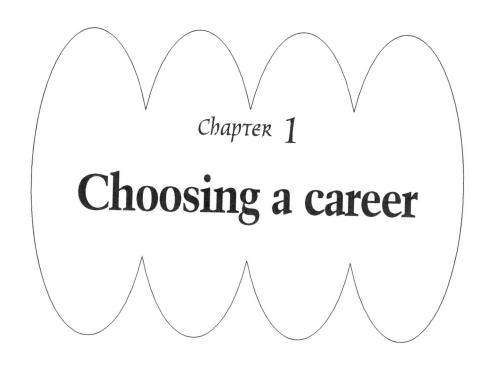

Chapter **1**

Choosing a career

Your career choice is a *process*—it will not occur overnight. Most people are not born knowing what occupations they want to pursue. Many continue to explore long after they have reached their 20s. Allowing time for sampling various jobs, sharing your thoughts with others and allowing time for researching information are all part of the process. Finding your occupational path can take 10 minutes or 10 years. There is no appropriate amount of time allotted to finding your ideal career. You have to be patient and allow yourself to do it at your own pace.

Most people go through three steps: self-assessment, exploration and training.

Step 1: Self-assessment

Step 1 is usually characterized by a fair amount of confusion, but at this stage, you have already admitted that there is a problem to be solved. Good! Congratulations for having the courage to entertain making a change and to get help with your planning.

If you are fairly certain about what fields you want to move your skills into, you may not need to read Chapter 4, at least for now. On the other hand, you may feel that you have no strong interests, no superior skills and no career ideas. If this is the case, you need to get reacquainted with yourself.

As you may have guessed, career choice is influenced by your values, temperament (your nature), your likes and dislikes, your interests, the life experiences you have had (including work experience), your class background and the expectations of others. In Chapter 4, you will have a chance to do a self-assessment that includes most of these factors and organizes them into a profile that will help you identify the right fields and jobs for you.

Confusion about a career is shared by many; in fact it is more the rule than the exception. Because you are confused doesn't mean that you will not have a successful work life. Take, for example, Thomas J. Watson, who created one of the most powerful corporations in the world, but originally wanted to become a teacher.

According to his biography by William Rogers, Watson decided to go into business but his father insisted first on a course in accounting. He graduated, got a bookkeeper's job and after a short time, decided bookkeeping was not the field for him either. Then he began to sell organs and pianos from a wagon. Several years later Watson started at what would become IBM. Notice the struggles this business genius had in finding out what he wanted. What's more, only the actual experience taught him anything; he didn't know what any of his jobs were going to be until he actually tried them out, which is what you'll learn in Step 2: Exploration.

Step 2: Exploration

At this stage you should have a basic idea which occupations interest you and which of your skills you want to use in your next job, but you need to shop around before making a decision. It may be necessary to live out one or more of your interests. For example, in high school Peter was told by a counselor that he was not college material, yet his high SAT scores changed the counselor's opinion. Peter wanted to be a professional musician, but as a compromise, he enrolled at the state university in music. He played with groups downtown in the evenings and soon found himself struggling in his classes.

After two years of academic failure, he dropped out of college. After leaving, he drove a truck, sold cameras, swept floors, worked at a photo lab, drove an ambulance as a volunteer, took training in operating a dialysis machine as well as some science courses at the local community college. At this point he realized that he did want to be a physician's assistant.

He applied to the certificate program at his community college—along with many other career-changers who had bachelor's, master's and Ph.D. degrees. Peter graduated with a two-year associate's degree and a certificate as a physician's assistant. Now Peter works at a first-rate hospital, making about $50,000 a year. He does some research, trains new residents and does all the computer programming for one of the hospital's departments.

Peter's Step 2 took a long time because he really needed to test out his interest in music before he was ready to choose training in medicine. A two- or three-year detour hardly compares to lifelong regret, so live out your interests. Finding exactly the right field for you may take a long time, but no time is really wasted if you are actively learning in an area about which you care.

According to a December 1992 article in *The New York Times*, Dr. Robert K. Jarvik, who designed the artificial heart for the first heart transplant patient, wanted to be a sculptor. He was a doctor's son and assisted his father in the operating room. Then he went to Syracuse University for architecture and mechanical drawing and graduated with a degree in zoology. With college grades not quite good enough for admission to American medical schools, he enrolled in the University of Bologna's School of Medicine in Italy. After two years he dropped out and received a master's degree in occupational biomechanics in 1971. Convinced that he was still interested in medicine, he earned his medical degree at the University of Utah College of Medicine in Salt Lake City in 1976. He finally landed exactly on target—sculpture and medicine.

In the Step 2 stage, courage is very important. You may be ambivalent, but people grow by standing up to their fears. Self-limiting ideas about what you can do can change, if you are willing to take risks to put yourself in a position where you can experience success. Self-esteem is built through accomplishment; your goal-setting should start with small steps.

All of the self-assessments included in Chapter 4 are designed to challenge your fixed ideas about your abilities; they will help you identify accomplishments and skills from both your life and work experiences.

In Step 2, you may want to do library research about occupations in which you are interested and get some insight into the occupations by talking to people in the occupations or industries that appeal to you. Exploring also includes interning, volunteering or working at the job.

According to *Particular Passions*, a book by Lynn Gilbert and Moore Gaylen, Louise Scott Brown, the architect, explained that she developed by being inspired by someone else's work and saying, "I want to study with that person." And that is what she did; she saw the work of an established architect and requested to study with him. He liked her work enough to take her on.

The founder of the Gray Panthers, a militant national organization for the elderly, Maggie Kuhn, started her social action career when a friend of her mother's who was on the board of the YWCA got her a volunteer committee appointment. She got involved in adult education for working women, then went to work for the social action division of a Protestant church. After retiring from a long and successful career, she began the Gray Panthers.

As mentioned earlier, researching, visiting workplaces, volunteering, interning and apprenticing ideally will lead to making a commitment to an occupation, but it will be every bit as useful if it shows you that the field is not for you before you invest in years of training.

It is difficult to decide on a career path because you can't foresee how you will manage the variety of tasks on even the simplest job. Getting a taste of several occupations is essential to making an informed decision.

Networking

Meeting successful people in the fields in which you are interested will be easier if you use contacts available through your family-friend network. Don't underestimate your contacts. If your aunt or your dry cleaner's wife has met someone in a field in which you are interested, pursue this contact. Make it clear that you are collecting information for planning purposes, not looking for a job. Does the contact know about any good training programs? What is needed for success in the field? Does he or she have the names of other people who might be willing to speak with you about the field? The ability to network in this way will be needed when it is time to look for work, so get all the practice you can.

When actually speaking with someone in a field in which you are interested, you must be ready to show the person what past experiences or skills you will bring to the field. (Your self-assessment will help you to organize this.) For example, in talking with an engineer, share information about summer jobs or engineering-related coursework. If you have any experience at all, let him or her know it.

When asking for help, you must believe that professionals want to talk about their work and want to encourage others to pursue careers in the field as well. In fact, most people love to help others when the relationship has no hidden agenda. As long as you make it clear that you are trying to learn firsthand about the occupation, you will get a good response. Always follow up with a thank-you letter, including any helpful bits of information that you might have for them or perhaps a clipping that might be of interest, to show you are interested in him or her.

Don't be afraid to show off your skills or interests to others. Step 2 may simply involve doing the things in which you are interested and then sharing or showing off the product. Julia Child, best known for her cooking show on television, says she started cooking elaborate meals to attract dinner guests. She went on to attend classes and write a cookbook on sauces.

According to Gilbert and Gaylen, Ellen Stewart, the director of LaMamma Theatre, was befriended by an Orchard Street store owner after she came to New York City to go to a fashion school. The merchant supplied her with fabric, from which she designed clothing. The shoppers at Saks Fifth Avenue, where she worked in alterations, saw these clothes and wanted to buy them. She was offered a job as one of the executive designers at Saks. After a successful career as a freelance designer, she moved into theatre design and production.

Step 2 should involve communication with those who know you best. Describe some of the ideas you are considering and how your career exploration is progressing. If those you love feel included in the process, they will be more supportive about your decision and more understanding of the time the process takes.

One very successful criminal lawyer left college in the first semester because he didn't know what he wanted to study. His parents reassured him that a decision would come in time. In the meantime, they asked him to earn his own expenses. He worked in the family business, then crossed the country with his friends. His parents never insulted him or doubted themselves for his indecision. They felt that their son could learn something positive from every experience. As a result, they never panicked and he never saw himself as a failure. Exploration—the gathering of experience and information—is necessary for planning. Don't feel like you are a quitter because you need to try out a variety of situations.

On the other hand, if you are one of the very lucky ones who is genuinely focused early, enjoy it. Clarity about wanting to be a naturalist or musician may appear in the very young. Try to consider this a gift and a blessing. A very strong interest in math or science or literature can only make your planning easier. Just because your peers have not made a career choice doesn't mean there is something wrong with you because you have one very obvious, very strong interest.

Getting help with the process

Certainly talking through your thoughts about jobs or careers with someone else—a career counselor at college, a friend who is a good listener, a relative or partner who will listen carefully—will help you clarify your thinking.

You can help organize this discussion by listing the advantages and disadvantages of each path you are considering. The hard part will be maintaining the objectivity to write down every possibility. In other words, people often hastily rule out careers. Don't be so quick to eliminate possibilities—slow down and consider everything in your interest area. There is no reason why you shouldn't be a doctor, starting at the age of 35. Or an architect, even if you have been out of high school for 10 years. Or a lawyer, even if you get average grades.

You don't have to rule out alternative or nontraditional employment. There is at least one career out there for your specific needs. John Holt, a contemporary educator, quotes the following article from *Sports Illustrated:* "One of the youngest and most successful design teams in contemporary ocean racing has Ron Holland as its equally unlikely chief. Holland failed the most elementary public exam for secondary schools in his native Auckland, New Zealand, repeatedly flunked math (considered by many to be a requisite in yacht design) and has no formal qualifications whatsoever in naval architecture. He even elected not to complete a boatbuilding apprenticeship." Yet today everybody wants a Holland design.

At 16, Holland dropped out of secondary school on the grounds that it was "too academic." He had been sailing since he was seven and his father bought him a seven-foot dinghy. Holland got into the boating industry as an apprentice, and quickly quit that job because it took time away from ocean racing. In 1973, after three years of intermittent design experience, Holland campaigned his own quarter-tonner, Eygthene, in the world championships at Weymouth, England. It was a radical design—based, Holland admits now, on intuition, not "plain arithmetic." Eygthene won.

In his book, *Teach Your Own*, Holt comments: "If you want someday to do something, go to where other people are doing it, find out as much as you can. When you've learned all they know, or will tell you, move on. Before long, even in the highly technical field of yacht design, you may find that you know as much as anyone, enough to do whatever you want to do." While Holt's career choice was yacht design, this is applicable to any field of interest.

Step 3: Training or job?

When you are ready to choose a path, you are taking Step 3, which may involve a training program, a program of higher education (college or graduate school) or actual job experience.

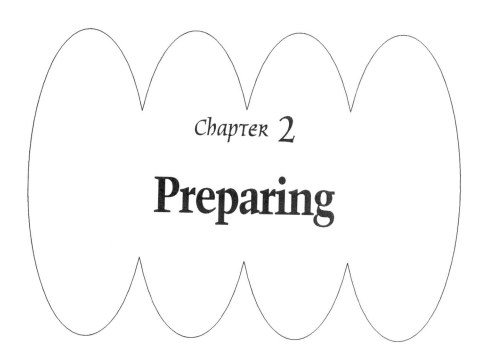

Chapter 2

Preparing

What's hot

According to a survey in the March 1995 issue of *Kiplinger's*, of the top 10 starting salaries, chemical engineers will start at the top, earning $40,000. Mechanical, electrical and industrial engineers follow, with beginning salaries averaging around $35,000. Computer science, nursing, civil engineering, geology, chemistry and accounting majors also are in the top 10. Individuals with undergraduate degrees in home economics, liberal arts, journalism and telecommunications generally have starting salaries below $22,000. However, this doesn't mean that all college graduates who don't go to graduate school start below $22,000. Many find very lucrative first jobs for themselves, as you will see in later chapters.

Of 50 corporations that will be hiring, most want technically trained people like engineers, computer scientists and accountants, or workers with advanced degrees, such as M.B.A.s (Masters of Business Administration) and doctorates. These startling statistics show why you need to choose the education necessary for your field of interest. You will be employable if you get the specific preparation required for success in your field. It is not possible to turn yourself into an engineer if your real interest lies in psychology, but if you focus and begin to prepare early for a career in psychology, you can be a very successful psychologist.

In a less competitive labor market, it was possible to wait until after college graduation to decide upon a career, but this cannot be done anymore; specializing is important in getting hired and the specialization must be in line with your interests and abilities. If you weren't focused during college, don't waste your time in regret or self-blame; instead, utilize the self-assessment in Chapter 4.

Planning ahead: high school coursework

This is a critical concern because to enter many colleges you will need specific math and science courses, and you will be competing with those who took advanced placement courses in subjects such as physics, precalculus, calculus, geometry, intermediate algebra and trigonometry. For example, see the requirements to apply to engineering programs in the section Solving Practical Problems beginning on page 99. All the information about the high school courses you need will be available in the college catalogues of the college programs you are considering. In addition to taking the Scholastic Aptitude Test (SAT) or American College Testing (ACT), you will want to take the Preliminary Scholastic Aptitude Test (PSAT) which is given to high school juniors; it is the qualifying test for the National Merit Scholarship and is good practice for the SAT.

Advice to parents

Support in the form of recognizing a child's unique interests and validating them is also important for success. For example, if a child expresses an interest in geology, arrange to visit a natural history museum—the display on geology will encourage him or her. Interests need to be recognized, deepened and expanded as children grow. Parents can help with this.

An article printed March 7, 1995 in *The New York Times*, states that parents who expect achievement from their children are a stronger predictor of school performance, earnings and job achievement than childhood IQ scores. If you are a parent unconcerned about academic achievement, your child's performance will be affected by this. If you want to be able to create an environment in which good grades are expected, you need to show your child that his or her education is important.

Parents need to make sure their child's high school offers the appropriate classes for his or her intended course of action. For example, if your child wants to apply to an engineering program, he or she probably needs to take high school courses like trigonometry, precalculus and calculus, physics and chemistry. College catalogues list specific course requirements; these catalogues can often be found in the public library. If the high school doesn't offer the necessary preparation, you need to make special arrangements with the district to provide the education your child needs to get into his or her desired program.

Parents should consider paying for a private secondary school. It makes sense to spend money on a good preparatory school experience. The skills that can be developed in small classes with experienced and caring teachers can enable your child to go to a better college and perhaps even get merit-based financial aid. Well-trained students will succeed in college. Children who experience difficulty in high school may lose interest in college, because the work level assumes students have good basic skills. If students don't have these, they won't be able to do actual college-level work and they won't be accepted into good programs.

Matching interests with college programs

You can be a smart shopper for your college education or post-high school training if you are willing to do a little research. First, you need to understand yourself; you will get help with self-assessment in Chapter 4. Then, after reading about occupations of interest to you, you can use MacMillan's *Degrees Offered* and MacMillan's *Occupational Programs,* two books that will help you connect your interests with the right schools. Connecting your interests with colleges will certainly provide you with appropriate choices.

For example, MacMillan's *Degrees Offered* lists all the engineering programs and all the chemistry degrees awarded at all levels in the country, including technical institutes, for example, Georgia Institute of Technology, California Institute of Technology and Carnegie Mellon University.

If you want to earn a graduate degree in the sciences, you might want to choose a large research university for your undergraduate training rather than a small college, no matter how elite, because larger universities offer more research experience opportunities. All of these will be listed in MacMillan's by subject. Getting these names, ordering the course catalogues and studying the course descriptions and the fine print will help you gain a better understanding of the field and make it easier to write the applications.

For a short-term training program, consult both volumes. For example, if you are a career-changer and you want culinary training, check both *Occupational Programs* and *Degrees Offered*. In the first volume, *Occupational Programs*, you will find private vocational schools; in the other volume, *Degrees Offered*, you will find community college programs that offer culinary training toward an associate's degree.

Liberal arts colleges

There are many areas of interest which will require a liberal arts bachelor's degree (a major in History, English or Biology, for example) and then specialized graduate training: law, social work or teaching, to name a few. MacMillan's will be less useful here (there are so many liberal arts colleges), but if you anticipate post-graduate study, see if the graduate school you are aiming for has some suggestions regarding your undergraduate coursework.

Ask the liberal arts college to show you information about the graduates of that school to see if they are successful; if this information does not appear at the end of the catalogue, you can request it. Some states, such as New York, require that this information be available to you, and good schools will proudly show you this information. Finally you will narrow down your search on the basis of school specialty, region, cost and size, among other personal preferences.

Remedy your deficiencies

If you have not completed the necessary prerequisite courses for admission to the school of your choice, go to your local community college, take the courses, then apply. Don't let a lack of courses hold you back. Many have completed this kind of preparation before you and then attended schools they otherwise would have had to rule out, so it is well worth the effort. For example, one nurse went back to college 10 years later for the courses that she needed to apply to medical school. A high school student took 12 credits of math and science at the local community college to apply to engineering school.

Using college to enhance employability

Today college graduates aren't finding jobs as easily as they did in the past because of the poor labor market and the increased need for technically trained workers. About a third don't find jobs that require a college degree, according to an article by Kristina Shelley in *Occupational Outlook Quarterly*, published by the Department of Labor. The solution to this is not to avoid college, but to use college well. One way to do this is to arrange an internship in your strongest area of interest. Internships will give you the skills and experience you need to make yourself more employable, and they look impressive on a resume. Most colleges have a career services office where alumni are contacted to provide internships for students. For example, a six-month, two-day-a-week stint at a publishing house or a full-time work experience at a museum between semesters will help you find out if you are really interested in the field. The internship could also offer networking opportunities to meet people who will later help in job hunting. Various internships are listed with the appropriate fields in the body of this book.

Participation in extracurricular activities in school is a way to sharpen your leadership and team-playing skills. Holding an officer position in your sorority or fraternity, for example, demonstrates that you can take responsibility for projects and motivate others. These people skills are critical for success in every field.

Make mentors of the faculty. Faculty can help you find a job, suggest places to look for work or just give you the support you need to guide you in the right direction.

Use the services of the career development office. This office has contacts with recruiters and can offer interest testing, counseling about career choice, and material on careers and contacts in the industries in which there are alumni working. The sole purpose of the career development counselor's job is to help you prepare for employment. Make an appointment early in your college years for interest inventories and counseling, so you can get the most out of the services offered.

Undergraduate degrees in marketing, social work and mass communications, to name a few, may not be the best option. In some cases, these majors have been created to attract enrollment and may not be good bets for employment because you are specializing too soon in fields that require you to specialize later. You will see that both undergraduate and graduate degrees in these areas are listed in MacMillan's; the graduate degrees are established, while the undergraduate degrees are relatively new.

The community college

The local community college offers two-year degrees in the liberal arts and sciences, called Associate of Arts and Associate in Science (A.A. and A.S.), as well as in many vocational areas. For the vocational programs, the degree will be the Associate in Applied Arts or Associate in Applied Science (A.A.A. or A.A.S.). These latter degrees contain many vocational courses that cannot be applied to an A.A. or A.S. or a B.A. or B.S. If you want to get a four-year degree at a later time and have completed these degrees, you will have to start over. (Community college catalogues are obligated by law to include this information. They must be read with extreme care.)

On the other hand, if you get an A.A. or an A.S. from a community college you can transfer these credits to a four-year school (if the four-year school has approved the course descriptions and your grades meet their requirements). If not, you may have to take some required courses for entrance. All this is explained in the catalogue of the four-year school. In other words, the community college can be used to get started if you think ahead.

It is important to know to what exactly you have been accepted. For example, are you in a degree program or a certificate program? A prenursing sequence or the nursing program itself? A program for the A.A.S. or the A.S.? Are you a degree candidate (matriculated) or a nonmatriculated student taking courses for credit which may or may not be applied to the degree? Are you a student taking courses for no credit in an adult or continuing education program?

Get all agreements in writing about course waivers, and as to which courses count for what. In other words, if a faculty member tells you a course will satisfy requirements, get it in writing, because you may later be informed otherwise. Noncredit remedial courses are obstacles for a surprising number of students applying to the less selective colleges. However, you will be asked to take basic skills or skills assessment tests, which could excuse you from these courses if you earn a high grade. If you transfer from one college to another, make sure the scores on these tests are forwarded to your new institution.

Using the private vocational school

Dental lab technology is an example of a field in which training may only be available at a private vocational school. Schools such as these are listed in the yellow pages. Care must be used in choosing the school. In your state there may be a law that the school must provide a printed statement showing how many started training, how many graduated and how many secured employment related to the training. When making a decision as important as this, you should be able to have all of your questions answered. Can you cancel the contract you sign with them? When? How long is it for? What is the refund policy? Is the program less expensive at the local community college?

Must you go to college?

For some people who have particular aptitudes, the answer is no. For example, John is a senior video editor at a cable network. He learned this field starting in the mailroom, using a relative's contacts after dropping out of a college film production program in the first year. He thought that college was not a wise investment of his time. He was willing and able to get started in the working world and learn everything he needed to know on the job.

On the other hand, Regina earned a bachelor's degree in liberal arts. She then worked for five years as a waitress after college, during which time she saved $50,000 to go to a good culinary institute where she is currently studying.

On-the-job training

You may decide to take a position because it offers on-the-job training. Health clubs, garden centers, nursing homes, restaurants and small businesses of all sorts are places where you can learn on the job and get some work experience for your resume. In fact, any entry-level job in a small to mid-sized business (15 to 50 employees) will allow a young person to learn a number of diverse jobs and move up. This may be preferable to attending a community college for several years without a focus.

Regional differences and career choice

Work in publishing, the entertainment industry, the arts, medical research—the list goes on and on—usually takes place in large urban areas. Beginners especially will have to be in these areas to get the training and experience they need. On the other hand, many occupations are only available in suburban or rural areas, such as farming, which requires large areas for harvesting, raising livestock, etc. Keep this in mind when narrowing down your career choices.

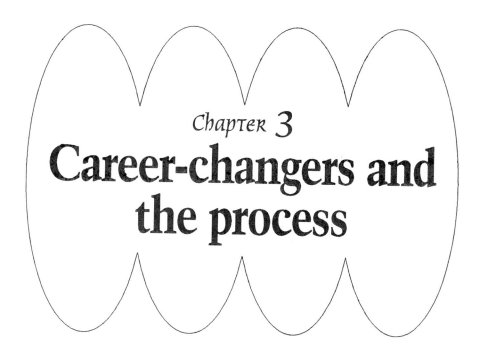

Chapter 3

Career-changers and the process

Career indecision

According to Richard Bolles's *What Color Is Your Parachute?*, the average adult tries out five jobs before making a longer-term commitment to one field; this is normal growing and should not be cause for alarm. Go ahead and sample occupations that interest you. If you want to be an artist, live it out. If you want to be an engineer, get a summer job working with engineers.

Most career-changers enter new occupations using old skills and experience. Most go through three steps of self-assessment in which they focus on what they enjoy doing, exploration in which they consider several possible occupations and pursuing either a job or training program.

Career change can be accomplished in one of several ways:

> **Entering a new field.** This often means retraining.
> **Transferring skills.** This may allow you to start in a new field in a position higher than entry-level.
> **Transferring hobby skills.**

One of the most disturbing parts of being a career-changer is the feeling that you are starting over and returning to the insecurities of the new graduate, as you contemplate entering a brand new field.

A knowledge of your options will help you plan a career move. Because career change will be a reality for most readers, we need to understand the appropriate action to take in making a change. Layoffs have created a huge pool of career-changers, many of whom had long periods of stable employment, and are relatively inexperienced at self-assessment and job hunting. Most Americans know very little about other people's occupations. This book unscrambles the mazes and points out alternative ways to enter your new field of choice.

The big leap

Valuing career satisfaction enough to take a risk is important for career-changers. Some adults who want to change careers have strong nonwork interests that they can use toward landing a job, after some training. For example, Jane works as a computer programmer, but her real interest has always been nature and animals. She decided to pursue a master's degree in biology. This degree will allow her to work as a naturalist, to teach, to work in a zoo or to work as a biological researcher.

Running for office or opening a small business are often-considered options, but career-changers can move, into any occupation they choose, and should examine all occupations in their areas of interest. As a career-changer, you may choose to go to work without training—as a driver, corrections guard, customer service representative, gardener or nursing aide. One IBMer-turned-window-washer enjoys the change and makes several hundred dollars a day.

Transferring skills

Other career-changers take skills they are using on one job and transfer them to a new job. Helena was a meeting and travel planner for a brokerage house. She quit her job, got an M.B.A., and interned through her school program at Colgate-Palmolive, managing the design, production, promotion and sales of a new suncare product. After finishing her internship, she did some travel consulting for American Express and, when an opening came up, she was hired as manager of sales planning and financial analysis. Recently she made a lateral move to corporate marketing.

Sara worked as a buyer of television time for 10 years, negotiating deals in top markets. She combined her skills in sales, promotion and negotiation, plus her interest in entertainment to make a career change into entertainment marketing. Many career-changers make lateral moves such as this.

Using hobby-related skills

Other career-changers take hobby-related skills and use them to gain employment. Bill, who was laid off from his banking job, had worked out for years and found the gym to be a very congenial environment. He combined both his hobby-related skills and his bookkeeping skills from banking when he was hired to do weight training and bookkeeping for the local gym.

Starting over

Career-changers should take advantage of free training in the form of an informal apprenticeship or on-the-job training in an entry-level job.

Other career-changers essentially start over in a new field, using their old skills to get in. Bob was a psychotherapist for 12 years. He had a master's degree in education, but closed his private practice because he found it too isolating. Out of work for nine months, he took a job interviewing home health care aides in order to learn about the health care field. Now he is working at a local HMO; his job involves answering members' questions and he hopes to move into member education.

Getting the facts

Step Two for the career-changer may involve collecting a number of options and then, by talking to people in the fields, assessing the labor market in the industry as well as the cost of retraining.

Career-changers should look at their options *before* they leave their current jobs. Kristin was a proposal writer for an educational agency. She wanted to make a change, but after exploring, found her possibilities were limited because she had never finished her four-year degree. Kristin decided she wanted to become an educational psychologist, so she chose to stay in her job and the money she earned eventually went toward getting a B.A. and a Ph.D.

Lilly was about to hand over her country inn to her husband in a divorce proceeding and she needed a new occupation. After learning through career counseling about the options for a 45-year-old innkeeper with a foreign degree in demographics and some cooking skills, she realized she had few choices. As a result, she told her husband that she was keeping the business she had built. Looking at options before she gave up the inn allowed Lilly to rethink her course of action.

Although many people change careers after exploring their options, many find that exploring options can be confirming. Sometimes people imagine that there is some obscure career out there they haven't thought of. By reviewing occupations and all their interests, they often come to realize that it's not an accident they are working in the field in which they find themselves.

Often career-changers go back to a path not taken. For example, Charles was a technical writer and manager of other technical writers. When circumstances in the industry made him fearful of layoffs, he decided to sit for the bar exam, a path he had turned his back on after graduation from law school 30 years ago.

Sometimes adults are surprised by the amount of hard work involved in changing careers. Long-term planning is often essential. Taking the prerequisites necessary to enter a graduate program, for example, can take many months before the application goes in. Becoming computer-literate or making a lateral move at your present job in preparation for the job you eventually want will also require many months of preparation. Remember, knowledge is power; getting the facts will help make your career dream come true.

Often career-changers need a skill that will make them immediately useful to employers. For example, the public relations specialist who wants to move from banking into cable television may have to do something he or she never had to do in the old job, such as get out correspondence or compose press releases on the computer. He or she may require training and an in-depth knowledge of the problems facing the cable industry, which can be gained from research, including networking and informational interviewing.

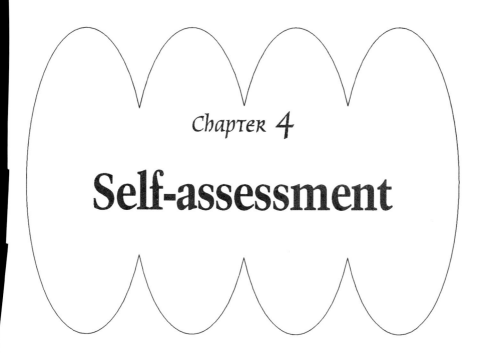

Chapter 4

Self-assessment

Your self-assessment, once finished, will be custom-made just for you. It appears at the end of this chapter. It is easy and fun, but best of all, you will learn things about yourself that will help you in your career search.

Exercise #1: Skill inventory

The following interest inventory from Barbara Scher's book, *Wishcraft,* is a challenging and useful exercise in self-reflection. List those activities that you do well, feel good about and enjoy. You should be able to say all three things about each activity—but don't be too exacting. Include hobbies, household tasks, activities from school and your childhood. Be sure to list verbs (writing, building) and be as specific as possible. Keep adding until you have written down 10 different activities.

Examples: writing papers for philosophy class, selling raffle tickets, counseling friends.

1. _____
2. _____
3. _____
4. _____
5. _____
6. _____
7. _____
8. _____
9. _____
10. _____

Are there any interesting patterns? Do some of the verbs repeat themselves? Do some of the activities seem related? Could any of the activities be work-related?

Now, go back to the list and link these traits to the occupations described in this book. For example, writing papers for philosophy class could be connected to several of the occupations in the Arts and Communications section, especially writing and education. Selling raffle tickets could be connected to occupations in the Selling and Managing section. Counseling friends could be connected to many of the following jobs in The Sciences section, under mental health/ fitness. Enter your answers on your profile at the end of the chapter.

Exercise #2: Interest inventory

Within each of the following groups, circle the activities that interest you most. You are likely to find that you have circled more activities in some groups that in others. Then choose one or two of the groups containing the activities you would enjoy most. For example, you might choose Group B and Group D. After you have selected a first and second choice, refer to the profile to see which two groups you have chosen. These two groups should be entered in the appropriate places on your profile.

Group A

Do a lab experiment.
Learn calculus and statistics.
Design a research plan to study the effects of vitamins.
Take readings at an observatory.
Measure the vital signs of a patient and record them.
Counsel a grieving widow.

Group B

Design and build a bridge.
Modify the design of a plane to increase its speed.
Build a computer.
Fix a toaster.
Cook a gourmet meal.
Plan and grow a garden.

Group C

Talk lawmakers into passing a law.
Plan a sales campaign and sell the product to retailers.
Be a diplomat in Europe.
Draft new accounting policies for your firm.
Study business trends in software.
Manage a business.

Group D

Edit a biography.
Write a magazine article.
Design a dress.
Act in a play.
Teach first grade.
Direct a movie.

Exercise #3: Identifying your skills

A skill is something you do well. You may have put some of these on the first interest inventory. Complete the section below by selecting five favorite skills—perhaps you have used them in the past for jobs or hobbies. Describe how, where, with what or whom you use or have used this skill. (It may help you to have a copy of

your resume beside you.) Here are a few verbs: designing, directing, programming, developing, etc. For example: I am good at writing descriptive articles for regional history magazines.

Transfer these to your profile and add the occupations suggested to your list. For example, writing articles suggests that you should look at the journalism and writing paths within the Arts and Communications section.

1. _____
2. _____
3. _____
4. _____
5. _____

Exercise #4: Your temperament

These exercises can introduce you to the importance of your personality and its impact on career happiness. In the book *Please Understand Me*, David Keirsey and Marilyn Bates explain that there are four dimensions of type:

Dimension #1: Extrovert (E) - Introvert (I)
Those who get energy from others versus those who get energy from within.

Dimension #2: Sensing (S) - Intuition (N)
Those with an interest in concrete facts versus those who trust inspiration, imagination and new ideas.

Dimension #3: Thinking (T) - Feeling (F)
Those who make decisions on the basis of logic versus those who make decisions on the basis of feelings and values.

Dimension #4: Judging (J) - Perceiving (P)
Those who need closure and structure versus those who keep their options open and sometimes delay.

Your temperament: choice #1

From the above four dimensions, you could make 16 possible combinations. Circle one choice from each set above. For example, ESFP (Extrovert, Sensing, Feeling and Perceiving) is one type. Write your own personal code here: _____.

Your temperament: choice #2

Choose only one of the following:

SP: Sensing Perceivers. They love freedom and the process, not the product. They are clever, facile, impulsive. They live in the moment and love action.

SJ: Sensing Judgers. They are product-oriented, thorough, loyal, responsible, tradition-minded. They are caretakers, maintainers and managers.

NT: Intuitive Thinkers. They love to learn. They are system builders and planners, striving for knowledge, competence and power.

NF: Intuitive Feelers. They seek meaning and have a very personal orientation. They want to help others, express their own uniqueness and be acknowledged for feelings and ideas.

Write your choice here: _____

Now, choose from the descriptions below, which are the same types as above but stated differently. This exercise may help clarify your type.

Your temperament: choice #3

Choose only one of the following:

#1: Not interested in day-to-day operations, loves long-term planning, emphasizes competence, can be critical. (NT)

#2: Idealistic and emotional, often impractical, focuses on future and possibilities, communicates in leaps, tries very hard to be helpful. (NF)

#3: Hates unplanned surprises, critical of the sloppiness of others, respectful of procedure, resists new ways, eager to make deadlines. (SJ)

#4: Trouble tolerating boredom, hates long-term planning, impulsive, has a play ethic and a wait-and-see attitude. (SP)

Write your choice here, using the letters at the end of each line (for example, SP):_____

Move your type onto the profile sheet, combining the results of your three attempts to make a four-letter type, such as ISTJ. If your three choices are all different, you may want to refer to *Please Understand Me* for more thorough testing, or you can take the Meyers-Briggs Type Indicator test with a psychologist.

All types are found in all industries and occupations. Paul and Barbara Tieger's book, *Do What You Are,* offers examples of this. Understanding your temperament will not tell you which occupation you should choose, but it will help you better understand your preferences.

Values

It is important for you to become conscious of what you value most. In the following exercise, put a number 1 by the value you feel is most important to you and rank order the rest:

____change and variety   ____helping others
____creativity   ____independence
____affluence   ____stability/security
____managerial authority   ____prestige/recognition
____adventure   ____working with others
____working alone

Move your top five values to your profile.

Ideal day

Another idea in *Wishcraft* is to describe your perfect work day. Talk about this day in the present tense and in detail from waking up until going to bed. Tell who is there at each stage, where you are, what you are doing. For this fantasy exercise, be the person you dream yourself to be. Assume you know everything and can do everything that you aspire to, right now.

_____
_____
_____
_____
_____
_____

Move the results of this exercise (any ideas you got about interests or jobs) to the profile.

Your profile
Exercise #1

Your top three verbs   Three related occupations

_____   _____
_____   _____
_____   _____

Exercise #2

A=The Sciences   C=Selling and Managing
B=Solving Practical Problems   D=Arts and Communications

Your first and second choices:

1. _____
2. _____

Jobs or fields related to your choices above (for example, if you chose Selling and Managing, review the fields and jobs in this division and then write down the ones that appeal to you):

_____
_____
_____
_____
_____
_____
_____

Exercise #3

Skills and related fields and jobs (write your **skills, then use** the index to find some related fields or jobs):

_____
_____
_____
_____
_____
_____

Exercise #4

Your temperament type (four-letter code): _____

The meaning for me in terms of strengths and weaknesses at work:

_____
_____
_____

and in terms of my choice of occupation:

_____
_____
_____

Values

1. _____
2. _____
3. _____
4. _____
5. _____

Ideal day

Any occupations identified? List below:

_____
_____
_____

Based on all of the above, I want to check carefully the following fields and jobs in this book:

_____
_____
_____
_____
_____
_____

After careful consideration, I would like to actively explore the following paths:

_____
_____
_____
_____

Date: _____

You have completed your profile.

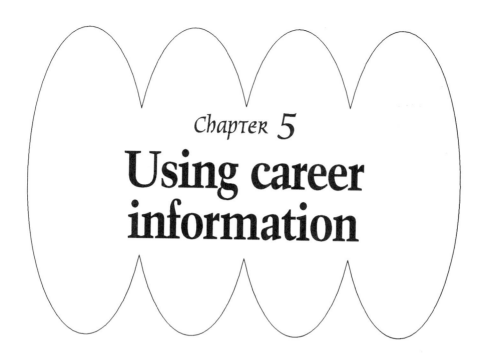

Chapter 5

Using career information

You need to compare occupations before ruling out one or another. Then you will be ready to look closely at specific occupations and how to prepare for them.

You will notice that for each job, there are several paths to obtain the necessary education and experience. It is important to understand how preparing for one job may help you get a better job later. For example, being a nurse's aide can give you an indication of whether or not you would enjoy being a nurse.

Why this arrangement of jobs and fields?

The occupations are arranged based on John Holland's lifelong research on the key attributes necessary for particular occupations. For example, to be a successful social worker, you need to have a high score on Holland's scale of social interests. To be a successful anthropologist, you need have a high score on the scale of investigative interests, even though anthropologists are "social scientists." Lawyers need to score high on the entrepreneurial scale, as do politicians. The jobs in this book are arranged in four major categories, based loosely on John Holland's grouping. The four categories are: The Sciences, Solving Practical Problems, Selling and Managing and Arts and Communications. Mathematics is split between math-based occupations in the Selling and Managing section, and math-based occupations in The Sciences section.

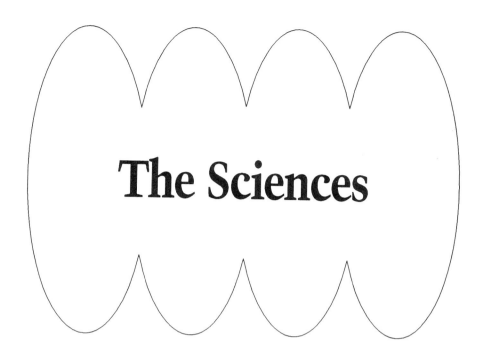

The Sciences

This section includes jobs for nurses, doctors, technicians in the health care field, physical scientists, mathematicians, animal scientists, biological research and environmental scientists and social scientists. The health care fields are included in this section because you must have an understanding of science to succeed in health care. This section includes the mathematically based physical sciences, the numbers fields and the social sciences. Many of these fields—for example, environmental science and the physical sciences—are very closely related to engineering so you should read that section, as well, if engineering is one of your interests.

Women in the sciences

There are lots of cultural signals that tell girls to stay away from science. According to a January 24, 1993 article in *The New York Times*, 35 to 40 percent of the graduating classes from graduate life science and medical programs are women, but only 19 percent of principal investigators for National Institute of Health (NIH) grants are women. In largely male classes, women are sometimes ignored by male professors and are not taken seriously, causing them to lose motivation. Many women with doctorates are in nontenure track positions in universities and medical schools.

If you are a woman interested in the life sciences, do realize that many more opportunities are opening up for women today; there is no telling where you could go or what you could contribute. Women may find they flourish in the sciences in women's colleges that expect women to be high achievers.

The following categories are included in The Sciences:

Biological and Environmental Sciences
Health Care
Mental Health/Fitness
Physical Sciences
Social Sciences
Mathematics

Biological and Environmental Science jobs

Biologist
Forest and Wildlife jobs
Animal Health Care

Some of the specialists in biology include botanists, who study plants; embryologists, who study the development of the individual organism; microbiologists, who study microscopic organisms; zoologists who study wild animals (see animal science for the study of domestic animals); physiologists, who study the internal processes of organisms; ecologists who study organisms in their environment; geneticists, who study how genes are inherited; anatomists and morphologists, who study the form and structure of organisms; pathologists who study plant and animal diseases; cytologists, who study cells; and pharmacologists and toxicologists, who study the effects of drugs and poisons. Horticulturalists and agronomists are discussed in the section, Solving Practical Problems.

Job: Biologist

Path #1: Laboratory technician

Private industry employs many biological technicians. The technician must be a high school graduate with good grades in biology, and some experience in handling laboratory animals, perhaps as a breeder of mice or as a worker in an animal shelter. Taking a technician's job will allow the college biology major to gain laboratory experience and understand the profit-making side of biological research.

For help locating the industries in your area that are hiring technicians, consult the *College Placement Annual* in your library. Be on the lookout also for firms seeking to hire biologists; these companies will also need technicians. Genetic research, drug and environmental companies are all in need of biological laboratory technicians. Some of these companies will even offer college tuition assistance.

Path #2: Internship

Because research requires many hands, college students have a variety of internships open to them. For example, get an internship in tropical research, oceanographic sorting or radiation biology.

Write to the Office of Fellowships and Grants, Smithsonian Institution, L'Infant Plaza, Suite 7300, Washington, DC 20560, 202-287-3271 for information about their science internships in fields such as ecology, animal behavior, tropical environmental science, earth sciences, evolutionary and systematic biology.

The Smithsonian also sponsors programs that offer college chemistry and biology students a chance to do environmental research for a semester or summer at a research center on the Rhode River Estuary near Annapolis, Md.

Students are needed in upland plant ecology, use of successional vegetation by birds, habitat utilization by migratory warblers, forest canopy studies, nutrient transport modeling, estuarine fish biology, benthic invertebrates, global change and vegetation and studies in ecological parasitology. Students are paid a weekly stipend and may earn college credit. Write to: Work/Learn Program, Smithsonian Environmental Research Center, P.O. Box 28, Edgewater, MD 21037, 301-261-4084.

The National Audubon Society's Expedition Institute offers accredited courses in the form of summer, semester or year-long trips across the country, focusing on environmental education. The Society also sponsors a naturalist training program for college students. For information about both programs, write to: National Audubon Society, 700 Broadway, New York, NY 10003, 212-979-3000.

The Environmental Careers Organization, 286 Congress St., Boston, MA 02210, 617-426-4375, offers paid internships to qualified students interested in environmental programs. In general, the students they accept have finished their junior year and have engineering, chemistry, biology or environmental science majors. This organization also places people in paid, short-term professional positions.

Community Jobs: The Employment Newspaper for the Non-Profit Sector, published by Access, 50 Beacon Street, Boston, MA 02108, 617-720-5627, lists many jobs in environmental advocacy organizations. Three issues cost $29.

Brookhaven National Laboratory offers summer research trainee appointments to undergraduates in the life sciences (chemistry, biology) interested in a career in teaching and research and who will pursue the doctorate. Write to Dr. Donald Metz, Office of Educational Programs, Brookhaven National Laboratory, Upton, NY 11973, 516-282-3054.

Most oceanographic institutions where marine biologists might intern are affiliated with academic institutions; students may have to register for courses at a particular academic institution. For example, for information about a 12-week Sea Semester, write to Sea Education Association, P.O. Box 6, Woods Hole, MA 02543, 617-540-3954. College credit can be arranged for this semester on an ocean-going schooner combined with shore work.

The Hudson Valley Raptor Center offers three-month internships in raptor rehabilitation and environmental education. Interns receive training in the care, handling and treatment of injured birds of prey, and handle hawks and owls in educational presentations. Write to Dona Tracy, Executive Director, Hudson Valley Raptor Center, RR 1 Box 437B, South Rd., Stanfordville, NY 12581 or call 914-758-6957.

Earthwatch, 680 Mt. Auburn St., Watertown, MA 02172, 800-776-0188, offers many two-week expeditions in which students pay their own costs and help scientists with their research. The locations are exotic and a wide range of archaeologists, paleontologists, primatologists, animal behaviorists, ornithologists and ecologists are represented.

Cindy Zipf, listed in *Vocational Biographies*, has a bachelor's degree in marine policies (a governmental policies specialty) from the University of Rhode Island. While in school, she held an internship with the National Maritime Fisheries Service. After graduation she landed an internship with the American Littoral Society in Highlands, N.J., where she organized a coalition of New Jersey groups against ocean dumping. Now this coalition, Clean Ocean Action, of which Cindy is the executive director, lobbies with state politicians and fights major chemical companies and polluters. This example shows the value that you can get from the internships available to college students.

Path #3: Bachelor's degree in environmental science

Degrees in environmental science are new creations and generally will not give you the depth of technical training you need. They are designed to appeal to young people who want to work for the environment. An undergraduate degree in environmental science may not hinder you from being an activist, but most activists, recyclers, regulators and conservationists are either engineers, lawyers or Ph.D.s in biology. If you are getting an advanced degree, an engineering, biology or law degree would be most useful, or you could look at the physical sciences for information about hydrology, chemistry and geology.

One of the major protectors of the global environment, Peter Raven (*Current Biography Yearbook*, 1994), is director of the Missouri Botanical Garden, the world's leading center of research on tropical rain forests. He made botanical discoveries at 14: a manzanita plant which was thought to be extinct, and a plant of the evening primrose family called *Clarkia franciscana* which had not been collected for 50 years. He received his Ph.D. from UCLA at Berkeley and got a post-doc at The British Museum. He then moved on to Stanford as a professor and continued his work with the evening primrose family, studying chemical defenses as part of the larger topic of coevolution (how a whole ecology evolves together). Raven has recruited 40 scientists to collect and catalog the world's remaining tropical plants (100,000 specimens a year) as quickly as possible to understand what we have before we lose it.

Path #4: Bachelor's degree in biology

The biology major in college will take chemistry, organic chemistry, mathematics, statistical methods, physics, developmental biology, ecology, genetics, evolutionary biology, physiology and computer applications.

The student with the bachelor's degree can work in a research laboratory as an assistant to a scientist with the doctorate. New college graduates can also start their careers in technical sales (sales that require scientific knowledge to effectively sell the product) or testing and inspecting in factories. The company for which you work may help you earn your Ph.D. through a tuition reimbursement program.

John, who has an undergraduate degree in biology, tests food for bacteria and spoilage. His title is quality control microbiologist and chemist. If there is a problem, he is responsible for stopping production in the factory.

Cynthia Moss, listed in the 1993 edition of *Current Biography Yearbook*, has been studying elephants for 25 years. After college, she traveled to Africa's wilderness areas. When she got there, she felt that she had found her home. She took a job as a research assistant. When the research ended, another zoologist suggested that Moss work with the elephants of Amboseli National Park. She and another researcher began to identify the 500 elephants. Her data about mating behavior will help in the conservation of elephants. In recent years, Moss has worked as an activist to protect the elephant, lobbying for a ban on the trade of ivory.

Lynn Rogers (*Current Biography Yearbook*, 1994), a more conventionally trained wildlife biologist, has spent the last 25 years studying the black bear. Lacking the funds to attend a university, he went to the local community college for biology. He then spent seven years as a letter carrier and wildlife photographer, during which time he raised the money to attend Michigan State University as a full-time student of wildlife biology.

One summer he got a job as a student aide with the Michigan Department of Natural Resources working with "nuisance" black bears—bears that go through garbage in dumps and linger around campsites. After graduation, Rogers followed the suggestion of another bear researcher, and went to Minnesota to gather more data about wild bears.

He started graduate work in ecology at the University of Minnesota and received an M.S. in 1970, midway through a four-year stint as a research assistant at the university's museum of natural history. Then he directed the university's wildlife research institute while earning his doctorate on social relationships, movements and population dynamics of black bears. Wildlife organizations supported his research before he went to the U.S. Forest Service in 1976, where he worked until his retirement in 1993.

Rogers has published three books about bears in addition to many articles and photographs. He was the first to draw blood from hibernating bears. He developed bear-proof containers for campsites and field-tested a bear repellent. He consulted on a major bear exhibit that will form the basis for an international bear center to be founded in 1998.

For more information about careers in biology, write to The American Institute of Biological Sciences, 730 11th St. NW, Washington, DC 20001, 202-628-1500. The institute can supply you with the names of specialized professional organizations within the field of biology. The organization for your special interest area will typically publish a journal and hold an annual conference.

Path #5: Ph.D. in biology

Getting a Ph.D. in biology will allow you to work in academia, government and corporate situations, as Walter Gilbert's career illustrates. Gilbert (*Current Biography Yearbook*, 1992) is a molecular biologist who showed an interest in science from his earliest years. His key discoveries have led to an improved understanding of the role of DNA, and he also has contributed to biotechnology by developing a method to "sequence" or define chemically long stretches of genetic material, for which he was awarded the Nobel Prize in 1980. Gilbert gave up his role as CEO at Biogen, a genetic engineering company, and now works at Harvard University. He said working for the company "distracted him from his deeper interests in science which are ultimately not the same as the company's." There is great tension between marketing commercial applications and pure research in biological research.

Francis Collins (*Current Biography Yearbook*, 1994), director of the National Center for Human Genome Research, is a medical geneticist. The National Center for Human Genome Research is a $3 billion, 15-year project to find the location of 100,000 human genes and to describe chemically all of the DNA found in the human genome. With collaborators, Collins has found genes that cause cystic fibrosis, neurofibromatosis (sometimes erroneously called Elephant Man's disease) and Huntington's chorea. Collins took a liking to chemistry in high school and studied it in college. He started a doctoral program in physical chemistry at Yale. Then after learning more about human genetics and consulting with Gilbert, who had left physics to become a molecular biologist, Collins was encouraged to leave physical chemistry.

Collins's doubts and concerns pointed him toward medicine. He completed medical school, and after finishing his residency, he joined the faculty of a medical school and rose quickly to full professor, and at the same time became a full investigator with the Howard Hughes Medical Institute, the largest biomedical philanthropy in the United States.

Sylvia Earle (*Current Biography Yearbook*, 1995), the daughter of an electrician and a nature-lover, was raised on a farm in New Jersey. At 17, she enrolled in a summer scuba diving course and went on to establish Deep Ocean Engineering, which manufactures submarines to be rented by the day for exploration. Sylvia has been a marine botanist for all of her career. She took an active role in studying the effects of the Exxon Valdez spill and was chief scientist of the National Oceanic and Atmospheric Administration. She left in protest when the Bush administration caused massive destruction of the Persian Gulf during the war on Iraq.

Zoologist Victor Scheffer (*Current Biography Yearbook*, 1994) got his start in college when he took a course in entomology. He entered the graduate program in zoology at the University of Washington, got a job as a research assistant in oceanography, and saw what he refers to as the "clean beauty of ocean wilderness." For his doctoral dissertation he studied the 107 species of plankton in Lake Washington, and his work served as a measure of purity when Seattle tried to clean up the lake.

For five summers Scheffer served as a ranger-naturalist at Mount Rainier National Park. He kept taking the civil service exams and finally was hired by the U.S. Biological Survey, now known as the Fish and Wildlife Service. He studied the various fur-bearing animals of Washington State and later joined the Aleutian Islands Expedition with Olaus Murie, who was one of the first to describe, in his own words, "mankind's unending need for wilderness." Scheffer describes this expedition in detail in *Adventures of a Zoologist*. Scheffer's work with whales, especially the publication of his book entitled *The Year of the Whale*, contributed to the passage of the Marine Mammal Protection Act in 1973.

For a copy of the booklet *Training and Careers in Marine Science*, send $5 to International Oceanographic Foundation, 4600 Rickenbacker Causeway, Miami, FL 33149or call the Foundation at 305-361-4888.

The 10 institutions that offer doctoral degrees in blue-water oceanography and carry out the majority of funded research in this field are: Columbia University (Lamont-Doherty Geological Observatory), Oregon State University, Scripps Institution of Oceanography, Texas A&M University, University of Hawaii, University of Miami (Rosentiel School), University of Rhode Island, University of Texas at Austin, University of Washington and Woods Hole Oceanographic Institution.

See the magazine *Science and Bioscience* for job leads and attend annual meetings of your specialty as a college student to get to know the major figures in biological research and where they are in universities.

According to a 1991 survey conducted by The Institute for Scientific Information, these are the top 25 science research universities:

Rockefeller University
California Institute of
  Technology
Massachusetts Institute of
  Technology
Stanford University
Princeton University
University of California at
  Berkeley
Harvard University
University of California at
  San Francisco
University of California at
  San Diego
University of Oregon
Yale University

University of California at
  Santa Cruz
Washington University
University of Colorado
University of Chicago
Brandeis University
University of Washington
Vanderbilt University
Columbia University
New York University
Johns Hopkins University
Duke University
University of California at
  Los Angeles
University of Massachusetts
Cornell University

These are the universities most often cited by scientists in published papers; this is just one way to measure quality of education, but perhaps it will suggest a few schools you hadn't considered. The job growth, according to *Jobs,* a book by Kathy and Ross Petras, will be in biotechnology and environmental positions.

Job: Forest and Wildlife jobs

Path #1: National park volunteers

The Student Conservation Association places volunteers to act as researchers and educators in national parks. For example, at the Moosehorn National Wildlife Refuge, you could greet and orient visitors, write news releases, provide tours, assist in banding animals, etc. You need a valid driver's license and an interest in communicating with the public. At the Denali National Park and Preserve, a six-million-acre wilderness park containing Mount McKinley, you could work in the visitor center, backcountry registration and information, collection of bear incident and observation data, backcountry statistics, backpacker campground programs and special projects and surveys, including patrols. These positions require basic first aid skills, maturity and the ability to work with minimal supervision. You should be a self-starter in good physical condition, with a knowledge of wilderness survival and minimum impact camping skills, and have good writing ability, computer literacy and a knowledge of German, French or Japanese. The positions, for three males or females, are available from May to September. You can arrange for college credit.

The agencies sponsoring such volunteer positions as backcountry patrol, interpretation, research or range management, or visitor assistance are the National Park Service, U.S. Forest Service, Bureau of Land Management, U.S. Fish and Wildlife Service, National Biological Survey and the U.S. Army and U.S. Navy Natural Resources Program. Some positions begin in the fall, but most are during the summer. For summer positions, selection begins March 1; for fall, June 1. There is no final deadline. You must be 18 and a high school graduate. There is no upper age limit. Free housing is provided plus a small stipend for basic expenses, a travel grant and a uniform grant. The catalog of volunteer positions is available from Student Conservation Association, Inc., P.O. Box 550, Charleston, NH 03603-0550, 603-543-1700.

Path #2: Seasonal work as a ranger

Full-time park ranger jobs at the National Park Service, the agency administering the nation's parks, are fiercely competitive and require a bachelor's degree. But the Park Service uses seasonal workers and the Bureau of Land Management, Bureau of Reclamation, Corps of Engineers, Forest Service and Fish and Wildlife Service also employ some seasonal workers.

Local offices of the state agencies typically handle ranger positions. In New York state, for example, fish and wildlife are handled by the Department of Environmental Conservation. This department has a number of regional offices. For minorities and women especially, the federal government's paid cooperative education program is another way to enter while getting the undergraduate degree, as are internships.

Path #3: Environmental science associate's degree

You can take the civil service exam in New York with a two-year degree in forestry or environmental science. If the degree is in environmental science, you need 15 credits in forestry-related topics like botany, dendrology, forest mensuration and nursery management. You must be over 18 to apply but there is no upper age limit. Pat worked for two years as a forest ranger for New York state. She spent the majority of her time checking trails and orienting hikers.

You can work as an environmental technician taking water samples or air quality samples for an environmental engineer or as a technician working for the Department of Health. Cathy started as an environmental health technician working for her local health department. Now she has advanced to sanitary inspector, visiting the homes of children who test high on the lead test that the health department administers. If she finds peeling paint, she contacts the landlord and works alongside the owner to remedy the situation. She has a bachelor's degree in health sciences but, in many regions of the country, she could have gotten the same job with a two-year degree in environmental science. She could move to food inspection, water inspection, indoor air and toxic control—all areas covered by the Department of Health. Community colleges have produced many environmental technicians over the last few years; whether there will be a market for this training depends on governmental regulations. Before signing up for a program, consult several environmental engineering firms in your region to determine the need for technicians or talk to graduates of the program you intend to enter.

The regional office of your state's Department of Environmental Conservation may hire wildlife technicians. The two-year community college program can supply you with ideas for local employment, but you should be sure there are jobs available in the wildlife area for technicians with two-year degrees before you make a commitment. If you want to continue in biology at a four-year school, be sure there is a transfer agreement or get advance approval for your courses from the four-year school.

You can be a ranger with a private conservation organization. Josh Crabtree is a High Peak Summit Steward in the Adirondack Park, meeting hikers at the top of Mt. Marcy and Algonquin Peak to explain the fragility of rare alpine vegetation found on the summits. This program is run by the state, the Adirondack Mountain Club and the Nature Conservancy.

Path #4: Nature and recreation guide

In many areas of the country, tourism is a major source of revenue. Helen organizes scenic cruises on the Hudson River between New York City and Troy, N.Y. More and more people make a living organizing things such as white water rafting in Costa Rica or mule trips through the Grand Canyon. Special skills, like wilderness medicine, will help you get a job with tour companies.

Path #5: Park manager

Employment in natural resource and park management will require a bachelor's degree in parks and recreation management, forestry, biology, ecology, geology or a related discipline. The National Recreation and Park Association, Resource Development Division, 2775 South Quincy St., Suite 300, Arlington, VA 22206-2204, 703-820-4940, will send you materials on recreation administration, therapeutic recreation, tourism management, natural resources and parks management.

The Pennsylvania Bureau of State Parks operates environmental education centers; those who educate usually have some experience in teaching and biology. School groups come to the center to learn about the natural world. Programs for the community, in-service workshops for teachers and training sessions are also offered throughout the year. Working in a center like this may be the ideal job for the environmentalist who wants to influence youth.

Path #6: Forester

Many foresters work for the U.S. Forest Service but many others have their own consulting firms, managing timberland for clients. They improve the timber stands and appraise forest land and timber. They may also do environmental impact studies concerning wildlife and soil type or help clients with estate and tax planning. Jobs in the forestry industry require logging, or supervising logging, inventory and administration.

Penny (*Vocational Biographies*) works for the U.S. Forest Service, primarily managing timber sales. She helps decide which trees will be sold, plans logging roads and supervises the crews that mark and sell the trees. Penny's boss, the district ranger, made sure she learned to monitor water quality, road management, recreation work, special permits, mining and firefighting, since she often works alone in the woods. Relocating as a requirement for promotion is standard practice in her field. Penny has a bachelor's degree in forestry management and was hired as a forester trainee because her school offered cooperative education with the U.S. Forest Service. This is frequently the way to get a job, so check if your desired undergraduate program has this relationship with the U.S. Forest Service. Contact U.S. Forest Service, U.S. Dept. of Agriculture, 14th St. and Independence Ave. SW, Washington, DC 20013.

Job: Animal Health Care

Path #1: Work as an assistant

Veterinarians' assistants, workers in humane centers and helpers in kennels, stables and pet stores all gain hands-on experience working with animals. Taking a job like one of these will help you decide how you want to earn a living and you will learn some valuable skills. For example, dog groomers often learn their trade as apprentices in kennels and vets hire beginners at low wages and train them. Animal lovers will not enjoy employment in laboratories that use animals for research, despite the fact that your job may include caring for animals.

Path #2: Getting training in raising farm animals

The county in which you live has agricultural extension services of some sort. You can find these listings in the white pages or blue (government) pages in the telephone book. Your county may offer a livestock program, which encourages the breeding of certain animals through giving young people animals, for example goats or sheep, and then helping to raise them. They may connect you with the association in the area devoted to the raising of a particular breed or they may know of farmers who are seeking summer workers.

Path #3: Volunteer work in animal conservation

Jobs with the National Park Service or National Forest Service require advanced degrees and are keenly competitive; even summer jobs are hard to get. *The Encyclopedia of Associations* lists wildlife biology groups in your region. Many of these outfits are not-for-profit and use volunteers as well. See Biological and Environmental Sciences above for several paths working with wildlife. Zoos also use volunteers, but you must demonstrate a long-standing interest; the market for working with zoo animals is very competitive.

Path #4: Training in animal welfare

The American Society for the Prevention of Cruelty to Animals (ASPCA) in your region may hold training courses sponsored by a community animal welfare agency for volunteering in such an agency, or for students of animal science. Animal welfare, by nature, deals with cases of animal abuse or neglect, so animal lovers may want to find a job in a less stressful field. Call for information about activities in the local area.

Path #5: Your own business

Boarding kennels care for dogs and cats while their owners are away. Your first step is to check with the town clerk to see if your property is zoned for kennel operation. Kennels can be constructed from garages, sheds or barns. To expand your business, grooming and training services can be added to the boarding service. Often professional handlers who are paid to show dogs by their owners at dog shows, and dog breeders, have boarding kennels to finance their other activities.

See the yellow pages or contact The American Boarding Kennels Association to get information about operating a kennel in your region. For information, write to: Executive Director, American Boarding Kennels Association, 4575 Galley Rd., Suite 400A, Colorado Springs, CO 80915, 719-591-1113. An informative book, *Building, Buying and Operating a Boarding Kennel*, is available through the association.

Path #6: Raise and sell animals

There are associations for the raising of almost every kind of animal including goats, mink, chinchilla, poultry, tropical fish and donkeys, as well as every breed of dog, horse and cow. See *The Encyclopedia of Associations* in your library. Write to the association to get a name in your local area and then visit to get help with your project.

Path #7: Veterinary science technician

Vets, labs and zoos hire animal health technicians to assist them in their practice. At the minimum, they are graduates of 18-month programs accredited by the American Veterinary Medical Association or registered by the state Education Department, although after graduation you are eligible to sit for the exam and get a state license. Technicians collect specimens, perform lab procedures, expose x-rays, administer medications, maintain anesthesia and are permitted to do the vet's work without the physical presence of the vet. For a list of these programs, contact the state or your local agricultural college. The agricultural college at Delhi (State University of New York College of Technology), for example, offers a two-year program in which students receive an associate's degree in applied science.

The courses for the A.A.S. will not be transferable into another program because they are too specific, so if you have any thoughts about becoming a veterinarian, you may want to pursue the A.S. program, which takes three years. You can choose a clinical option or a lab animal option in the second year of the technician program.

Doris is an animal health technician. She always loved animals and finds her job very satisfying. She didn't want too much more school after high school graduation, but she was able to complete a two-year program. She works alongside a veterinarian, assisting in the surgery, giving medications prescribed by the vet and doing laboratory work. Another technician was hired by a medical lab to care for monkeys used in research; she found that this job paid more than working with a vet.

Path #8: Veterinary school

Animal science is one specialization you may choose when you get an undergraduate degree in agriculture. This is the kind of training that farmers get to help them manage their livestock in the most advanced way.

Another path is to get an undergraduate degree in biology, chemistry or animal science, then go to veterinary school. These schools are almost as competitive as medical school but vets earn on the average about one quarter of what doctors earn ($41,000 a year). Foreign schools may be easier to get into and the degrees can be used in the United States. Many vets are employed by the beef industry, milk producers or horse racing farms. Caring for pets seems currently to be quite a competitive branch of the veterinary business.

Write to: American Veterinary Medical Association, 1931 North Meacham, Suite 100, Schaumburg, IL 60173.

Health Care jobs

Nurse	Dental Hygienist
Optician	Dental Laboratory Technologist
Medical Records	Pharmacist
Health Care Administrator	Emergency Medical Worker
Medical Technologist	Physician's Assistant
(includes 17 specialties)	Physician

This section includes traditional jobs as well as some of the newer wellness specialties like yoga. Mental health occupations and physical fitness jobs are also included; the mind-body connection and its importance in maintaining and restoring good health is increasingly recognized.

Job: Nurse

Path #1: Volunteer hospital experience

Hospitals are always in need of volunteers and use them to do work formerly done by nurse's aides. Their duties include feeding patients, transporting them for tests, taking specimens to the medical laboratory and making beds. Volunteers get the opportunity to view the operations of the whole hospital. Contact the head of volunteers at the hospital that interests you.

Barry is a retired tax attorney who made an appointment with the director of volunteers. He wanted to do something for the community but he also learned in the interview that his interest in medicine is very limited and specific. He rejected work in the emergency room, afraid he would get ill at the sight of all that blood, but he was interested in being a receptionist. He was oriented with a group of volunteers so that he would know about hospital safety and procedures, and now answers the telephone and helps visitors find patients.

Path #2: Free training as a home health aide

Agencies that provide home health aides to families often offer training and certification. See the employment section of the newspaper for local agencies and their training programs. You will need a driver's license and a car, fifth-grade mathematics and reading, and a lot of compassion. This may be a good option for you if you are comfortable with caring for others in their own homes or if your English is limited. You will be asked to cook, clean and perhaps do grocery shopping, as well as care for the patient, including bathing and supervising the taking of medicine.

Path #3: Nurse's aide

A nurse's aide or orderly job in a hospital or nursing home doesn't pay very well (the median according to the *Occupational Outlook Handbook* is $13,800 to start), but the union, if the hospital is unionized, may offer you training for advancement in a career ladder program.

A nursing home may hire inexperienced workers and then offer them 75 hours of training. After four months of experience and passing a competency evaluation, the aide is registered with a state registry. Hospitals often look for aides with experience in a nursing home or as home health aides.

Ida is a nurse's aide in a nursing home. She finds the work to be deeply satisfying; as a religious person she believes that the ideal job is one in which you have the privilege of serving those in need. Ida enjoyed the training the nursing home offered and is considering going to community college and studying nursing after her children go to college.

Path #4: Training as a Licensed Practical Nurse

According to the *Occupational Outlook Handbook*, L.P.N.s earn about $21,000 a year. The training program takes a year and is often offered through a public adult education program. It might be a better idea to take courses toward your R.N. at the community college because, unlike the L.P.N., additional training can be added to the two-year nursing degree.

Path #5: Nursing school

The two-year associate's degree program is a good bet for the student who needs to begin work as soon as possible. Joan tried college when she was young but decided it was unnecessary. Then she got married, had two children and took her associate's degree in nursing after her children started school. Now, her children are in college and she has gone back to school to get her bachelor's degree in nursing. She has worked as a nurse in her present job for 10 years (working two 12-hour days per week); her long-term goal is to be involved in research projects as a nurse or to do health education for Planned Parenthood.

Nursing is changing and new kinds of nurses will be needed, which means there will be jobs available. Despite the downsizing of acute care hospital capacity, the number of ambulatory (out of hospital) services, primary care clinics and home health care, nursing jobs will be expanding. In 1994, according to an article by Peter Kilborn in *The New York Times,* nursing graduates of four-year programs started at $32,858.

Courses in microbiology, pharmacology, anatomy and physiology, and nursing practice itself will be included in your course of study. Students with the two-year degree are eligible to sit for the Registered Nurse (R.N.) examination. They start at a slightly lower salary than nurses with four-year degrees, but both take exactly the same exam and their credential, R.N., is the same regardless of the length of the training. The R.N. credential also opens up other doors.

If you have the two-year degree, you can return to school after working for a while by entering an R.N. Pathway program, a bachelor's degree program for Registered Nurses. These programs are for the employed nurse who wants to get the B.S.

Because nursing schools are expensive to operate, some schools give an examination to their nursing applicants for entrance into a prenursing program; the program is obligated to find the student a seat in the nursing program itself if the student meets the grade requirements in prenursing.

Write to the State Board of Nursing in your state for a list of approved schools. The National League for Nursing, Career

Information Department, 350 Hudson St., New York, NY 10014, 212-989-9393, will send you information about nursing careers.

Path #6: Nurse practitioner

The bachelor's degree in nursing will allow you to get a better job initially and go on for your master's degree. Many nursing jobs these days require you to operate independently. Nurses who get the master's degree can work as nurse practitioners, taking responsibility for many doctors' tasks, especially in rural areas and clinic settings. A nurse practitioner operates under the supervision of a doctor, but writes prescriptions, performs exams and makes referrals without the doctor being present.

With the master's degree, the nurse practitioner can also operate as a clinical specialist, administrator, researcher or teacher of nursing. In the state of Maine, nurse practitioners can medicate psychiatric patients without the doctor's supervision, and this may be the direction in which medicine is going: increasing the responsibility of primary caregivers without the M.D. Psychiatric nurse-practitioners, in some states, can medicate and have a private practice.

For assistance in paying for training, contact the National Health Service Corps Scholarship Program, 1010 Wayne Ave., Suite 240, Silver Spring, MD, 20910, 800-638-0824.

Path #7: Nurse-midwife

A nurse can become a midwife by entering a master's degree program in midwifery or completing a certificate program of the American College of Nurse-Midwives. You could apply for a scholarship through the National Health Service Corps Scholarship Program. (See address under "Nurse practitioner.")

In most states, nurse-midwives can prescribe medicines. They also offer contraceptive counseling, gynecological screening and treatment as well as preconception and maternity care.

In 1982, Maureen Rayson was the first certified nurse-midwife to obtain admitting privileges at Beth Israel Hospital, where she also established the first independent practice with hospital privileges. She was the acting director of the midwifery service, which she established as an independent service, and she became the first nurse-midwife to obtain third party reimbursement by insurance companies in New York. Her eight percent cesarean section rate is very low compared to rates for physician-assisted births.

Midwifery is a growing profession; the number of births these primary care providers attend has grown steadily. With the current effort to cut costs, the need for certified nurse-midwives (CNMs) should continue to grow. They work in hospitals, HMOs, private practices, birth centers and clinics. Insurance companies prefer midwives, as they are less expensive than doctors.

For more information, write to the American College of Nurse-Midwives, 818 Connecticut Ave. NW, Suite 900, Washington, DC 20006, 202-728-9860.

Path #8: Nurse-entrepreneur

Many nurses set up their own health services. For example, some nurses operate home health care agencies. They train the service providers, work with the families needing the service and evaluate the care given. This kind of entrepreneurial role for the nurse is new.

Path #9: Rehabilitation nurse

A rehabilitation nurse works for an insurance company to manage the rehabilitation of the patient and act as liaison between the injured employee, the doctor, the employer and medical care providers. This is another new kind of nursing.

Path #10: Organ transplant coordinator

Donna (*Vocational Biographies*) is one of about 400 organ transplant coordinators in the United States. She finds people waiting for the organs and coordinates the organ preservation and transportation from the operating room of one hospital to the operating room of the hospital where a patient will receive the organ. She counsels all of the families involved, especially the donor family, and works with organ recipients after transplantation.

Liver and heart transplants are being done much more frequently now than in the past. Donna does public education about organ donation and shares in the joy of those who have received organs. She took a special course offered to nurses by the Professional Association of Transplant Coordinators. Some other health practitioner-coordinators in hospitals might be weight management program coordinators, wellness center directors, AIDS researchers, and day-care center coordinators for Alzheimer's patients.

Path #11: Nurse anesthetist

To do this you need to be an R.N. with a bachelor's degree and have a year of experience in acute care. You need to participate in the CRNA (certified registered nurse anesthetist) program for two to three years, part-time, and pass a certification exam. Many programs also award the master's degree. According to the American Association of Nurse Anesthetists, starting salary is $50,000 and average annual salary is $80,900.

Send for CRNA program information, including a list of schools through the American Association of Nurse Anesthetists, 222 South Prospect Ave., Park Ridge, IL 60068-4001, 708-692-7050.

Job: Optician

Path #1: Optician's assistant

Major retail eyeglass chains offer training programs for new employees. You will learn to measure customers for glasses, write up work orders and make the glasses.

Path #2: Licensed optician

Many states require dispensing opticians to be licensed. After several years of on-the-job training as an apprentice, you could take the exams for a license and operate your own optical store. Paid training is not recommended, because you will not earn enough as an employee to compensate for it, and you can train on the job to open your own shop if you can pass the exams.

Those who specialize in optical mechanics or benchwork (making the glasses) are called ophthalmic laboratory technicians. High school graduates with good mathematics and science grades are hired to train if they have the ability to do precision work. Apprenticeships supervised by the state are sometimes available and, by federal law, must be posted at the state's Job Services offices. For information about requirements, write to the agency in your state responsible for occupational licensing. See the information on doctors below if you are interested in the fields of ophthalmology (treatment of eye diseases) or optometry (prescribing corrective lenses).

Mary (*Vocational Biographies*) is an optician's assistant. She does office work, customer service and does benchwork. She learned everything on the job. Mary makes a modest wage but likes the work and is not interested in taking the exams for licensure as an optician. Her boss's income is limited because he cannot write prescriptions; instead fills prescriptions written by an optometrist.

Job: Medical Records

Path #1: On-the-job training

This field is essentially data entry and coding. You need to learn some medical vocabulary so you can read the charts, code them and input the information. The field has grown tremendously, but it may be currently shrinking because all health care agencies are cutting costs.

Don't invest money in training until you have tried to get a clerical job in medical records for data entry, or perhaps you can study on your own through the programs of the American Health Information Management Association. Write to them at 919 N. Michigan Ave., Suite 1400, Chicago, IL 60611-1683, 312-787-2672, ext. 402.

Path #2: Medical records administrator

You can get a four-year degree in medical records administration or a one-year certificate if you have any undergraduate degree. According to the American Medical Association, the average starting salary is $19,000.

Job: Health Care Administrator

To get upper-level jobs in hospitals, health care administrators need training in strategic planning (usually offered in business school) and a knowledge of state government health care legislation, as well as experience in hospital administration.

Gloria worked for a department of health as a director of licensing and inspector of hospitals and nursing homes, while getting her master's degree in health facility management and taking courses in business administration.

Marketing is a large part of health care administration. The administrator deals with doctors, cuts in Medicaid and increasing costs and lawsuits. Many administrative positions are currently being cut to save hospitals money, so you may not want to invest your time and money in the specialized education of a B.S. in health care administration. You may be better off getting a less specific undergraduate degree, then getting experience and a master's degree.

Gary Hoffman, who works for an HMO, had a health sciences (biology, chemistry, etc.) undergraduate degree and a good sales and marketing record with another HMO before getting his current job. While he was at the first HMO, he earned a business degree at night. He says the growth areas in health care administration are in HMO management and health education. For sales positions, he likes to interview those with insurance experience or those with education and experience in business. He doesn't want someone with an M.B.A. because it focuses too much on finance, but wants someone who knows how to negotiate and finalize a deal.

There are many enterprises that need administrators. Hospitals, however, are currently going through a very stressful period. Downsizing and merging result in the layoff of middle managers.

Medical Technology specialties

The health care field is currently turbulent and the various technicians in the health field will be the first group to be affected when hospitals and medical services have to cut back. For example, if the states limit Medicaid expenses, fewer medical tests will be given. Managed care is growing rapidly and it seems safe to assume that managed care also means less work for technologists. Before making an investment in training, talk to technicians and technologists in your region. See how they feel about the future of medical technology specialties.

The American Medical Association's *Allied Health Education Directory* lists the AMA-accredited academic programs for medical technology jobs in your state. Check your local library or, to order, contact the AMA at 505 N. State St., Chicago, IL 60610, 312-464-5000. For most of these occupations, you must graduate from an accredited school in order to take the state licensing exams. Check your state's licensing requirements. You can request written material on each area it regulates.

The following are medical support jobs for which the AMA accredits school programs. Depending on the state in which you live, you may be able to work without going to an AMA-accredited program, or there may be other accrediting bodies in particular fields.

Job #1: Anesthesiologist's assistant

This is a two-year program for bachelor's degree graduates or respiratory therapists or nurses. It consists of the same work and has the same salary level as nurse anesthetists, $60,000 to $70,000. There are two accredited programs in the country: Emory University School of Medicine in Atlanta, Georgia, and Case-Western Reserve University in Cleveland, Ohio. See also nurse anesthetist.

Job #2: Cardiovascular technologist

This worker does invasive and noninvasive diagnostic examinations. There are four accredited programs in the country: Grossmont College, El Cajon, Calif.; SUNY Health Science Center at Stony Brook, N.Y.; Sentara Norfolk General Hospital, Va.; and Spokane Community College, Wash. A high school diploma or experience are required to enter a program which may be from one to four years. Average starting salary is $28,490.

Job #3: Cytotechnologist

This technologist works with pathologists studying cells. You need basic college biology and chemistry plus one year of specialized training. There are many accredited programs. Starting salary on the average is $34,057. Contact the American Society of Clinical Pathologists (ASCP) Board of Registry, P.O. Box 12277, Chicago, IL 60612 or call 312-738-1336.

Job #4: Diagnostic medical sonographer

Training involves one- or two-year programs after high school. There are many accredited programs. Average starting salary is $27,706.

Job #5: Electroneurodiagnostic technologist

EEG techniques. Programs require one year after high school. A few programs in the country are accredited by the AMA. Average starting salary is $22,926.

Job #6: Histologic technician/technologist

One-year program for technicians or four-year program for technologists. This technologist processes body tissues in the lab. Average starting salary is $21,641. Hospitals may offer a certificate program or you can earn an associate's degree at a community college. Graduates of the four-year program are called histotechnologists and can do more complex techniques or supervise others. Write to the American Society of Clinical Pathologists (ASCP) Board of Registry. (See address under "Cytotechnologist.")

Job #7: Medical laboratory technician: five options

1. In some cities, you can graduate from high school and take the city Department of Health's technician exam after six months of work at an approved training laboratory.

2. Some medical labs hire responsible people with high school diplomas and train them. However, if the lab is not approved, they will not be able to take the exams.

3. After five years of employment in a lab, you can get certified by the ASCP Board of Registry or the National Certification Agency for Medical Lab Personnel.

4. Hospital labs may offer a certificate for technicians.

5. Often medical laboratory technicians have a certificate (after on-the-job training and examination) and the associate's degree.

Talk to medical technicians in your area to get input on which of these options seems the most promising. According to the AMA, the average starting salary is $20,059.

Drug manufacturing companies hire new employees with good grades in high school biology and math. Jim (*Vocational Biographies*) worked as a lab technician for several years before getting his current job at a drug company which manufactures antibiotics. Now he produces bacteria to make an antibiotic for chicken and cattle. If he had a degree in microbiology, he could get a supervisory position in production. Jim says his chief benefit is the chance to work four 12-hour shifts a week. Two agencies certify medical lab workers: ASCP Board of Registry, and National Certification Agency for Medical Lab Personnel, 7910 Woodmont Ave., Suite 1301, Bethesda, MD 20814, 301-654-1622.

Job #8: Medical technologist

You will need basic college-level science courses plus one year of specific training; often students earn a bachelor's degree along the way. Medical technologists are usually employed in hospital laboratories and supervise medical laboratory technicians. The average starting salary is $25,815. Write to ASCP Board of Registry for more information.

Job #9: Nuclear medicine technologist

You will need basic college science courses plus one year of specific training in nuclear medicine. Average starting salary is $28,696.

Job #10: Ophthalmic medical technician/technologist

You assist ophthalmologists after completing a one-year program. There are a few accredited programs.

Job #11: Perfusionist

In this new specialty you operate circulation equipment during surgery. You will need college basic sciences plus two years of special training. There are a number of accredited programs.

Job #12: Specialist, blood bank technology

Available to the medical technologist with one additional year of training or to someone with the bachelor's degree plus one year of special training. Entry-level salary averages $31,713. Phlebotomist training is much shorter and available to the high school graduate. It may be available through your local public adult education program.

Job #13: Radiation therapist/technologist

Programs are one to four years in length after high school. Starting salary averages $30,705 and there are many accredited programs.

Job #14: Radiographer

Requires two to four years of training. Radiographers use imaging equipment. Starting salary averages $22,532. There are many accredited programs.

Job #15: Respiratory therapist/technician

A respiratory therapist participates in a two-year training program and a technician has one year of training. There are many accredited programs. Starting salary averages $24,934.

Job #17: Surgical technologist

This position requires a high school diploma plus nine to 24 months of special training. There are many accredited programs. Average entry-level salary is $17,945.

This concludes the list of medical technology specialties listed in the *Allied Health Education Directory*.

Job: Dental Hygienist

A survey by the American Dental Association revealed that the mean weekly salaries of full-time dental hygienists range from $654 to $707. Part-time hygienists make more per hour, (approximately $22), but receive no benefits. Often dentists prefer to hire part-timers because of this. Training for dental hygiene can be completed in two years after high school; you earn an associate's degree, then take a national examination and a state clinical examination before getting your Registered Dental Hygienist (RDH) and state license. Besides basic science, you take courses such as dental anatomy, oral embryology and histology and oral pathology. Write or call the American Dental Hygienists' Association, 444 N. Michigan Ave., Chicago, IL 60611, 312-440-8900.

Job: Dental Laboratory Technologist

Dental laboratory technicians work mostly with experts in ceramics and orthodontics and are often hired on their ability to sculpt a tooth from clay. A beginner who sculpts well can often learn better on the job than at a school. Entry-level wages are low, but an apprentice can learn all the areas of dental technology well enough to go into business for himself or herself, doing work for several dentists. A commercial dental laboratory is a good place to start looking for a job.

Job: Pharmacist

Pharmacists have five-year bachelor's degrees from schools of pharmacy. Working for a chain store as a pharmacist is not as rewarding as having your own pharmacy; however, independently owned and managed pharmacies are less and less able to compete with the chains. Many pharmacists sell drugs for a drug company and become the preferred salespersons. For more information, contact the agency in your state that regulates pharmacies.

For information about training programs in your region, write to the American Association of Colleges of Pharmacy, 1426 Prince St., Alexandria, VA 22314, 703-739-2330.

Job: Emergency Medical Worker

Emergency medical technicians (EMTs) are required to complete 300 hours of training before they sit for the examination. They must have a driver's license and be 18 years of age. Your local rescue squad may offer training. EMTs work either as dispatchers, on ambulance corps in cities or as volunteers on squads in the suburbs or in rural areas. Your local Emergency Medical Services should be able to provide information about training. If not, contact the Director of EMS for your state to find training.

Job: Physician's Assistant

Physicians' assistants work in hospitals, clinics and doctors' offices. The physician's assistant treats patients under the supervision of a doctor, much like the nurse practitioner. Average starting salary is $35,000 to $40,000, but earnings can exceed $100,000. To take the certification examination, you must graduate from an AMA-accredited P.A. program have four years of experience as a P.A. or be a nurse practitioner. Laws regarding the conditions of practice for the P.A. vary from state to state. In rural areas, P.A.s operate as doctors, under the supervision of a doctor. Your state will give you the requirements for practice and the list of what you will be allowed to do as well as what insurance companies will allow. Target a few programs of interest and write to them for their catalog. They will require college science but you may be able to do the science beforehand and then apply.

Most physician's-assistant programs require two years of college science for students seeking admission and two years of training. Some programs award a two- or four-year degree or a master's degree and a certificate (for those who have already earned a degree).

For AMA-accredited schools, write to the Committee on Allied Health Education and Accreditation (CAHEA) of the AMA, 515 North State St., Chicago, IL 60610, 312-464-5000, or see the directory in the library.

The Association of Physician Assistant Programs and the American Academy of Physician Assistants (two different organizations under one roof), 950 N. Washington St., Arlington, VA 22314, 703-836-2272, publish a $25 directory of programs. You may be able to locate it in the library or use MacMillan's *Blue Books, Degrees Offered.*

For funding, contact the National Health Service Corps Scholarship Program, 1010 Wayne Ave., Suite 240, Silver Spring, MD 20910, 800-638-0824.

Job: Physician

Path #1: Medical school

Family physicians are in great demand now because insurance companies will drive down the specialists' numbers and require that everybody see a primary caregiver first (in many cases this will be a nurse practitioner or a P.A.).

Normally, medical school requires four additional years after college, but there are schools that offer a combined six-year program. State-operated schools generally do not admit many out-of-state applicants into their programs, according to the AMA.

Introductory calculus, biology, physics, chemistry, English and social studies are required for admission, although the student should check the requirements of particular schools of interest. Here is a list provided by the AMA that includes both six- and eight-year combined programs:

Union College and Albany Medical College, Schenectady, N.Y.
Case-Western Reserve University, Cleveland, Ohio
Northeastern Ohio Universities, College of Medicine,
    Rootstown, Ohio
Gannon University and Hahnemann University School of
    Medicine, Erie, Pa.
Lehigh University and Medical College of Pennsylvania,
    Bethlehem, Pa.
Villanova University and Medical College of Pennsylvania,
    Villanova, Pa.
Pennsylvania State University and Jefferson Medical College,
    University Park, Pa.
Brown University, Providence, R.I.
East Tennessee State University, Johnson City, Tenn.
University of Wisconsin Medical School, Madison, Wis.
University of South Alabama, Mobile, Ala.
University of California—Riverside and University of
    California—Los Angeles, Riverside, Calif.
Howard University, Washington, D.C.
University of Miami, Coral Gables, Fla.
University of Health Sciences/The Chicago Medical School and
    Illinois Institute of Technology, Chicago, Ill.
Northwestern University, Evanston, Ill.
Louisiana State University, Shreveport, La.
Boston University, Boston, Mass.
University of Michigan, Ann Arbor, Mich.
University of Missouri—Kansas City, Kansas City, Mo.

If you can't get into a medical school in the United States, look into accredited foreign medical schools, listed in the *World Health Directory*. Upon return to this country, you will need certification from the Educational Commission for Foreign Medical Graduates before you start your residency. You may wish to contact this group before starting medical school. You can reach the commission at 3624 Market St., Philadelphia, PA 19104-2685. Write to the attention of William Kelly.

You could apply for a scholarship through the National Health Service Corps Scholarship Program, 1010 Wayne Ave., Suite 240, Silver Spring, MD 20910, 800-638-0824. This program also gives scholarships to midwives, physician's assistants and nurse practitioners. The emphasis is on financing primary care training. They pay a stipend of almost $800 a month plus full tuition. For each year they finance, you serve a year. They are looking for those who can make a sincere commitment to giving primary care to the disadvantaged.

Path #2: Career-change to doctor

There are programs that prepare career-changers to get into medical school; in other words, you would take the science and math that you didn't take in college, and get special prepping to take the exam required for medical school application. One young nurse, Carol, decided to go back to school to become a doctor. She took organic chemistry twice until she got an A and then applied to medical school; she got into three schools and is now a psychiatrist with a flourishing practice.

Because medicine pays an average of $134,000 a year full-time, you can afford to work part-time and/or get help with childcare and household duties. The average age of entrance now is over 30 and people even older are accepted, so don't rule yourself out because of your age.

Medical specialties

Specialties include general and family practice, cardiovascular medicine, dermatology, gastroenterology, internal medicine, pediatrics, pulmonary disease, ophthalmology, obstetrics, surgery, anesthesiology, psychiatry, diagnostic radiology, emergency medicine, neurology, occupational medicine, pathology, physical and rehabilitation medicine, public health and radiology.

Job: Osteopath

Osteopaths put an emphasis on the musculoskeletal system. There are 16 colleges that train osteopaths. According to the *Occupational Outlook Handbook*, osteopathic physicians are located chiefly in states that have osteopathic hospitals. This is because a residency training program is required after the degree is earned and doctors need to be affiliated with a hospital to practice. Most doctors of osteopathy are located in Florida, Michigan,

Pennsylvania, Ohio, Texas and Missouri. Write to the American Association of Colleges of Osteopathic Medicine, 6110 Executive Blvd., Suite 405, Rockville, MD 20852, for a list of schools, or call 301-468-2037.

Job: Podiatrist

There are seven schools of podiatry in the United States. To enter a college of podiatry, you need at least 90 undergraduate credits, but most entrants have earned a bachelor's degree. The training is very similar to the four-year medical school program in which physicians are trained. For a list of six colleges, write to American Association of Colleges of Podiatric Medicine, 1350 Piccard Drive, Suite 322, Rockville, MD 20850, 301-990-7400. The New York School of Podiatric Medicine, in New York City, is not part of the association.

Job: Optometrist

There are 17 accredited schools of optometry in the United States. The four-year degree program usually admits only students with college degrees, although two or three years of college may be acceptable. Optometrists treat vision problems and may, in 23 states, treat eye diseases with drugs.

Write or call the American Optometric Association, Educational Services, 243 North Lindbergh Blvd., St. Louis, MO 63141, 314-991-4100, for a list of accredited schools. Their materials include college course requirements for admissions to each school of optometry, percentage of out-of-state applicants admitted, etc., plus a profile on each school.

Job: Dentist

Write to SELECT Program, Department of Career Guidance, American Dental Association, 211 East Chicago Ave., Chicago IL 60611, 312-440-2500, to ask for the list of accredited schools of dentistry. You usually enter these after college, but some dental schools only require two years of college.

Mental Health/Fitness jobs

Counselor/Therapist	Chiropractor
Social Worker	Acupuncturist
Probation Officer	Fitness Trainer/
Pastoral Counselor and	Health Club Manager
Spiritual Advisor	Coach
Massage Therapist	Physical Therapist
Yoga Instructor	Activities Therapist

These jobs have been grouped together because they concern mind-body wellness. None of these practitioners can write prescriptions, so they are all dependent on doctors if medication is a part of the treatment.

Job: Counselor/Therapist

Path #1: Volunteer counselor

If you enjoy helping people express their feelings and sort out their options, you may want to further test your interest in becoming a clinical psychologist or clinical social worker by getting a job as a volunteer. Homes for mentally ill/neglected children, settlement houses or community centers and psychiatric hospitals all need volunteers. In these settings, you will have the opportunity to meet clinical psychologists and social workers as well as the population you will be training to serve.

Almost every community offers hotline services. Suicide-prevention hotlines, hotlines for runaways and switchboards that handle requests for all sorts of services are usually staffed with trained volunteers and offer a good way to gain counseling experience while getting free training. Your county mental health agency will help you locate hotlines. A reference from the hotline director will be useful if you want to go on in the mental health field.

Path #2: Work as an aide, direct care worker or residence counselor

Homes for the developmentally disabled are often in need of direct care workers to bathe, dress and feed residents. Homes for the mentally ill also need counselors who help the residents prepare meals, clean and provide transportation. These handicapped populations are housed in group homes in the community rather than in large institutions. Often a clean driver's license and a high school diploma are the only requirements.

Mental health aide positions in most state and city mental hospitals require a high school diploma and some experience. Trainees must be able to speak English or Spanish and pass a written test. They work regular nurses' hours (either day, evening or night shifts), and assist the nursing staff with patient care. After a period of employment you could move up the career ladder and take an exam to become a community client services assistant, mental health staff development specialist, mental health therapy assistant, psychiatric social work assistant, or recreation or rehabilitation assistant. The state's job service can help you locate positions in the mental health, correctional services, drug abuse and youth fields. Although some jobs do not require training, it is important that you get some training because it will help you to cope with the demands of the job.

Aides may earn a dollar or two above minimum wage to start. They help patients get dressed, counsel them and socialize with them. You can do this work with or without a two-year degree in human services from a community college; the two-year human services degree may not be a good idea because many of the courses will not be transferable if you decide to continue your education.

Path #3: Mental health counselor

In some counties, case managers don't need master's degrees; with a year of experience and related undergraduate course work, they can coordinate the care of the mentally ill. To give an example in the nonprofit sector, the New York Council of Churches is looking for a substance abuse/mental health counselor with good interpersonal skills, a B.A. in psychology or a related field and three years of relevant experience. This experience could mean either three years of work in a rehabilitation center after being a resident—often rehabs hire ex-clients as counselors—or three years of experience as a residence counselor in a group home for the mentally ill. The salary is in the mid-20s.

Path #4: Clinical mental health counselor

Sometimes school guidance counselors work outside the school and become clinical mental health counselors. They may have master's degrees in clinical psychology, counseling psychology, mental health counseling or education (with a specialty in mental health counseling). Some states do not license these workers.

Path #5: Certified Alcoholism Counselor or Certified Substance Abuse Counselor

New York state gives a credential to counselors of alcoholics and substance abusers who have a year of experience and 650 clock hours of college credit or training in the field. This credential may help in getting a job as a counselor or a job in prevention and education. A college education is not required, but a high school diploma or GED is needed to sit for the examination. Most states have similar programs.

Path #6: Marriage and family counselor

Marriage and family counselors have master's degrees or Ph.D.s in marriage and family therapy (these are often offered in schools of education), or at least a master's degree in another area and further training in marriage and family counseling.

Write to the American Association for Marriage and Family Therapy, 1100 17th St. NW, 10th Fl., Washington, DC 20036, or call 202-452-0109 for a list of schools offering accredited programs.

Path #7: Clinical and counseling psychologist

This job requires graduate training beyond the four-year college degree. Some graduate programs in psychology require that the undergraduate degree be in psychology; other programs prefer broader preparation, such as a liberal arts background. You can receive the master's degree en route to earning the doctorate. A master's degree in psychology will qualify you for jobs in teaching and research, but Ph.D. students often get them. Depending on state requirements, you may be able to have a private practice and collect insurance payments with the doctorate. The program usually takes five years, the last year being an internship. You must complete a dissertation on a piece of original experimental research for the Doctor of Philosophy (Ph.D.), unless you are in a Doctor of Psychology (Psy.D.)

program, which takes four years to complete, including the internship, and does not require a thesis.

If you are interested in having a private practice as a psychologist, you must get up-to-date information on how the insurance companies reimburse psychologists for therapy as opposed to social workers, nurses and psychiatrists, and of course on licensing requirements in your state.

States generally require a doctorate in psychology and two years of professional experience before the license or certificate for independent practice in psychotherapy is awarded. Psychologists cannot prescribe drugs; they work with psychiatrists if patients need medication.

Counseling psychologists or educational psychologists generally work in educational settings and have doctorates in education. School psychologists, who have a doctorate in education, and guidance counselors (also called school counselors), who have education master's degrees, are other school-based workers in child and family psychology.

You can also get a Ph.D. in experimental psychology (a degree for research and teaching). According to a May 30, 1995 article in *The New York Times*, Martha McClintock is a professor of biopsychology who studies animal behavior in the laboratory. She is interested in the way behavior affects physiology. For example, rats generate pheromones that enhance or suppress the fertility of their neighbors. Her research revealed the exact way that rats' surroundings impact the individual rat's birth cycles. She is getting adequate funding for her work to build a $12 million research institute at the University of Chicago. Other researchers include a primatologist who studies yellow baboons' hormones and their struggles over rank and status, an immunologist who looks at the impact of behaviors on the immune system and a molecular biologist specializing in the genetic aspects of behavior. Write to The American Psychological Association, 750 First St. NE, Washington, DC 20002, 202-336-5500.

Job: Social Worker

Path #1: Social work volunteer

Hospitals often use volunteers to do social work functions—for example, calling nursing homes in order to find a bed for a patient.

Organizations such as Catholic Charities may use volunteers. See the library's directory of social welfare agencies in your region.

Path #2: Social work aide or assistant

The Bachelor of Arts in social work may qualify you for a job as a case aide; however, a master's degree is a prerequisite to obtaining a license. The agencies and insurance companies that pay social workers must hire only those with licenses if the agencies are going to get paid for services to clients.

Community organization is one area of concentration in the social work curriculum. For example, community organizing jobs are available through organizations like ACORN. This organization is involved with housing, toxic chemicals, school reform, lending, health care and other issues concerning low- and moderate-income families. ACORN organizes neighborhoods, identifies and develops leadership, researches issues and works with community groups to plan strategies for local, city-wide and national campaigns. Training is provided and salary is $12,000 to $15,000 a year.

The Public Interest Research Groups of Ralph Nader, the Northwest Neighborhood Federation in Chicago, Citizens for Community Improvement in Des Moines and many other organizations offer these types of positions. Often some prior experience is the only credential needed for these jobs. They are listed in *Community Jobs: The Employment Newspaper for the Non-Profit Sector*, Access, 40 Beacon St., Boston, MA 02108.

Path #3: Master of Social Work

Master's degree programs will accept a variety of undergraduate majors, but currently even social workers with advanced degrees are relocating to find acceptable employment. Hiring is strongly influenced by government social service funding.

Social workers can specialize in administration, casework (which includes individual counseling or therapy), community organization or group work. To be a psychiatric social worker and be eligible for insurance company reimbursements for your patients, you must do some years of work under a supervisor who is certified in the psychiatric field. Social workers are licensed by the state and each state is different; look into the requirements for licensing in your state. Write to the National Association of Social Workers, 750 First St. NE, Suite 700, Washington, DC 20002-4241, 202-408-8600.

Rose became a social worker because her own family was dysfunctional and she wanted to help others from similar backgrounds. Her graduate school training was paid for by the federal government because she was bilingual (Spanish and English), and Spanish-speaking social workers were desperately needed in the city where she was working. She worked for many years with the county mental health agency. The caseload was quite challenging but she liked the security of agency work rather than private practice work.

Job: Probation Officer

Probation officers can work for the judicial branch or the executive branch of the government. In New York state they work for the executive branch of the county and sit for civil service examinations. In other states they can intern as college students and get hired without further examination. You need a college degree in criminal justice, sociology, teaching or psychology.

As a probation officer you make recommendations in sentencing, supervise those on probation and do substance abuse evaluations. This job includes a lot of social work; probationers and parolees often have emergencies, so you have to be available sometimes after work hours, but you also have an enforcement role. You must be willing to go into potentially dangerous neighborhoods and homes.

Sean studied sociology in college and realized that criminology was his real interest. He participated in a college program that involved working in a courthouse and attending seminars on criminal justice with a teacher who later became a mentor. After getting his bachelor's degree in the social sciences, (sociology, psychology and economics), he sat for a civil service exam and started as a trainee in the probation department. Now he is director of the county's probation officers.

Job: Pastoral Counselor and Spiritual Advisor

The first step here is to establish a strong connection over time with a denomination or church. To become a Protestant minister, for example, you will need to attend seminary after college, but more importantly, you need to establish a strong relationship with the church so they will understand the seriousness of your commitment. You need to find out what the requirements are for seminary admission and for ordination while you are in college. Some evangelical churches are not concerned with educational credentials and ordain ministers entirely on the basis of their spiritual leadership qualities. Some Protestant churches will not ordain women. No women may become priests in the Catholic church.

Pastoral counseling is something that many church leaders are trained in seminary to do as a specialty. They see individuals who want counseling from a person with psychological and spiritual training. Other ministers, priests and rabbis counsel informally and, more often, on a crisis basis.

Rosalind is a part-time interim minister in a small church. She went to seminary after working for some years as a flight attendant. When her airline closed down, she took advantage of the opportunity to get training in a seminary. She uses her pastoral counseling training, which she got in seminary, for individual clients and does church duties—the sermon, funerals and weddings, youth group and other church business—20 hours a week in one church, for about $20,000 a year. It is quite a busy and stressful life; she is on call all the time and has a young child.

According to the *Occupational Outlook Handbook*, there were an estimated 290,000 Protestant ministers, approximately 4,000 rabbis and 53,000 priests in 1992. Contact the Association of Theological Schools in the United States, 10 Summit Park Dr., Pittsburgh, PA 15275-1103, 412-788-6505.

Job: Massage Therapist

Most massage therapists have private practices. Others work in spas, health clubs, Y's, hospitals and nursing homes. Although many people work as masseuses without formal training, your state may have particular requirements to obtain a license as a massage therapist.

The American Massage Therapy Association can help you locate accredited schools and give requirements for licensure in each state. Or you can call the state agency regulating professions and get the requirements for your state. Training in a formal program for massage usually requires a full year of study. Write to The American Massage Therapy Association, 820 Davis St., Suite 100, Evanston, IL 60201-4444, or call 708-864-0123.

Job: Yoga Instructor

Yoga has proven to be a valuable mental and physical practice. Teachers of yoga find employment in Y's, adult education programs, health clubs, wellness programs, senior citizen centers and even psychiatric hospitals. Teacher training programs are offered by many groups and include anatomy, physiology, philosophy of yoga, meditation practices, vegetarian nutrition and the teaching of yoga. The magazine *Yoga International*, available from the Himalayan Institute, lists many different training programs. Write to *Yoga International*, RR 1 Box 407, Honesdale, PA 18431.

Job: Chiropractor

Chiropractors treat physical problems by manipulating the spine. Chiropractic schools may be overenrolled and earning a living in the field may be difficult because there are so many practitioners. Recently, however, some employers have started paying chiropractors to train their back-injury prone employees to avoid further problems through a program called Back Power, licensed in the U.S. by the National Safety Council. Programs such as this one may create more work for chiropractors. Training involves four years of specialized schooling after two or four years of college.

Write to the Council on Chiropractic Education, 4401 Westown Parkway, Suite 120, West Des Moines, IA 50266, for a list of approved schools.

Job: Acupuncturist

Acupuncturists use needles to stimulate nerves deep inside the body. The World Health Organization recognizes acupuncture in the treatment of a wide range of medical problems. Each state has different requirements for licensing but there is also a national level accreditation. This commission will assist students in locating an accredited school in your area.

National Board examinations are offered to graduates of schools accredited by the National Commission for the Certification of

Acupuncturists. Contact the chairperson at the address below. The certification requirements are quite rigorous, so make sure of your state's licensing requirements before undertaking this path. Some insurance companies require certification before they will pay for acupuncture. To sit for the certification exam you need three years of schooling, an apprenticeship and four years of professional practice. Write to the National Council of Acupuncture Schools and Colleges, 1424 16th St. NW, Suite 501, Washington, DC 20036, 202-232-1404.

Job: Fitness Trainer/Health Club Manager
Path #1: Exercise trainer in a health club

Fitness instructors, dance-exercise teachers, aerobic teachers and weight room trainers are hired because of their appearance and past experience. It is stated by one expert, Peg Angsten, that most clubs hire without asking for a certification.

To lead exercise classes, you must be physically fit and have some experience with exercise routines. This can be volunteer experience in a senior center or with a group of Girl Scouts. Often the fitness chains will audition leading candidates and train them after hire. Sometimes simply discussing related experience may be all that is required of the applicant. The audition may be of the same sort given to dancers, in which you will be asked to learn and repeat some steps.

The International Association of Fitness Professionals, 6190 Cornerstone Court East, Suite 204, San Diego, CA 92121, 619-535-8979; The American Council on Exercise, 5820 Oberlin Drive, Suite 102, San Diego, CA 92121-3787, 800-825-3636; the Aerobics and Fitness Association of America, 15250 Ventura Blvd., Suite 200, Sherman Oaks, CA 91403, 818-905-0040; the American College of Sports Medicine, P.O. Box 1440, Indianapolis, IN 46206-1440, 317-637-9200; the National Academy of Sports Medicine, 2434 N. Greenview Ave., Chicago, IL 60614, 312-929-5101; and the National Dance Exercise Instructors Training Association, 1503 S. Washington Ave., Suite 208, Minneapolis, MN 55454, 612-340-1306, offer certification exams. Find out which group will be recognized in your local area.

Employee wellness programs, sponsored by the Personnel Departments of major corporations, and local Y's and adult education programs, are good places to get started, but health clubs are the major employers. If you have had some courses in physiology, experience with nautilus conditioning or weight training and an athletic appearance and manner you may be able to get a job in the weight room. Another credentialing program for trainers is the National Strength and Conditioning Association, P.O. Box 81410, Lincoln, NE 68501, 402-472-3000.

Path #2: Trainer-salesperson

If you have the ability to sell and teach classes, you should look into a management position, which involves supervision of the facilities and selling memberships. According to health club employee Melanie, members of the club are considered first to teach exercise if they are in shape and outgoing. She was hired as an instructor at minimum wage and is now club manager. She gets commissions on all memberships she sells and can eventually own stock in the chain.

Job: Coach

Path #1: Volunteering

Experience coaching a children's team will give you a chance to learn about the training of athletes, the conditioning of bodies and sports injuries. You can volunteer through your town's recreation department or through the local athletic league.

Path #2: Athletic training

More and more high schools are hiring certified sports trainers to work with their athletes, coaches and doctors to prevent sports injuries; large health clubs and sports medicine clinics also hire sports trainers. Certified trainers enter the field either through physical therapy courses, college courses in athletic training or paramedic or nurse training, then add EMT training and an internship under a certified athletic trainer. The American Sports Medicine Association and Certification Board encourages young people to become involved in sports medicine training while in high school.

For more information about being a trainer, write to the American Sports Medicine Association and Certification Board, 660 West Duarte Rd., Arcadia, CA 91007, 818-445-1978 or the National Athletic Trainers' Association (NATA), 2952 Stemmons Freeway,

....

Dallas, TX 75247, 214-637-6282, for more information. This last organization has received approval by the AMA for their certification program for athletic trainers. According to NATA, trainers at colleges and universities average about $34,000 per year. Trainers in professional sports earn $50,000 to $110,000.

Path #3: Physical education degree

Schools of education offer bachelor's degrees in physical education. These graduates become coaches for elementary and secondary public schools because they must have teaching credentials to work in public schools. Some of these high school coaches go on to work with college or professional teams. Coach Dwain Painter got an offer from the Pittsburgh Steelers after 23 years on the high school and college circuit; he was a college player himself who went into coaching. According to *Current Biography Yearbook*, Dean Smith, the very successful basketball coach at the University of North Carolina, also went from player to coach. After graduating with a B.S. in physical education and mathematics, Smith stayed on at Kansas University as an assistant coach. After several years in the military and three years coaching at the Air Force Academy, he went to the University of North Carolina. He has trained many of the top players in college and professional basketball, including Michael Jordan.

Great professional players get jobs as coaches for colleges or professional teams. Sometimes a college player will move into coaching. Jimmy Johnson is the first coach to have won both a college national championship and back-to-back Super Bowls. He went into coaching after members of the Louisiana Tech coaching staff visited Arkansas during his senior season at Arkansas. Asked to explain the principles of defensive strategies, Johnson so impressed the coaches that they hired him as a fill-in for a defensive line coach. After a year at a high school, Johnson was signed as an assistant at Wichita State University, then at Iowa State University, Pittsburgh and Oklahoma State University (as head coach). Then he went to the University of Miami, again as head coach, and then to the Dallas Cowboys to win the Super Bowl twice. After stepping down, Johnson went on to be a studio analyst for Sunday NFL games for Fox and HBO.

In times of limited budgets, high school coaching jobs may be part-time. For example, one classified advertisement read that the Pine Plains Central School District in New York state was looking for a part-time football head coach, for $2,694 per year. Coaches for soccer, cross country, field hockey and volleyball were also listed.

Job: Physical Therapist

Path #1: Volunteering

The physical therapy departments of hospitals and nursing homes welcome volunteers who are willing to help patients do the exercises recommended by the physical therapist on staff. Do mention that you want to test your interest in a career in physical therapy by helping in a volunteer capacity.

Path #2: Associate's degree

Physical therapy assistants with the two-year associate's degree and experience work directly with the patient. Returning for the bachelor's degree in physical therapy may be nearly as difficult as starting from the beginning. Almost none of the courses taken for the associate's degree will be accepted toward the bachelor's degree in physical therapy. There is no provision for the person working in the field to take the physical therapy exam, as there is in occupational therapy.

Path #3: Bachelor's degree

Physical therapists are eligible to take the essential licensing examination if they have either a bachelor's degree from an accredited physical therapy program, a master's degree in physical therapy or a certificate in physical therapy from an accredited program. Good grades in high school science and college chemistry, physiology, anatomy, neuroanatomy, neurophysiology, biomechanics of motion and human growth and development are important.

Evelyn has a master's degree in physical therapy. She majored in biology in college and then decided to apply to physical therapy schools because she wanted to help people with their problems. Now she has a private practice in a country environment and a second practice in New York City. She gets her referrals by word of mouth. One interest of hers is counseling, which gives her a good understanding and appreciation of the mind-body connection.

For more information, write to the American Physical Therapy Association, 1111 North Fairfax St., Alexandria, VA 22314.

Job: Activities Therapist

Path #1: Assist an occupational therapist

Occupational therapists or activities therapists select activities which are designed to improve a patient's functioning and help the patient adjust to a physical or mental disability. If you can lead the patients in activities, you may be able to get a job as an assistant in a hospital, nursing home or residential treatment center.

An assistant to an occupational therapist can get a two-year degree or certificate or take the examination for licensure as an assistant occupational therapist after four years of work experience, depending on the experience, as stipulated by the American Occupational Therapy Association.

You can't use occupational therapy assistant courses or the one-year occupational therapy assistant certificate to enter a four-year occupational therapy program. The average starting salary is $20,954.

Path #2: Bachelor's or master's degree in occupational therapy

If you get the bachelor's or master's degree in occupational therapy, you will be eligible to take the licensing examination. Fifteen states require licensure for occupational therapists. Entrance is competitive, especially after the freshman year in accredited bachelor's degree programs. The student with a certificate from an accredited program is also eligible to sit for the licensing examination.

Human anatomy and physiology, psychology, sociology or cultural anthropology, statistics and studio arts are some of the courses required for entrance into a master's degree program in occupational therapy. According to the American Occupational Therapy Association, in 1994, half of all new occupational therapists earned an average of $34,500 in their first position. The average starting salary is $30,737. Most occupational therapists work in general, psychiatric and pediatric hospitals, public and private schools and rehabilitation centers.

There will be many occupational therapists needed for the expanding aging population. Some tasks of occupational therapists in gerontology include cognitive retraining in the skill of dressing with stroke patients, helping patients get the kind of wheelchair they need to maintain their lifestyle and studying the prevention of falls among the elderly.

For more information, write to American Occupational Therapy Association, 4720 Montgomery Lane, P.O. Box 31220, Bethesda, MD 20824-1220, or call 301-652-2682.

Path #3: Vocational rehabilitation

Vocational rehabilitation counseling follows roughly the same career path as occupational therapy. Programs in vocational rehabilitation are offered at undergraduate and graduate schools of education. Rehabilitation counselors are licensed by their state and certified by a national organization.

Write to the Council on Rehabilitation Education, 1835 Rohlwing Rd., Suite E, Rolling Meadows, IL 60008, 708-394-1785, or the American Academy of Orthotists and Prosthetists, 1650 King St., Suite 500, Alexandria, VA 22314, 703-836-7118.

Path #4: Recreational therapist

Recreational therapists, sometimes called activities therapists, have an especially hard time finding work in this age of budget cuts. Nursing homes may hire recreational therapists with bachelor's degrees to direct their activities programs. The bachelor's degree in parks and recreation is available at many colleges, although you may not need the degree to work in recreation. You can also get a taste of this field by volunteering.

For a list of accredited schools, write to the National Recreation and Park Association, Division of Professional Services, 3101 Park Center Dr., Alexandria, VA 22303, or call 703-820-4940.

Physical Science jobs

Chemist   Meteorologist
Geologist   Astronomer
Physicist   Science Teacher

The physical sciences include chemistry, physics, geology, meteorology and astronomy. Whether you study the nature of the universe, the atmosphere, the ocean, the earth's crust or chemical elements, you will be describing the physical world in mathematical terms.

The Department of Energy (DOE) offers the following experiences for physical sciences students; however, budget constraints may affect the future of some of these programs. Write to Laboratory

Infrastructure, Office of Energy Research, U.S. Department of Energy, 1000 Independence Ave. SW, Washington, DC 20585 or call the program director, Ms. Toni Joseph, at 202-586-5447.

Pre-Freshman Enrichment Program (PREP). Summer institutes for sixth- to tenth-grade students provide lab work, field trips, tutoring and counseling for 6,000 students each year.

High School Student Research Apprenticeship Program. This program is for freshman and sophomore high school minority and female students who are considering careers in science. Participating students get together at one of several labs, do research, attend lectures and seminars, and participate in field activities.

High School Science Student Honors Program. This national program sponsored by the DOE brings the very best high school science and mathematics students together for two weeks in the summer to perform energy-related research under the guidance of DOE laboratory scientists.

Environmental Restoration and Waste Management Scholarship Program. Scholarships are available to college students to study in scientific fields supportive of DOE's environmental-restoration and waste-management activities.

Fusion Research Fellowships; Science and Engineering Research Semester. Financial support is available for research appointments for one term at one of the seven DOE labs throughout the United States.

Co-op Education Programs at Brookhaven. Brookhaven National Laboratory offers co-ops to college students after their sophomore year. Contact Lisa Saracino in the Personnel Division, BNL, Upton, NY 11973. The lab also has an internship program with the Massachusetts Institute of Technology, a 12-week paid summer program for women and minorities, the Summer Student Program, the Summer Intern Program for high school students and a technician training program for minorities and women. Request their booklet, "Educational Programs."

Summer government jobs. Physical science aides are hired for summer jobs by The National Bureau of Standards, National Oceanic and Atmospheric Administration, Department of Energy, Environmental Protection Agency, U.S. Geological Survey, National

Aeronautics and Space Administration and Naval Research Laboratory of the Department of the Navy. Students are required to have a high school diploma, and one or two years of college. See U.S. Government, Office of Personnel Management, in the blue pages of the telephone directory for the address of the Federal Jobs Information Center in your region. Write for their booklet, "Summer Jobs," and the forms you need to apply. Some of these agencies above also offer internships.

Job: Chemist

Path #1: Chemical technician

Private industry employs most of the technicians in the physical sciences. If you have good grades and some laboratory experience, you could get a job as a technician, aide or assistant that will let you see how scientists and engineers work. You may be employed in a research or development laboratory or in the manufacturing plant itself.

Technicians in research and development build instruments, monitor experiments and record results. In manufacturing, they check to see that the product meets the specifications of the engineer. Many technicians have previously worked in factory production and have shown an aptitude or interest in the work as a career.

Sometimes a cooperative education program at a community college or a private technical institute will allow the student to get work experience as a technician. Physical science students in college get laboratory experience and, if they go to a research university, they may be able to assist in the funded research of their professors.

Path #2: Bachelor's degree

If you can get the bachelor's degree you can often find a job analyzing or testing products. For example, chemists are employed in the manufacture of practically everything organic—drugs, food, cosmetics. Or you could go to work in technical sales (sales in which technical knowledge is important), or assist a senior chemist. Food processing and pharmaceutical industries employ chemistry graduates as assistants, and your company may pay for your graduate school tuition.

Judy's listing in *Vocational Biographies* says she took chemistry courses for five years as an employee benefit from Eastman Kodak, where she worked first as a technician and then as a professional chemist. She now works for Eastman Kodak and an environmental information center, where she helps people understand environmental risk and mediates potential environmental conflicts. For example, she may help to work out solutions to environmental problems like the siting of a waste disposal facility or land use disputes. Judy also has a master's degree in environmental studies.

Chemists can make a substantial contribution to solving some of this country's major problems. For example, a January 17, 1995 article in *The New York Times* said that seven scientists at Catalytica Inc., in Mountain View, Calif., discovered a cheaper way to turn natural gas into methanol, which can power automobiles. Smog and global warming could be substantially reduced if gas is replaced by this cleaner fuel. A new class of drugs for the treatment of schizophrenia, clozaril, has made a great difference in the lives of thousands of people. Chemists working in the research and development labs of pharmaceutical companies produced this new medicine.

Forensic science is a sub-specialty in the field of biochemistry (the chemistry of living matter). An article printed in *The Times* on December 9, 1994 says that Dr. Henry Lee started his career in criminal justice, then got several degrees in biochemistry and trained in forensic science at Yale. He attended the Taiwan Police Academy, but was not interested in police work. He came to the United States at the insistence of his sister, who was a biochemistry professor at New York University. Working as a waiter, a stock boy and a groundskeeper, he paid for his education. Lee was hired by the defense on the O.J. Simpson case as well as many other major cases. He has transformed the Connecticut State Police Crime Laboratory into a $40 million research center.

According to the December 18, 1994 issue of *New York Times Magazine*, Eloy Rodriguez got a job cleaning a plant biochemistry lab in college. As he worked, two of the research assistants trained him to use the equipment. Plant biochemistry or chemical ecology is now the specialty of Rodriguez, a Cornell professor who, in order to find useful plants, examines certain plant species and the animals that rely on them. For example, Rodriguez studies a bird in Venezuela that eats a very poisonous plant to learn how the animal's system handles the poison. He has invented a whole new field—zoopharmacognosy, the study of how animals use plants as medicine. Rodriguez discovered a potent antibiotic and solved a medical crisis in India, when thousands were hospitalized due to the toxin in a common weed.

Job: Geologist

Jane (*Vocational Biographies*) used her bachelor's degree in geology to start as a field geologist for an engineering firm. Her duties included testing wells and soil for contaminants and checking underground fuel tanks for leakage. She went on to do site assessment and then opened her own consulting company. She advises property buyers about possible problems with contamination.

Hydrologists specialize in the earth's water. Currently jobs are plentiful. Emma was able to apply her knowledge of landfill hazards (water pollution from landfills is an issue in her locality). With her master's degree in hydrology, she landed a job with a resource recovery agency.

Job: Physicist

The field of physics presents a difficult job market, even for those with the Ph.D., and this is likely to continue because of decreased budgets and decreased hiring in defense and government research. Teaching positions, according to Kathy and Ross Petras, are also scarce. With this degree you could consider engineering, or other related fields like mathematics, astronomy and chemistry before you make a commitment to the field.

Abraham Pais (*Current Biography Yearbook*) is one of the founding fathers of particle physics and one of the leading theoretical physicists of his generation. As an undergraduate he majored in mathematics and chemistry but after hearing a lecture about how electrons spin on their axes, he knew what he was going to do for the rest of his life.

Pais got several postdoctoral fellowships, at the Institute for Advanced Study in Princeton and at the Niels Bohr Institute in Copenhagen. He worked all his life on, as he put it, "the search for an ever more refined description of matter and forces in the physical world." This is the subtitle of his book *Inward Bound*. He also wrote a scientific biography of Albert Einstein, called *Subtle Is the Lord*.

....

Leon Lederman (*Current Biography Yearbook*), who graduated from City College with a degree in chemistry, realized, when he was about to go to graduate school, that he had enjoyed his physics courses more than his chemistry courses, got a Ph.D. at Columbia and stayed on to work with their particle accelerator, and received the Nobel Prize in 1988 for his work in particle physics. Lederman describes what it is to be a scientist, "looking at the reams of paper spewing out of the computer. You look, and look, and suddenly you see some numbers that aren't like the rest—a spike in the data. You apply some statistical tests and look for errors, but no matter what you do, the spike's still there. It's real. You've found something. There's just no feeling like it in the world."

Chien-Shiung Wu is an experimental physicist and a professor at Columbia University. In 1956, her most celebrated experiment overturned one of the basic laws of physics, the law of conservation of parity, which held that a phenomenon of nature is symmetrical and looks the same whether observed directly or in a mirror. She got her start when her father encouraged her to prepare for university-level physics by bringing home textbooks on algebra, physics and chemistry. She enjoyed mastering mathematics and science, and studied these texts on her own.

Write to The American Institute of Physics, One Physics Ellipse, College Park, MD 20740-3843, or call 301-209-3100 for information.

Job: Meteorologist

The National Weather Service is expanding, according to occupational projections of the U.S. Government, and a bachelor's degree can get you started. Although the field itself is small (6,000 people), the National Weather Service expects to hire at least 100 meteorologists with bachelor's degrees each year. Most schools offer some courses in meteorology; the degree is in physics or chemistry, usually with mathematics courses including calculus. Working for The National Weather Service requires at least 20 semester hours of courses in meteorology. Given the lack of diversity in employment, preparing in a second field may be a good bet.

Job: Astronomer

Astronomy requires the Ph.D. It is a specialty of physics. Mae Jemison (*Current Biography Yearbook*) is a doctor, an astronaut and a chemical engineer. She was the first African-American woman in space. The Apollo 11 mission inspired her. She decided in high school to pursue a career in biomedical engineering. She entered Stanford University at 16 on a National Achievement Scholarship, majored in chemical engineering and African and Afro-American studies, later completed medical school and then joined the Peace Corps in West Africa. Upon returning, she took engineering courses. In 1987, she went to Houston and five years later got her place on a mission. During the eight days the space shuttle Endeavour was in orbit, Jemison conducted experiments dealing with weightlessness, tissue growth and the development of semiconductor materials.

For a pamphlet on careers in astronomy, send 50¢ to the Education Office, American Astronomical Society, Department of Astronomy, University of Texas, Building RLM15.308, Austin, TX 78712-1083. The Education Office can be reached by phone at 512-471-1309.

Job: Science Teacher

One way to teach science is through a science museum. For example, at the New York Hall of Science college students are offered paid internships explaining exhibits in exchange for tuition waivers at local colleges. Graduates of the program agree to teach in New York state schools for two years. Most science and technology centers work with local schools to train teachers to teach science and offer the schools field trips to the science center. Many teachers in residence programs become science education experts. The Exploratorium in San Francisco trains teachers in an intensive summer program.

The Association of Science Technology Centers in Washington, D.C., also trains science teachers. Write to them at 1025 Vermont Ave. NW, Suite 500, Washington, DC 20005, or call 202-783-7200.

Social Science jobs

Political Scientist
Sociologist
Anthropologist

Psychologists study individuals. Economists study money and people. Political scientists, anthropologists and sociologists study groups of people. These fields require the Ph.D. to teach full-time, and opportunities for academic and nonacademic employment are limited. Because of cutbacks in academia, all these fields may be shrinking at colleges and universities, and the universities themselves are shrinking, especially in the liberal arts areas.

Job: Political Scientist

Political campaigns may employ political scientists to design, administer and analyze polling results because they have a background in statistics and understand American politics and the factors that are operating at particular historical moments. The American Political Science Association can send you information on teaching jobs that will be available when you graduate and information on employment in the field. Contact them at 1527 New Hampshire Ave. NW, Washington, DC 20036, 202-483-2512.

Job: Sociologist

Sociologists study social problems like crime, teenage pregnancy, welfare, alcoholism, etc. Taking sociology courses at the undergraduate level will help you see if the field interests you enough to go to graduate school and then try to get a tenure track teaching job that will guarantee you job security. The American Sociological Association advises considering nonacademic employment as a sociologist and says that a double major in college and a dual focus for the graduate with a Ph.D. will be necessary to get work. In other words, you will be hired for your specialization in the second field of concentration—either business or health, for example. Write to the association at 1722 N St., NW, Washington, DC 20036, or call 202-833-3410.

Job: Anthropologist

Physical anthropology (the study of human ancestors), cultural anthropology (the study of living cultures), linguistics (the study of the human languages) and archaeology (the study of the physical remains of cultures) are the four subfields or specialties in anthropology. There are further subdivisions like medical anthropology or urban anthropology. Undergraduate work will help clarify your interest, but like sociology, you will need a dual major to work in applied fields with the Ph.D. Very few teaching jobs are available.

If you do field research with living cultures, be very careful that you don't end up working as an informal "spy"; often anthropologists are used either directly or indirectly in this way. Information that you collect about a group can be used against them, no matter how good your intentions are. Some believe that the study of non-U.S. groups should be left to the country's own academics. Write to the American Anthropological Association, 4350 N. Fairfax Drive, Suite 640, Arlington, VA 22203 or call 703-528-1902.

Mathematics jobs

Computer Programmer
Underwriter
Actuary
Statistician
Economist

Job: Computer Programmer
Path #1: Two-year degree

Community colleges offer two-year data-processing courses, but a more focused program, perhaps in accounting, may give the student better employment prospects. Two-year degrees in computer science are hard to use because you will be competing with four-year college graduates in computer science. (Word processing on the computer requires a solid 60 word per minute typing speed and can be learned quickly and often free of charge though a temporary secretarial agency or the local adult education program.) In many areas of the country there are too many programmers, but this may not be true in your region. Proceed with caution; remember, engineers, scientists and actuaries also program. Software has also eliminated many programming jobs.

Unless you want to be the computer specialist on the job (in charge of all the programming and computers), you will need to learn about computers as they apply to a particular field. If you do want to be the specialist, see the engineering section first, as this is a more desirable background to have in computers.

Path #2: Bachelor's degree

A computer science degree from the sciences division of the undergraduate school may be too limited for you to enter the field. The question to ask yourself is where (in what industry or environment) you want to be a programmer. Whatever environment you choose, you may find computer training built into the program. For example, accountants learn all the computer applications for their field from their academic programs.

Some programmers find the job tedious. Matthew got a computer science degree because computers were a growing field and he was skilled at math. He is unhappy in the state budget office doing payroll reports. He is trying to use his contacts to get out of budget and into something more people-oriented like employee relations.

Let me show you an example of someone who succeeded with a computer science degree. According to an article printed May 1, 1994 in *The New York Times*, one graduate with a computer science degree from the University of Delaware found a job programming for a computer consulting company starting at $29,000 a year; she had interned for three summers beforehand at Giant Foods, a supermarket chain, in their operating systems department.

Information specialists often are librarians with master's degrees. This training offers them a lot of computer courses. They work in many settings including corporation libraries. See librarian in Arts and Communications.

Designers and writers of software create games, educational interactive videos on cooking, genealogy software, interactive encyclopedias of the human body—all materials for the home market. In this field, you unlock the potential of the computer to solve problems. For industries, there are also hundreds of software products from inventory control to diagnostic tools for doctors. These are written by those knowledgeable about the industry and about programming.

Job: Underwriter

Path #1: Internship

The insurance industry hires many clerks, claim examiners, programmers, underwriters, actuaries, statisticians, mathematicians and economists. An internship, summer job or part-time job is recommended to give you a taste of the business. Most insurance companies accept interns and often keep them on as full-time employees. For internship information write to the Society of Actuaries.

Path #2: Bachelor's degree

To do underwriting, you don't need to be a math expert; the job entails doing research—the number of times a doctor has been sued, for example—and then, using the actuarial tables, making a recommendation about what the doctor should pay for a malpractice policy. Jobs like this are available for students coming out of college, so doing a college internship will help. Your librarian or college placement officer will be able to help you find a directory of insurance companies. For more information, write to the American Institute for Property and Liability Underwriters, 720 Providence Rd., Malvern, PA 19355.

Job: Actuary

Actuaries predict what might influence the amount of the claims and therefore help set the terms of policies and their rates by studying past figures. Actuaries apply mathematical models to the risk problems of insurance companies and government pension plans. The major specialty areas are life, health, pensions and casualty insurance.

There are 10 examinations to be taken in the process of becoming a Fellow in the Actuarial Society. After passing the first exam you can get a summer internship during college with an insurance company. See the Society of Actuaries booklet, "Actuarial Training Programs," which lists internships jobs that offer further training for actuaries after college.

Although a college degree is not required to sit for the examinations, a keen interest and ability in statistics, calculus and probability is necessary. Employers prefer the applicant to have a college degree and to have passed the first two examinations in the sequence. To sit for the civil service examination to work for New York state, as an assistant actuary, for example, you need only pass Parts I and II of the examination sequence.

Here is one job listing from *The New York Times*:

> *"Chubb Life Insurance Company in Concord, N.H. Require B.S. in math or comparable field. Working knowledge of BASIC or LOTUS desired. Must be able to write reports of a technical nature and communicate effectively with all levels. Should have 2-3 exams passed or equivalent. Offer rotation program, study time, exam raises, study notes, textbooks and reimbursement of exam fees when passed. $ competitive."*

According to *Vocational Biographies*, there are only about 1,000 casualty actuaries in the United States. In college, Paul majored in math and studied calculus, compound interest, probability, statistics and computer science, and now he works for the American Automobile Association as underwriting director. He started at AAA as an actuarial assistant. Then he moved to several insurance companies to broaden his experience and returned to AAA as an area manager. He feels he should have taken the first two of the 10 exams required to become a fellow in the Casualty Actuarial Society while in college, because the knowledge tested on the exams is fresher if you have just finished the coursework. He is an associate member of the society and has completed seven of the 10 exams. Write to the Society of Actuaries, 475 N. Martingale Rd., Schaumburg, IL 60173, 708-706-3500 or the American Academy of Actuaries, 1720 I St. NW, 7th Floor, Washington, DC 20006, 202-223-8196.

Job: Statistician

Path #1: Government work

Some state governments are so eager to hire "numbers crunchers" that they will hire you if you have only two years of college statistics courses, but most professional statisticians receive the major part of their training at the graduate level. The undergraduate degree may be in the area in which they will use the statistics, such as business, engineering, biology or mathematics. See "Careers in Statistics" from the American Statistical Association.

Path #2: Bachelor's degree

The college graduate with a major in statistics can begin work at a government agency, corporation, investment brokerage house, public opinion or market research company or insurance company (as an underwriter). Here is one example from *The New York Times*, printed February 14, 1995:

> *"Biostatistician: You will be involved in a full range of statistical activities, including the design and analysis of clinical studies, analysis of efficiency and safety data, bioavailablity and pharmacokinetics. A master's degree or Ph.D. in Biostatistics and three or more years of related pharmaceutical industry experience are required." This job at a drug company in Jersey City pays about $85,000.*

As quality becomes the watchword in manufacturing, statistics provides the means to measure quality and achieve it. Statistics allows for the analysis of market trends. The development of new drugs to fight deadly disease depends heavily upon statisticians.

The demand for statisticians is currently high and the field is projected to grow. The field of statistics is crucial to the space program and efforts to save endangered species. Statistics support research in global warming and the greenhouse effect. The federal government uses statisticians in many different agencies, For example, statisticians for the National Oceanic and Atmospheric Administration do crop forecasting.

The statistician Sharon LeDuc worked on the EPA's Sahelian Project. The Sahel, a region in north central Africa, has experienced severe drought for more than a decade. According to a 1990 article in *Occupational Outlook Quarterly*, the project developed a system that could point out future famine areas and encourage the introduction of better land use methods. Contact the American Statistical Association, 1429 Duke St., Alexandria, VA 22314-3402, 703-684-1221, for a list of colleges offering degrees in statistics.

Job: Economist

Although the bachelor's degree in economics and high grades may allow you to get a job in business, the doctorate is essential to gaining employment as an economist. In addition to the required courses in economics, you should have a background in finance, cost and financial accounting, business administration, statistics, mathematics, English and computers. English is a more important asset than a highly technical knowledge of statistics and mathematics. You may be able to obtain a full-time job as a junior business economist after completing undergraduate study and carry on graduate work on a part-time basis.

Economics is the largest and most highly paid of the basic social sciences, quantitative techniques to analyze data. In business, economists supply management with information with which to make decisions. Dave became the chief economist for a large petroleum firm after gaining experience as a financial economist for a large bank. He shows his firm how it will be impacted by the larger economy, playing the role of skeptic to protect investments, serving on task forces of industry trade groups and acting as a spokesperson.

Another economist worked on a development plan for the government of Guam, then for an international company as a corporate economist. This job included forecasting product demand, prices and sales, conducting plant site location studies and market research and lobbying at the state and national level, which became formalized into the Tokyo GATT, a trade agreement.

Economists also are employed by brokerage houses, banks, insurance companies, government and universities. According to an article by Nancy Chambers in the July 1995 issue of *Working Woman*, pharmaco-economists, new to the industry, do cost-benefit analyses of drug therapies for hospital chains, government agencies, insurance companies and HMOs. For their booklet, contact: National Association of Business Economists, 1233 20th St. NW, Suite 505, Washington, DC 20036, 202-463-6223.

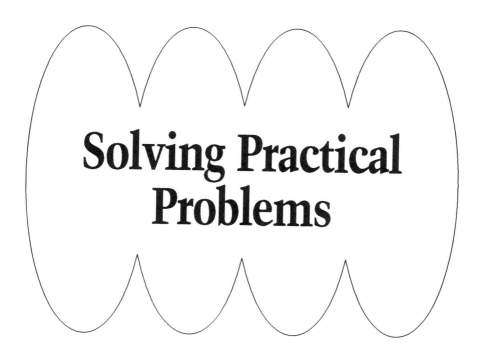

Solving Practical Problems

These occupations require an interest in solving real-life problems. These are fields for the practical, no-nonsense, "just the facts, please" types, people who score high on sensing in the temperament tests in Chapter 4, people who want to produce an excellent product.

Engineering and Related Fields
Marine, Fire, Law Enforcement and Transportation
Building Trades
Hospitality
Horticulture

Engineering and Related Fields

Electronic Technician   Auto Mechanic
Land Surveyor   Airplane Mechanic
Engineer   Pilot

Job: Electronic Technician

Path #1: Free training

Check out your local, free Jobs Training Partnership Act (JTPA) programs at the unemployment office for photocopy machine repair technician or telecommunications technician (installation and repair of telephones). A high school diploma may not be required, but you will be required to have at least ninth-grade math and reading and a low income to qualify for free training. These programs are likely to offer free training if there is a shortage of repair people in your area. See if this is true before you invest your time and effort. Avoid training for draftsperson, because most engineers now do their own drafting on computers.

Path #2: Training as a computer repair technician

Private vocational schools offer short training (several months) in computer maintenance and repair. These programs require at least ninth-grade math and reading and/or a high school diploma. You can use student loans and grants at these private schools.

The placement rate of the school you choose is very important. By New York state law, the placement rates of colleges and training schools must appear at the end of their catalogs. Look at these rates and then talk to some of the graduates. Use MacMillan's *Blue Books, Occupational Education*, in the library, to find private schools. *The Degrees Offered* volume will have local college programs.

An industry has to be growing quite rapidly to employ fresh graduates right out of school with no experience. Make sure that you are interested in dealing with customers, usually in their workplaces, and that you wouldn't mind driving from customer to customer.

Companies that sell photocopy equipment may be able to help you find good local training because they sell service contracts, requiring technicians.

Path #3: Short-term training

Keith attended a one-year private vocational school electronics program and started to install and service computerized electronic security systems. After doing this for a few years, he and his friend George, who was a salesman for the company, decided to borrow $50,000 from George's father-in-law and go out on their own. Many of the clients of the old company became their clients and now they have nearly 100 employees and each makes a comfortable living. Because of new technologies emerging in electronics, short training and hard work can result in success. See above for information about finding the ideal school program in your region.

Path #4: Recording engineer (technician)

Most radio and television stations, including college stations, have internship programs for students, or they take volunteers. You may have to do some unrelated tasks, including getting coffee and sweeping floors, but overall, this experience will help you understand the duties of the recording engineer. Television work, at least in areas where a high degree of electronic training is not essential, includes the operation of cameras, lights, microphone booms and tape machines. An entering technician with an associate's degree in electronics and experience at a radio or television station may be able to find a job in this very competitive field.

In the past, the technician was required to have the FCC (Federal Communications Commission) Second Class license and anyone who worked in a station was required to have a Third Class restricted permit. Now the FCC has made the station responsible for all training requirements for personnel.

To repair transmitting equipment, you must have the Second Class license, but employees of the station do not need to be licensed. The Second Class license examination is given at your FCC Field Operations Bureau on a quarterly basis. Consult the blue pages at the back of the telephone directory for the location in your region.

Many chief engineers at major stations have at least the bachelor's degree in engineering. For more information about this field, contact: Society of Motion Picture and Television Engineers, 595 W. Hartsdale Ave., White Plains, NY 10607, 914-761-1100.

Path #5: Studio recording engineer

To be a recording engineer in a studio, you need training in a private technical school and a job placement in a studio where you will work as an assistant, acting as a runner. This advice comes from Al Schmitt, who has won three Grammy awards for his work in the studio. He learned everything on the job because there were no schools at the time. Today, audio technology technical schools exist, but they can be very expensive. No matter which school you choose, you need to find out if they will be able to place you.

Most cities don't have very many recording studios; the business is concentrated in areas like Los Angeles, New York and Nashville. Many people are interested in this field, so exercise caution; you will have trouble getting into a studio if your school doesn't offer placement services.

Some recording engineers learned how to operate the equipment by working with transmitters or installing and repairing other electronic audio equipment (intercoms, for example). They used these experiences to get into studios.

See "Mastering the Mix" in *The Recording Industry Career Handbook*, which can be obtained by writing to: The NARAS Foundation, 3402 Pico Blvd., Santa Monica, CA 90405.

Path #6: Telecommunications technician

Helen Paxson Waicunas is a senior telecommunications analyst for the *Los Angeles Times*. She started as a telephone operator at another newspaper, where her duties included voice and data communications, budget, evaluation, selection, purchase, implementation and management of all telecommunication-related products in more than 40 locations. She can install a phone system, connect a conference call or assist new employees with voice mail in addition to many more complex tasks. She got a lot of on-the-job training and learned a lot just by doing. For the last five years she has worked for the *Los Angeles Times*, providing all telecommunications services to six field offices. She also works on special projects such as installing the voice, data and fiber network for the printing plant.

You can learn a lot about this field as an intern or assistant. Newspapers will not hire engineers for these jobs; rather, they promote from within the company. Newspapers use a lot of telecommunications equipment, so they are good places to learn about telecommunications.

Write for the Newspaper Association of America Foundation booklet, "Newspaper: What's in It for Me?" at 11600 Sunrise Valley Dr., Reston, VA 22091. This booklet gives information about various newspaper jobs.

Path #7: On-the-job training

You may be able to get a job in production in a large company that does the kind of engineering in which you are interested. A high school diploma and evidence of interest, in the form of a hobby for example, will be required to get an assembly-line job, and the employer will test your math skills before hiring you. If you stay with the company, you may be upgraded to technician. The technician performs calculations, sets up tests, calibrates instruments and writes reports. On the job, you will be able to observe teams of scientists, engineers and technicians working together; this will help you decide which role you would like to play on the team.

Many technicians have learned on the job, or have been trained at the employer's expense. You can find companies which may be potential employers in the yellow pages and in employer directories in the public library. Manufacturing cut three million jobs overseas between 1972 and 1992 but it still provides employment for more than 18 million workers, according to Mark Mittelhauser, an economist in the Office of Employment Projections, Bureau of Labor Statistics.

Path #8: Associate's or bachelor's degree in engineering technology

Training for technicians is offered in associate's degree programs. Some technicians work in research and development in major corporations, others work in the repair or customer service field. If you decide to earn an associate's degree, it is wise to choose courses that will be accepted if you transfer to an undergraduate, four-year engineering program or a four-year engineering technology program. The four-year engineering school will advise you about which community college courses you should take.

You will learn computer assisted design (CAD) while in the community college, but preparing as a drafter is probably not a good bet, because engineers can do their own drafting on computer.

Sometimes two-year programs offer cooperative education (alternating periods of school and work). The associate's degree programs may offer paid work experience for credit. Sometimes having this experience will give you an edge in the job market. For a list of accredited two-year programs that offer co-ops, write to the Accreditation Board for Engineering and Technology (ABET), 345 East 47th St., New York, NY 10017, 212-705-7000.

Engineering technicians and technologists often work as engineers, but at a much lower pay rate than those with engineering degrees.

Tom (*Vocational Biographies*) is a technical aide for Sandia National Laboratories in Albuquerque, N.M. He signed up for a five-year apprenticeship in this firm, which does nuclear research services for the defense and energy departments of the federal government. In the beginning Tom was trained on instrumentation and refrigeration, although he had come to the job with 15 years of mechanical training in aircraft mechanics and some computer operator experience. Now he researches the impact of storing nuclear waste inside mountains. Tom designs and supervises the data acquisition systems and the making of computer hardware items required by the project. The in-house training offered in computers, geology and math contributed greatly to his ability to do this job. His employer would like to see an associate's degree in engineering technology as a minimum education requirement for this job.

Job: Land Surveyor

The courses needed to become a surveyor are offered in engineering technology programs. The local agency that regulates the licensing of professionals can give you the requirements for land surveyors in the state. Surveyor's helpers who have experience and some formal training can advance to licensed surveyors. These workers are in greater demand in regions of the country where there is a lot of new construction.

Job: Engineer

Despite the fact that an increasing amount of manufacturing workers have been laid off over the last 30 years, America is still a major manufacturer and there is always a need for engineers. Here are the manufacturing industries projected to have the fastest annual output growth between 1992 and 2005, according to economist Mark Mittelhauser at the Bureau of Labor Statistics, with the annual percent increase in parentheses to the right of the industry:

railroad equipment (3.4)
electronic components (3.5)
measuring and controlling devices, watches (3.7)
electromedical apparatus (3.7)
chemical products (3.9)
publishing (3.9)
metal services (4.1)
plastic products (4.2)
aircraft and missile parts (4.2)
broadcasting communications equipment (4.4)
truck and bus bodies, trailers, motor homes (4.8)
semiconductors (5.6)
boat building and repairing (5.9)
medical instruments and supplies (6.1)
computer equipment (8.1)

Remember these fields vary in size, so although computer equipment is growing quickly, it will produce fewer jobs than some larger fields such as commercial printing, medical instruments, aircraft/ missile parts and plastic products. A total of 466,000 jobs will be created in these four categories alone from 1992 to 2005.

Kinds of engineers. Electrical/electronic engineers working in telecommunications can put the branches of a chain supermarket's stores on one computer network. Electric power engineers can design power plants. Biomedical engineers can fix an MRI (magnetic resonance imaging) machine. Industrial or chemical engineers can design drug factories. Mechanical engineers can design car parts. Industrial engineers can organize an assembly line using robots. Materials engineers can design skin for a spacecraft. You don't have to know which of these specialties you want before applying to engineering school. To get into an engineering program, you should complete a college preparatory program that includes physics, chemistry, four units of mathematics, (normally covering intermediate algebra, trigonometry and plane geometry) and English.

More advanced study in math and science (precalculus or calculus, etc.) in high school is recommended. Some schools, such as Rensselaer Polytechnic Institute (RPI), in Troy, N.Y., strongly recommend achievement tests in English composition, advanced mathematics and either physics or chemistry. These will give you a chance to show your skills. If possible, you should also take advanced placement tests, because good performance on these can exempt you from certain courses.

Women in high school and college should consider engineering because schools are looking for qualified women and engineering is an opportunity to make a good living. The National Association for Women in Education has a two-part series in their journal *Initiatives* called "Gender Equity in Math and Science." In the second issue they describe Purdue University's mentor program for women engineering students. Contact NAWE, Suite 210, 1325 18th St. NW, Washington, DC 20036-6511, 202-659-9330.

Engineering can be a stepping stone to management. According to a December, 1994 article in *Working Woman,* Ursala Burns is an African-American woman and engineer working for Xerox. Ursala was chosen for management because of her nimble mind and good communications skills. She moved through a series of jobs: strategic planning in 1984, then systems engineering manager on a design team, then executive assistant to two CEOs. Then, when they reorganized in 1992, she leapfrogged from her staff job to vice-president and general manager for fax machines and color copiers. Her unit was expanded to include all digital office products, including developing a new high-tech copier, managing a troubled fax business and creating new digital products.

Louis Gerstner, Jr., (*Current Biography Yearbook*) the current head of IBM, got an engineering degree from Dartmouth and an M.B.A. from Harvard. At 31, he was a senior partner for McKinsey and Company, a management consulting company, then CEO of American Express, RJR Nabisco and IBM.

If you do not want to be an executive, many companies reward their engineers for increased experience. Professional Engineers (P.E.s) have the master's degree in engineering; this credential is needed for major engineering jobs.

Engineers can be self-employed if they are entrepreneurial, too. According to a July 5, 1995 article in *The New York Times*, Paul Gerst, an electrical engineer, built a cogeneration plant in Escondido, Calif. He sells electrical power to the local utility under a 30-year contract. The utility is required to buy the electricity he produces. They signed a bad contract so they pay Gerst several cents above the going rate; he had to sue the utility to get paid. He built the power plant in an enterprise zone so the city gives him tax breaks. He financed the complex largely through California Alternative Energy funding bonds. Gerst built cogeneration plants around the country for others; this one was for him.

Here are the four-year engineering programs at RPI. You can major in one branch and take a concentration, which is like a minor, in another branch:

Biomedical engineering includes systems physiology, clinical medicine and surgery, cellular bioengineering and impedance imaging.

Chemical engineering includes fluid mechanics, heat transfer, polymers and high temperature kinetics.

Civil and environmental engineering includes structural engineering, transportation engineering, solid and hazardous wastes.

Electric power engineering includes power switching, electric and magnetic field computation, and semi-conductor power electronics.

Materials engineering includes glass and ceramics, composites, electronic materials, metallurgy, polymers and surfaces.

Electrical, computer and systems engineering
includes control, robotics and automation, communications,
information and signal processing, computer engineering,
plasma engineering and electromagnetics, solid state and
integrated electronics.

**Mechanical engineering, aeronautical engineering
and mechanics** includes aeronautics, design,
manufacturing and space technology.

Engineering physics includes nuclear engineering.

Path #1: Co-op education

Engineering schools offer co-ops. This refers to full-time work for
between $11 and $14 an hour as an engineer, alternating with
school semesters. Gaining practical experience, learning about career options, acquiring employment contacts and earning money are
a few reasons for doing co-ops. Many schools allow you to co-op after
the first year; some schools alternate semesters of co-op and school.
Smaller schools cannot offer all of their courses each semester, so a
longer co-op period is advantageous. The nature of the work is negotiated with the employer and then approved by the faculty. Obtaining a co-op assignment is a competitive process.

Candy worked as an environmental engineer for an environmental engineering consulting firm in Virginia. As a co-op student,
the first thing she did was OSHA Training Standard 1910.120, a 40-
hour training period for engineers at hazardous waste sites. She
learned how to maintain monitoring equipment and sample a site.
She did support and development of effluent guidelines for the pulp
and paper industry, and collected the data and analyzed answers to
a questionnaire on waste water treatment. She found this experience to be very confirming of her interest.

John did a mechanical engineering co-op experience, working for
a company that manufactures surgical instruments for eye doctors.
He scaled up drawings for new parts for a surgical instrument
called the Otoscope, worked on AutoCAD software and interacted
with the engineering department within the company where the
prototypes of the parts were made.

Jim's biomedical co-op was at a major medical center where he did a combination of technical equipment repair and research and development. For example, he worked on automation of medical records using monitored charting of vital signs, tested circuit board designs and ran the computer program controlling the infusion pumps for cardiac bypass surgeries.

In the pharmaceutical, cement, coal and polymer industries, solid waste is a concern. Ann spent many months at a major chemical company, figuring out which kind of processing worked best, and included in her research a specific system then in use to see if it was the most efficient device available. She found this work to be a little isolating and plans to look for something in production for her next co-op experience so that she will have the opportunity to interact with people.

The International Association of Students for Technical Experience offers summer work placements in foreign countries for college students in science, math and engineering programs. Write to IASTE/US, 10400 Little Patuxent Parkway, Suite 250, Columbia, MD 21044-3510, or call 410-997-3068.

Job: Auto Mechanic

Path #1: Informal apprenticeship

You can test your interest in auto mechanics through an informal apprenticeship. Sherry had always worked on her motorcycle and automobile; her father was a mechanic and taught her how to fix these vehicles. She started working in her family's garage as the receptionist and, for three years, scheduled repair appointments and ordered parts from suppliers. Finally, there was an opening in the shop and she was offered a chance to work as a mechanic. Now she is in her second year of repair work. She plans to open an all-women-mechanics repair shop in five years.

Training informally, starting with oil and tire changes, and gradually doing more complicated repairs, is a real option. Often, school will speed up the hands-on learning process, but for young people who are patient, work hard, have a good mechanical aptitude and would prefer avoiding further schooling, the small shop is an ideal place to learn.

To get a job as a trainee or apprentice, make it clear to the garage owner that you are responsible, dependable, hard-working, cooperative and interested in the field and give an example of each trait. If you feel it will work to your benefit, show the employer the work you have done on your own car.

Sometimes beginners get jobs helping customers find auto parts. These jobs may help you learn auto mechanics (Sherry feels ordering parts helped her); they don't require any particular training or education beyond perhaps a high school diploma and you could go on to own an auto parts store.

Path #2: Formal training

Your high school or local adult education program probably offers a course in auto mechanics. This course may be free or very inexpensive. In addition, your educational district may offer a two-year mechanics program to high school students and adults. Programs require eighth-grade reading and math levels for course admission. This course may prepare you to take the National Institute for Automotive Service Excellence (ASE) exams. When you pass one or more of the following tests and meet the two-year experience requirement, you become an ASE Certified Automobile Technician:

Engine repair	Brakes
Automatic transmission/	Electrical/electronic systems
transaxle	Heating and air conditioning
Manual drive train and axles	Engine performance
Suspension and steering	

When you pass all of them you become an ASE Certified Master Automobile Technician. For more information, contact the National Institute for Automotive Excellence, 13505 Dulles Technology Dr., Herndon, VA 22071-3415. You can pick up a booklet about the exam at many auto parts stores.

Certification by ASE is required to be considered for employment as a mechanic at many auto dealerships, such as Subaru and Ford. Graduation from a high school course is not adequate preparation. However, graduates of the high school course often get entry-level work in the industry at places such as Sears, Midas, etc., even though they are not ready for dealership work. Often they go on to technical schools, or either private or community college.

Path #3: Two-year program

Local community colleges may offer two-year programs in auto technology; choose a program which has training for a specific manufacturer. For example, in New York, Hudson Valley Community College has General Motors training and Columbia-Greene Community College trains for Toyota and Ford. To work for a dealer, it is desirable to have been trained in one of their programs. There are also private two-year technical schools (see MacMillan's *Blue Books* for a list).

Path #4: Manufacturers' schools

A job at a dealership will give you further training. The dealer sponsors the employee in the program. For example, Stewart now instructs high school students and adults who want vocational training.

He got the job because he had 15 years of experience as a mechanic, graduated from a two-year community college and went to work for a dealership from which he was sent to the manufacturer's schools one or two days a month for training in a specific area. Some mechanics in dealerships earn between $40,000 and $60,000 a year; investing in two-year college programs to get a dealership job will insure that your earnings increase with your experience.

Job: Airplane Mechanic

Path #1: Apprentice mechanic/lineperson

All work done on planes must be done by a licensed airframe and power plant (A & P) mechanic who signs his or her name in the plane's log after doing work on it. If the job gives experience repairing both airplane engines (power plants) and airframes (the structural parts of the airplane), you are eligible to take the combined A & P examination for the A & P license after 30 months on the job. The mechanic who trains you vouches for the breadth of your experience. Airplane mechanics for the major airlines earn around $22 an hour.

Jim is preparing to take his A & P exam to become a licensed mechanic, and he also works at a private airport as a mechanic's helper and a lineperson on the ground, moving, parking, fueling and towing aircraft. In some jobs, the linepersons will service and maintain the interiors of corporate jets and do customer service jobs like having rental cars available, putting ice and coffee on the plane, etc. He is learning quickly because he has had a great deal of experience and training on automobiles. According to Daniel Sherman, Director of Facilities for Clay Lacy Aviation at Van Nuys Airport in California, some experience with jets will allow you to work at a Fixed Base Operation (FBO), which services jets and does repairs.

FAPA, 4959 Massachusetts Blvd., Atlanta, GA 30337, 770-997-8097, has a monthly aviation maintenance job report. According to the report, mechanics are currently having a difficult time finding jobs in many areas of the country. You may want to visit your local airports and talk to mechanics about local conditions.

For more information, the "Aviation Careers Series" includes a booklet, *Airport Careers*, available from the Federal Aviation Administration, Aviation Education Program, Superintendent of Documents, Retail Distribution Division, Consigned Branch, 8610 Cherry Lane, Laurel, MD 20707.

Path #2: Approved school for mechanics

If you graduate from a Federal Aviation Administration (FAA) approved school, you can sit for the A & P examination. School programs typically last 12 to 24 months. You can complete the requirements in one year if you work eight-hour days.

A list of certified approved schools is available in Advisory Circular 147/2X. Send $1 to: Superintendent of Documents, U.S. Government Printing Office, Washington, DC 20402, or consult the circular at your regional U.S. Government Printing Office. For more information about training, write to the Office of Aviation Education, FAA, 400 7th St. SW, Washington, DC 20590, or call 202-366-7500.

Job: Pilot

Path #1: Private pilot

Your local adult education program may offer training for private pilots. There is a written exam and a flight test. The standards to pass the exam are available from the FAA and may be distributed in the course. Only 40 hours of flying time are required to take the test, but this can cost several thousand dollars. You will need to pay an instructor and rent a plane. Most pilots train in the military for this reason.

Path #2: Military pilot

Many people enter aviation through the military. For example, Jennifer Dormire is a West Point cadet who plans to become a helicopter pilot. After leaving the military, she will have the flying experience and licenses necessary to be considered for employment with a major airline, perhaps beginning as flight engineer and moving up to pilot or captain.

According to Joseph Berger (*The New York Times*), there are 473 women and 4,055 men at West Point. Women have been at the academy for 18 years, so the military should be considered an option for all women interested in aviation or aeronautical engineering. You are obligated to spend five years in the Army after graduating from the Academy at West Point. The Air Force and Coast Guard pilot training program is described in the section on Marine occupations.

Path #3: Commercial pilot

Commercial pilots need to complete 250 hours of flying time and earn a second-class medical rating. The FAA administers the examination for commercial pilot to men and women over the age of 18. The exam covers meteorology, physics, algebra, trigonometry, geometry and mechanical drawing.

John is an airport manager, pilot, licensed mechanic and licensed inspector. He contracts with a partner to operate a small airport. Because he has a commercial pilot's license and a mechanic's license, he can do such things as take up a district attorney who wants to view a crime scene, do a demonstration on a plane for sale and supervise repairs on a plane. With a commercial pilot's license you can fly cargo and passengers for hire (the private pilot can have passengers, but not for hire). Some airport managers study at Embry-Riddle Aeronautical University in Daytona Beach, Fla., and get a degree in aeronautical studies/aviation management, then start as operations agents at airports, but this school also graduates many pilots.

Path #4: Jet pilot

To fly corporate jets, you need a commercial or Air Transport (ATP) license, multi-engine and instrument ratings and a physical exam. Corporate pilots are in demand because 75 percent of general flying is done by business aircraft. Average mid-range salary for a corporate pilot is $50,000 a year, according to the FAA.

To be a major airline captain, you need the ATP license and instrument rating, a more rigorous physical exam than is required to fly corporate jets, and you must be 21 to 35 years of age. Both corporate pilots and pilots for major airlines often have degrees in aeronautical engineering. Major airline captains earn approximately $140,000 a year, according to the FAA. Corporate flight departments often hire aeronautical engineers who can do both engineering tasks and fly executives to meetings.

Write to the FAA for their *Aviation Careers Series,* at the address above, or call for help in planning. You could call the headquarters of the FAA aviation education program in Washington, DC, at 202-366-7500 and ask for the name and phone number of the person in your region. Keep in mind that the FAA may be going through a period of reorganization because of the deregulation of the industry in the mid-1990s.

Marine, Fire, Law Enforcement and Transportation jobs

Sailor
Diver
Firefighter
Police Officer

Corrections Officer
Security Worker
Transportation Manager

Job: Sailor

Path #1: Seaman's apprentice, Coast Guard

Matt worked his way up through the ranks, from seaman's apprentice to boatswain's mate. After 10 years he was placed in charge of his own lighthouse station, marking the river for mariners. He loves his choice, but he also could have worked toward heading up a search and rescue station.

The Coast Guard is part of the Department of Transportation, although it is a military operation. In the case of war, it becomes part of the Navy. The U.S. Coast Guard licenses those who work on ships that carry the U.S. flag and are part of our merchant marine (all commercial boats that carry passengers or cargo). Three to six months is the usual sign-up time for merchant mariners.

Keith started as a seaman's apprentice in the Coast Guard and worked his way up to chief petty officer and assistant navigator or quartermaster, mostly in New York City. He started collecting a pension at 39 when he retired and now has a civilian job with the Coast Guard.

When you take the tests for promotion, the Coast Guard provides on-the-job training and study guides. You are competing with everyone else in your pay grade. Through an elaborate system of tests and licenses, you can achieve Master Chief (the senior enlisted man or woman on the ship), second and third mate (deck positions) or chief, second or third engineer (power plant positions).

On a large ship there might be eight to 10 licensed positions, (commissioned and enlisted) and many unlicensed helpers, for a total of 45 to 50 people on a large cutter. The U.S. Government Printing Office will have materials on the licenses offered by the Coast Guard, but the first step is to see a recruiter. As in all military areas, you can take the tests with no obligation and then see what type of training they will offer before you sign a contract. To take the aptitude tests, you must be 17, have a high school diploma or GED, have no felony arrests and pass the physical tests and basic aptitude tests in reading, reasoning and arithmetic on the AFVAB (Armed Forces Vocational Aptitude Battery). The Arco Publishing Company publishes review books for these tests.

Make sure the contract specifies the area you desire. Here are the ratings (or training areas) from which you can choose when you enlist: Deck and Ordnance Group (boatswain's mate, quartermaster or navigator, radarman, gunner's mate, fire control technician); Engineering and Hull Group (damage controlman, machinery technician, electronics technician, telephone technician, electrician's mate); Aviation Group (aviation machinist mate, aviation survivalman, aviation electrician's mate, aviation structural mechanic, aviation electronics technician); Administrative and Scientific Group (marine science technician, yeoman or personnel clerk, storekeeper, public affairs specialist, radioman, subsistence specialist or cook, health services technician). Enlisted people enter after high school. Those who enter after college are commissioned as officers.

Everybody starts as an apprentice. You can advance to petty officer status by choosing a school when you enlist. This is called the Guaranteed School Program. For example, to be an aviation electronics technician, you could choose 24 weeks in intensive training in a school in Elizabeth City, N.C., or 12 weeks in a school in Yorktown, Va., to be a machinery technician.

You will be tested at enlistment to see if you are qualified for training. Or you can take correspondence courses in your specialty and then sit for examinations in conjunction with on-the-job training after enlistment. You can get money for college through the Veteran's Program if you don't reenlist.

In the civilian environment, the boatswain's mate is qualified to be a pier superintendent, a tugboat crewman, marina supervisor, marina operator or a ship's pilot.

Path #2: Enter as an officer with a college degree

You can apply to the four-year Coast Guard Academy until you are 22, or you can advance to commissioned officer by applying to Officer Candidate School as an enlisted person (nonofficer). The Navy and Air Force offer similar programs and opportunities for those who want to be at sea. If you are willing to join the Naval Reserve as a midshipman, you can receive a $3,000-a-year stipend for your study at a maritime academy, which will give you an engineering degree and prepare you to sit for licenses in the merchant marine or in the Coast Guard, Navy or National Oceanographic and Atmospheric Administration.

MacMillan's *Blue Books, Degrees Offered* lists these under Marine Engineering or Marine Science. Contact the local recruiting station for current information.

Getting the Third Mate and Third Assistant Engineer Licenses—two officer titles—show that you have learned about ship systems including the steam or diesel power plant, communications, navigation, etc. The Coast Guard gives these licensing examinations, and graduates of the maritime academies are eligible to sit for them.

Job: Diver

Path #1: Scuba diving classes

All diving students are asked to fill out a medical questionnaire. If there are areas of concern, a doctor makes the determination about the student's fitness to dive. Don't treat this lightly; there are certain heart defects that shouldn't be discovered under water.

Jeff is an ex-school teacher who has been teaching scuba diving for many years. Now he combines teaching at his own school with work as an administrator in his local police department. There are many national associations that certify instructors in the diving field, and certificates issued by these associations are accepted around the world. As you train to dive, you will get the certificate offered by your instructor.

Path #2: Commercial diving school

There are commercial diving schools that train student divers, usually between 25 and 35 years of age, to work under water as divers and tenders off of oil rigs (offshore diving). You can make $80,000 as an established diver in a good season.

Inland diving involves a variety of work including structural inspection, concrete construction and repair, piling work, hull inspection and repair, salvage work and sea harvest. The yearly salary is between $25,000 and $40,000 for an established diver. See MacMillan's *Blue Books, Occupational Education* for the names of schools that train divers.

Path #3: Diving instructor

Diving instructors hold a rank beyond advanced scuba, rescue and dive master. They can teach in a school or open their own, and may also salvage valuables, explore wrecks and recover boats or vehicles. Some instructors offer special credentials in ice diving or wreck diving. Diving instructors who work at diving equipment stores or resorts in exotic locations are often paid with room, board, free equipment and perhaps a small stipend. Often police or sheriffs' departments use diving teams, composed of policemen who are also divers. This inland diving may not require commercial diving preparation because most of it will be done in less than 100 feet of water and it uses air diving procedures, whereas deep sea diving uses helium and oxygen gasses.

Job: Firefighter

Here are the requirements to work for one city in upstate New York: have a high school diploma or GED; pass a physical which includes hearing, vision, agility, strength, endurance, weight and blood pressure; pass an exam which tests reading comprehension; and pass exams in math, reasoning in firefighting situations, mechanical reasoning, reading graphs and diagrams and following written instructions. Volunteer experience is very helpful.

Heidi has been with the force almost two years. She started 10 years ago with the rescue squad and joined the volunteer firefighters. She volunteered for eight years, then took the test to get paid working for the city's fire department. The fire department handles medical emergencies in addition to fires, so her earlier paramedic training is helpful.

Heidi enjoys helping people and this is what she values most about the job. She cautions women considering the occupation not to apply in order to make a political statement; you need to be interested in firefighting and medical emergencies. The work is very physically demanding and you will, because of your smaller size, work harder than the men. Volunteer fire departments are wonderful places to test your interest, and they often have a cadet branch for teenagers. Heidi is married; her husband is also a firefighter so he understands the scheduling problems. The nature of the job requires her to work 12-hour shifts, nights and holidays.

Job: Police Officer

Police officers and sheriffs' deputies are employed by cities, towns or states. You can get specific requirements for the positions from the personnel office of the local unit.

Path #1: Cadet

Some departments train and employ cadets who enter the force when they are 21 years of age—the usual age required by departments.

Path #2: After high school

Usually, applicants who have a high school diploma and meet the physical and character requirements are eligible to sit for the civil service examinations. All police officers are expected to be working toward a college degree. The John Jay College of Criminal Justice, for example, offers courses in which the same professor presents the same materials in both day and evening classes. This allows those working rotating shifts to continue their classes.

Special agents for the Federal Bureau of Investigation (FBI) and the Central Intelligence Agency (CIA), part of the State Department, are required to have college degrees. Alcohol, Tobacco and Firearms Agents, customs agents, U.S. Marshals, drug enforcement officers and secret service workers also need to have college degrees. (See the instructions for getting jobs with the federal government in Politics and Civil Service, Selling and Managing.)

The job requires many of the skills of a social worker, especially a desire to protect and help people. An appreciation for the importance of stress management is critical to success and to continued good health on the job.

Criminologists may be civilians working in the police department who become specialists in arson, ballistics, controlled substances or fingerprinting.

A November 30, 1994 article in *The New York Times* says that, at age 43, Beverly Harvard is the only African-American woman to head a major police department. She took the tests for police officer after graduating from college, and passed. In Atlanta she represents a new breed of police officer—college educated, trained in management and very politically savvy.

Job: Corrections Officer

Corrections is a part of criminal justice and law enforcement, but salaries are generally lower than elsewhere in law enforcement. Wardens make around $70,000 a year in New York state. Corrections departments hire both counselors and child welfare case workers with bachelor's degrees, parole officers and interviewers.

Executive leadership training for women in corrections is offered in some state systems, because about 30 percent of guards are women. Cheryl Clark trains correction officers and directs an incarceration division for the New York State Department of Correctional Services. She teaches inmates "how to live as successful citizens by teaching them how to learn," as she puts it. Prisons also hire support service personnel.

Often guards come out of the military. Joseph Young was an enlisted and commissioned marine who rapidly advanced in the federal prison system. He views corrections as a chance to manage a community.

For more information about these and other jobs in corrections, write to The American Correctional Association, 8025 Laurel Lakes Ct., Laurel, MD 20707, 301-206-5100 or 800-ACA-JOIN. This association offers an unpaid internship program in corrections and a magazine, *Corrections Today*.

The courts also hire administrators, probation officers, pre-trial services workers, victim services workers and mediators.

Job: Security Worker

With some experience, work in security may be available to you. Alarm investigator, credit investigator, security detective, loss prevention worker and security manager are jobs that are often held by experienced people who may not have a degree, although they may be ex-police officers or ex-military members. According to the Bureau of Labor Statistics, this is a growing field all across the United States.

Job: Transportation Manager

Path #1: Entry-level position

The following are entry-level positions with one transit company in New Jersey: accounting clerk, computer operator, electronics technician, equipment maintenance worker, bus operator, transit information clerk, revenue clerk, secretary, ticket seller and trainperson. If you are hired for one of these positions you will have the opportunity to gain experience; read the personnel bulletin board on which openings are posted, think about where you would like to go next and what further training and education you will need to get there.

One path in transportation might be to work full-time and take evening college courses, including computer and logistics courses in an engineering program. Transportation offers opportunities to the hard worker and can be entered with a minimum of credentials. For example, engineers and other train workers get on-the-job training and move up, based on their performance.

Path #2: Working your way up to manager

Railroads, transit systems and trucking and shipping companies all need good managers with computer backgrounds. Some have engineering degrees and are logistics specialists, but this is not a requirement.

According to a May 9, 1992 article in *The New York Times*, Shirley DeLibero, the head of New Jersey Transit, oversees 1,800 buses on 154 routes and 642 trains on 12 rail lines. She is a mechanic and can take a bus apart and put it back together. She studied for her associate's degrees in engineering and business administration and then took a job as a maintenance supervisor for a fleet of trolley cars for the Green Line, part of the Boston subway. She then moved to the Washington, D.C., transit system as an assistant general manager/administrator, then to Dallas's transit system and finally to New Jersey Transit. As of 1992, she was one of eight women in the country heading transit systems. She works 12- to 18-hour days, earning $150,000 a year.

These publications may help you learn about major employers and job openings in the industry: *Railway Age*, 345 Hudson St., New York, NY 10014, 212-620-7200; *American Shipper: The Monthly Journal of International Logistics*, P.O. Box 4728, Jacksonville, FL 32201, 800-874-6422; *Shipping Digest: The National Shipping Weekly of Export Transportation*, 51 Madison Ave., New York, NY 10010, 212-689-4411; and *Chilton's Commercial Carrier Journal for Professional Fleet Managers*, 1 Chilton Way, Radnor, PA 19089, 610-964-4524.

Building jobs

Electrician
Plumber
Carpenter

Job: Electrician

You must have good color vision for electrical work (be able to distinguish green from red); school and apprenticeship programs will test your vision. You must be bondable (no felony convictions), so your employer can take out insurance on you when you work alone in a house, and you must have a driver's license and a car. Employers will require the high school diploma or equivalent. You need to have had at least a B average in mathematics.

Path #1: Training in electrical subjects

Your board of education's adult education department may offer inexpensive training. These programs may require an eighth grade math and reading level. For example, say your local adult education program offers trade math, blueprint reading, electrical theory, electrical code and semiconductor theory of electrical, motor and generator theory. If you complete all the courses, meeting two nights a week for five years, you will be ready to sit for the licensing exams to become an electrician. Service repair technicians for appliances; oil burner repair technicians; and heating, refrigeration and air conditioning installers and repairers are all jobs for which you might be able to get training at local adult education programs. Or, you can find on-the-job training and study at night.

Path #2: Union apprenticeships

Electricians are licensed by and sit for exams given by the locality. The union and the local library have review books for you to use in preparing for the apprenticeship tests. Studying for them will be easier if you get someone in the union to guide you. However, you don't have to be in the union to take the exams.

Union apprenticeships for electricians must be posted at the state unemployment office. Of the construction and maintenance electricians employed in the U.S., 70 percent served an apprenticeship in a union-sponsored apprenticeship program. To enter a program you must have a high school diploma.

The apprentice completes four years of training and related classroom instruction. Over the years, the apprentice earns half to nearly full journeyman's wages. In many localities a license is not required to do electrical work on a home, but you will need a certificate showing the locality that you have insurance to cover your customer in the event of a fire, for example.

Path #3: On-the-job training

Power companies and manufacturers also use electricians. A course in industrial electricity covers some elementary physics, fundamentals of direct current, alternating currents and circuits, electric power generation and industry electrical controls for persons servicing power plant processes.

Often, power companies hire plant cleaners, maintenance people or even clerks who, after a period of employment, become eligible to take the exam for apprentice electrician. If you pass, you become eligible for on-the-job training and can move up to full electrician.

These are union shops, but the employer provides the training. This type of employment is more secure than work as a residential electrician Because there is little new home construction. Power plants are not hiring many people either, but they offer job security if you can get in.

Job: Plumber

Air conditioning, heating and refrigeration are parts of the plumbing field. You may be able to get an informal apprenticeship as a plumber's helper. In many localities, plumbers need to pass license examinations, so if you decide to pursue an informal apprenticeship, you may want to study on your own to pass the license examination. In the meantime, you will be dependent on a licensed plumber. There are union-sponsored apprenticeship programs, which must be posted at the state employment office. The tests for entrance will include math up to and including trigonometry. Find a plumber in the area who can help you with the union procedure.

Job: Carpenter

If you enjoy building structures and the outdoors, you should consider carpentry. If very skilled woodcraft work or the restoration of beautiful furniture are your interests, you should consider cabinetmaking or restoration.

Path #1: Brief training in carpentry/building maintenance

The adult division of the local board of education, the YMCA or YWCA or community college may offer carpentry or cabinetmaking training, which might give you enough skills and vocabulary to get an informal apprenticeship as a carpenter's helper.

If it is a building maintenance program, it will include carpentry, along with some basic electricity and plumbing. Building maintenance is a growing field, and can lead to better paying work as a building superintendent. Your vocational high school program may also offer a more detailed course in carpentry or building maintenance.

Path #2: Other specialized carpentry training

Sometimes apprenticeships in stringed instrument-making are listed in the magazine *The American Luthier*, prepared by the Guild of American Luthiers, 8222 South Park Ave., Tacoma, WA 98408, 206-472-7853. The magazine also provides a list of schools where you can find a 12-week program for acoustic and electric guitar construction and repair in Tennessee, or a four-year apprenticeship with a family of violin makers in Pennsylvania. It also gives advice about helpful books and sells instrument plans.

Woodwind instruments, like bassoons, are also made by hand. Katrina played the bassoon for years and then began assisting an instrument maker. Now she has her own shop; she and her teacher are the only bassoon makers on the East Coast.

The architect Paolo Soleri offers a chance to participate in the construction of Arcosanti in Arizona. Arcosanti, an urban habitat north of Phoenix, is the prototype for an energy-efficient town combining architectural and ecological concepts. The cost is $560 for room and board, registration and seminars for five weeks. Write to: Cosanti Foundation, 6433 Doubletree Rd., Scottsdale, AZ 85253, or call 602-948-6145.

The Shelter Institute, 38 Center St., Bath, ME 04530, 207-442-7938, offers a combination of lectures, skills workshops and actual building experience on homes-in-progress. Students learn to survey a property lot, pour a foundation and design and build every inch of a house. They receive instruction in the concept of heat, the physics of materials, engineering, framing and financing. This course is for do-it-yourself home builders, and it also serves as a wonderful introduction to construction. According to a 1994 article in *Time* magazine, graduates leave knowing how to build a house. Three-week sessions are scheduled several times from May to October and cost $725.

Path #3: Informal apprenticeship

Most carpenters learn their trade informally as carpenters' helpers. Nearly one carpenter out of every three is self-employed, so there are many non-union carpenters who need assistants. The assistant watches, works and learns. Perhaps one day, when a worker doesn't show up, the gofer may get the opportunity to show that he or she can do carpenter's work. Large, general contractors offer the best training because the helper is asked to do a greater variety of tasks. Contractors always need apprentices who have reliable transportation, come to the job site regularly and perhaps have their own tools. Write to The Apprentice Alliance, 151 Potrero Ave., San Francisco, CA 94103, or call 415-863-8661. This organization has sponsored almost 8,000 apprenticeships.

Path #4: Apprenticeships in skilled carpentry or woodworking

Skilled craftsmen and women in the field of furniture-making, cabinetmaking and antique furniture restoration are in short supply.

Outside of a few hobby courses in furniture-making or antique restoration, though, there is no thorough training program in this country for fine cabinetmaking.

Students must instead train by working as apprentices in antique restoration, fine cabinetmaking or furniture-making shops. Shops will want apprentices to have graduated from high school and to have demonstrated an interest, either through prior study or work samples. They are seeking hardworking and dedicated students who are artistically inclined and will stay with the shop for several years after they have been trained. See the yellow pages under Antiques Restoration or Cabinetmakers to locate employers, who are often craftsmen trained in Europe.

Path #5: Furniture design

Apprenticeships in furniture design studios can be found through: *American Woodturner*, 667 Harriet Ave., Shoreview, MN 55126, 614-484-9094; *American Woodworker*, 33 E. Minor St., Emmaus, PA 18098, 215-967-5171; or *Fine Woodworking*, 63 South Main St., P.O. Box 5506, Newtown, CT 06470-5506, 203-426-8171.

Fine cabinetmakers build special made-to-order units, do wood reproductions, veneering and fancy mill work (e.g., moldings and lattices). They take apprentices who can demonstrate their long-term interest in wood crafts. Big cities have the greatest number of employers in this field because of the increased market for antiques and fine cabinetmaking. Consult the yellow pages for names of employers.

Path #6: Restoration

Your local museum's Objects Conservation Department may be able to give you the names of skilled restorers in the region. The restoration of furniture and buildings is one use for skills in cabinetmaking. Doing an apprenticeship at the museum is very good training, but if there are no positions for assistants to the restorer, names of others in the local area will be helpful.

Path #7: Formal apprenticeship

The union-sponsored program for an apprenticeship requires four years of on-the-job training and related classroom instruction. If local unions are recruiting carpenter apprentices, they must post this information at the state unemployment office. Completion of the ninth grade may be a requirement and the test to be accepted as an apprentice includes a lot of mathematics and drafting. After you locate a union that is recruiting and fill out an application, the union will send you to a job site with a letter saying you will be taken into the union and trained if the employer hires you. Apprentices are paid at least half of full union members' wages to start so you will be learning and earning at the same time. The median weekly earnings of carpenters who were not self-employed were $425 in 1992, according to the *Occupational Outlook Handbook.*

Path #8: On-the-job training in boat building

Boat building and repair is a viable way to make a living in certain geographical locations. One of the youngest and most successful design teams in contemporary ocean racing has Ron Holland as its chief. A longer version of his story appears in Chapter 1. He learned everything on the job. Holland spent nearly three years working with American designers, first with Gary Mull and then with the flamboyant Charlie Morgan. Holland left Morgan to campaign his own quarter-tonner, Eygthene, in the world championships at Weymouth, England. It was a radical design—based, Holland admits now, on intuition, not "plain arithmetic." Eygthene won.

Eric Goetz, the shipwright, is another self-taught boat builder. According to a January 22, 1995 article in *The New York Times*, there are three syndicates vying for the right to represent the U.S. in defending the America's Cup and he built the boats for all three. He was raised in Port Washington, N.Y. His father was a shipping broker and an amateur sailor and woodworker.

Goetz sailed in college and spent his summers crewing on sailboats. He learned to build boats by doing it; he got his first break from Art Paine, who commissioned him to build one of his designs.

"The hardest thing is selling the first boat," says Goetz. He has 30 workers at his boatyard on Narragansett Bay, Mass., and he builds four or five boats a year, including yachts, cruising boats, power boats and ocean-racing maxi-boats.

Hospitality jobs

Cook/Chef
Hotel-Restaurant Manager
Dietician

Job: Cook/Chef

There is always a need for talented people in this field. Most chefs work unusual hours and actual food production is a high-stress job; making a gourmet dinner for 500 over the course of a few hours is quite a challenge, even if you have two other people on the line with you and a few helpers. To do it five nights a week is very demanding.

Path #1: Learn on the job

Cooks' assistants and kitchen helpers such as dishwashers learn a lot about cooking, and are soon ready to take over for the cook in a small restaurant. Two other positions in the kitchen are the *saucier* who prepares the sauces and the *garde-manger* who keeps tabs on supplies and prepares cold dishes. In a large hotel, one section may have several cooks who are supervised by a *chef de partie*. Most executive chefs were trained on the job and worked their way up.

"News from the Beard House," a newsletter published for members of The James Beard Foundation (167 West 12th St., New York, NY 10011, 212-675-4984) reports on the winners of the America's Best Chefs award. The winners are listed below; try to get to one of them so you can better understand the level of food preparation in an award-winning restaurant. Perhaps you have a comparable restaurant in your area.

America's Best Chefs are: Johanne Killeen and George Germon of Al Forno, Providence, R.I.; Alfred Portale of Gotham Bar and Grill, New York, N.Y.; Marcel Desaulniers of The Trellis, Williamsburg, Va.; Susan Spicer of Bayona, New Orleans, La.; Jimmy Schmidt of Rattlesnake Club, Detroit, Mich.; Vincent Guerithault of Camelback,

Phoenix, Ariz.; Bradley Ogden of Lark Creek Inn, Larkspur, Calif.; Jeremiah Tower of Stars, San Francisco, Calif.; Roy Yamaguchi of Roy's, Honolulu, Hawaii; Christian Delouvrier of Les Celebrities at the Essex House, New York, N.Y.; and Johnny Earles of Criolla's, Grayton Beach, Fla. One of your tasks as a student of cooking is to experience a restaurant like one of these in order to develop your own ideas about excellent cooking.

Path #2: Cruise line jobs

George Reilly spent 15 years as a chief purser and hotel manager on a cruise ship. His booklet, *Guide to Cruise Ship Jobs,* describes all the different jobs on a ship. It is $5.95 plus $1 for postage and handling from Pilot Books, 103 Cooper St., Babylon, NY 11707, 516-422-2225.

Or you could simply get the names of cruise lines from the newspaper and write directly to the Director of Marine Personnel. Small yacht owners also hire chefs. These boats might have six guests and six crew members.

Path #3: A.C.F. training

The American Culinary Federation has a three-year on-the-job training program complemented by related classroom instruction. You work full-time under a qualified supervising chef while attending school part-time. Local chefs get together and choose a few of their employees for the training; the student-apprentices receive certificates as A.C.F. cooks at the end of the program. There are currently 1,600 men and women enrolled in 110 apprenticeship programs nationwide. If you are starting as an apprentice in a restaurant, you will make at least $5 an hour to start, with a modest raise every six months.

Paul, a local restaurant owner, got his start through the Denver A.C.F. program. The chef in the restaurant where Paul was working got together with other local chefs, found an empty college classroom and began a local A.C.F. program by offering instruction.

Paul remembers participating in food display events—chocolate sculpture, tallow sculpture, ice sculpture, hot and cold buffets, cakes—staged by the chefs and their apprentices at the local convention center. He says most of the learning occurred on the job but he was happy to have the book learning as well. Compared to the tuition at a private two-year school for chefs, working toward the certificate is well worth it.

Write to the American Culinary Federation at P.O. Box 3466, St. Augustine, FL 32085-3466, 904-824-4468, for a list of the contact persons within your state.

Path #4: Associate's degree

There are many two-year programs that train you to become a cook, an assistant chef (*sous-chef*) or kitchen manager of a hotel or restaurant. You are trained in the school's kitchens and then in an internship. Programs which emphasize culinary training are the best bets; management is hard to enter with an associate's degree. Some programs offer a semester abroad to their students. You can find the programs in MacMillan's *Blue Books, Degrees Offered* (at community colleges) and in *Occupational Education*. Cooking schools sometimes have poor placement records, so make sure you check the figures, which are required by state law to be listed in the catalog.

One young woman earned her bachelor's degree from a liberal arts school, worked as a waitress for five years after college at a very fancy restaurant in Manhattan and saved $50,000 to attend a two-year program, in which she was required to do several internships. She started as a kitchen manager working under an executive chef, earning $25,000 to $30,000 a year. She understands the realities of corporate restaurant and hotel cooking: excellent wages, frequent relocation and hard work in a business-like environment.

Before paying a great deal of money or using federal grants to attend a school (there is a lifetime undergraduate limit on the amount of federal Pell awards), you may want to work in the field as a cook's helper to make sure the field is right for you. The better programs ask you to work in food service and get letters of recommendation before application.

Clarify where you want to work and what you want to do. If you want to be a fancy chef, you could learn in the kitchen of a chef, starting out chopping vegetables. Often this kind of training is what the executive chef prefers for his successor. If you want to open your own restaurant, you may want to train with a chef and save money to get started on your own. Hotel, cruise ship and convention center work requires a broader training than a single restaurant experience can provide—schooling may be necessary.

According to an April 27, 1988 article in *The New York Times,* experienced chefs working for the season in the Hamptons on Long Island can make $50,000 for the summer. Some chefs in very good New York City restaurants can make more than $100,000 a year, although most experienced chefs make between $24,000 and $60,000 a year depending on the region, their qualifications and place of employment. Cooks average about $8 an hour. The Bureau of Labor Statistics estimates that through the year 2005, 200,000 new chefs and cooks will be needed each year.

Job: Hotel-Restaurant Manager

Path #1: Internship

Many hotel-restaurant chains have internship programs. For example, Marriott has an internship for college students and a co-op/work experience program, both of which are paid. Marriott offers these to interest students in management. They are looking for majors in Hotel and Restaurant Management (bachelor's degree program) or Business (bachelor's or master's degree), except in the food area where they will accept culinary training. For information about their internship programs, contact Marriott Corporation, Marriott Dr., Washington, DC 20058, 800-638-8108.

If you want to do an internship at a specific place, it is best to get the name of the owner, which may be a conglomerate in another state. If you are in a college program in hotel and restaurant management, the head of your program will most probably have internship possibilities. Hotel-restaurant chains see these internship opportunities as management training and like students to have completed at least two years of college before interning. To work internationally, language skills will be important.

Path #2: On-the-job training assisting a convention services manager

As an assistant to a convention services manager, you will be required to attend to the many details. You need good social skills, and an ability to work long hours and handle various crises resulting from changes of plans, groups overstaying their designated time slot, cancellations, etc. You will have day-to-day administrative responsibilities, working with representatives of groups as well as with sales and marketing staff, rooms-division, catering, food and beverage, housekeeping, conventions, security and accounting.

Marriott has established a management training track for people to become convention-services managers and directors at the firm's hotels. The average salary revealed by a survey in the *Cornell Hotel and Restaurant Quarterly* was $40,000 for a work week of 60 to 70 hours.

According to a Michael Stanton article in *Occupational Outlook Quarterly*, meeting planners for large organizations may get their start managing conventions for one particular organization. Tina Hochberg worked for one group and now she is in charge of meeting operations for an organization of associations. This group has several major conventions each year and she and her staff handle the logistics.

Path #3: Bachelor's degree in hotel management or business

Four-year programs offering degrees in restaurant or institutional management include training in the kitchen and courses in business management. Purchasing, accounting, hotel management practices, baking, food control, beverage control, merchandising, housekeeping, sales promotion, statistics and computer applications are some of the courses offered in these programs.

The sales department, accounting department and food and beverage department are all good divisions to enter within large hotels and their heads report to the manager. Banking, business administration and accounting are also good avenues into hotel administration provided you have some experience, perhaps in the form of an internship or cooperative work.

Anthony (*Vocational Biographies*) is the manager of a hotel-casino in Las Vegas. He was accounting manager for another resort, then spent some time as an accountant for his present employer. To move into management, he volunteered weekends as a shift manager to prove he could handle the responsibilities. He then progressed to hotel front office manager and then hotel manager, where he now supervises 250 people.

Path #4: Your own restaurant

Misty started her career by selling sandwiches from the back of her car, then rented a small space behind the local art gallery. She was always noted for her taste and style and she served interesting food at reasonable prices. She related well to her staff. She trained many young people by being clear, yet patient with them about what was expected. Interpersonal skills like these are essential in supervising the kitchen/dining room team; untrained employees often need tactful handling. Misty made a living for 20 years serving only breakfast and lunch.

In *How to Turn a Passion for Food into a Profit,* Elayne J. Kleeman and Jeanne A. Voltz give information about food-related businesses including selling mail order, establishing a gourmet shop, restaurant or catering service and selling bottled specialties. Keep in mind that each state has its own licensing process, fee structure and inspection program for home food manufacturing, so you need to call the state and find the right agency.

Being a personal chef who cooks for families is another employment possibility. Sometimes this service takes the form of delivery of meals. One cook prepares meals for 15 families and delivers them. Nancy Davis, who operates Chef on the Run in Austin, Texas, goes from kitchen to kitchen, leaving 10 entrees and side dishes for two in her clients' refrigerators every other week. She charges $260 for 10 meals for two. Another chef makes $25 an hour plus food costs. She has clients for whom she leaves 30 meals in the freezer once a month. The United States Personal Chef Association has 650 members in 46 states. Members of the association charge $8 to $13 a person for each meal. The names of personal chefs in your area can be obtained by calling the association at 800-995-2138.

Jeff Smith was an ordained Methodist minister who left his job as a chaplain to open the Chaplain's Pantry, a deli and catering service. Then he wrote *The Frugal Gourmet* and started doing cooking shows on television, from which he promoted his books. A bold career change really paid off for Jeff Smith.

Job: Dietician

Path #1: Associate's degree

Gross annual incomes between $15,000 and $20,000 are reported by 30 percent of dietician technicians. Incomes between $20,000 and $30,000 (employed from one to five years) are reported by 55 percent. These salaries suggest that formal training as a technician may not pay off; you can get a job in a kitchen and aim for dietician (not technician) if you want to go to school. Two dietetic technician programs are available through independent study. More information is available about these through the American Dietetic Association, address and phone below.

Path #2: Bachelor's degree

Laws governing dietetics exist in 30 states. In many states, dieticians are required to have the bachelor's degree. To sit for the registration exam, you need both an academic and a clinical (experience) component. These requirements can be fulfilled in a number of ways, including year-long, full-time, unpaid clinical internships, part-time work or experience through the academic program.

Dieticians work in institutions like hospitals, planning menus, or in the food industry, developing new foods, or with individuals who need help with their diets. Gross annual incomes between $25,000 and $35,000 are reported by 65 percent of dieticians employed from one to five years after registration, and incomes between $35,000 and $45,000 are reported by 16 percent. A nutritionist may or may not be a registered dietician. Some nutritionists do have a B.A. in nutrition; they may have wanted to be registered dieticians but did not go to a school that had the proper internship available.

For more information, write to The American Dietetic Association, 216 West Jackson Blvd., Chicago, IL 60606-6995, 312-899-0040. The association will send you a list of accredited programs that combine classroom and practical experience, as well as a list of programs that meet their academic requirements but do not include the practice or internship required for the registration exam.

Horticulture jobs

Floral Designer	Landscape Architect
Arborist	Farmer
Gardener	

Job: Floral Designer

Your city's department of employment may offer a free training program in floral design for the economically disadvantaged. This short-term program will prepare you to work at a retail florist or for a wholesaler. A knowledge of the field may be important in getting work, but you may also be able to get a position as an assistant and learn on the job.

Many florists work as floral designers in private studios catering to clients by appointment. They specialize in keeping homes, offices, restaurants or shops filled with fresh flowers, designing flowers for parties and weddings, and landscaping terraces and gardens. According to a June 26, 1987 article in *The New York Times*, one designer, Giacomo, prepares miniature meadows for a client. His forte is reproducing Flemish paintings for buffets—mixtures of fruits and flowers spilling out of containers. He studied landscape architecture in Europe and Japan.

Job: Arborist

Arborists fertilize, strengthen, remove, prune and diagnose sick trees. In suburban areas, people value their trees and want expert help to save them. Employers accept trainees without the high school diploma. See the yellow pages for tree maintenance services.

Kent (*Vocational Biographies*) owns his own tree service. He has a high school diploma and is a certified arborist through his state's arborist association which offers an exam for certification. He started with a $400 chainsaw and now employs large crews of workers. He would like to add a small lumbering operation.

Job: Gardener

Path #1: On-the-job-training with a nursery or garden center

Nursery operators fill orders for shrubs and plants from landscape architects and retail florists, or they sell directly to the public through a garden center. The assistant production manager of a wholesale nursery may have a four-year college degree in nursery management. A helper's job at a nursery is a way for you to test your interest, while learning how to operate a nursery. Some people begin by operating an open-air lot, where they sell plants until they have enough saved to start a garden center. Greenhouses attached to historic houses or resorts may also provide employment and learning.

Path #2: Parks Department gardener

If you have a high school diploma, working for the Parks Department can lead, in three or four years, to taking the gardener's examination for the city. Gardeners start at around $30,000 a year in some regions.

Many people in parks administration have gotten their jobs because of volunteer work, interest in plants or fund-raising skills. According to a September 30, 1993 article in *The New York Times*, Betsy Rogers, the administrator for Central Park in New York City, was interested in landscape architecture but took a degree in city planning because the school she had to attend didn't have a landscape architecture program. Then she wrote several books on forests, wetlands and one on Frederick Olmstead, the designer of Central Park. She has become an expert on public-private partnerships (getting the private sector to give money to save the park) and travels around the world talking to park groups on this topic.

Path #3: Gardener-plant maintenance

Services that maintain plants for businesses also need helpers, basically to make certain that plants are watered. You must have experience with plants, proper etiquette for an office environment and good communication skills. Be able to write and speak well, so you can interact with the customer well.

Path #4: Apprentice to a gardener

The magazine *The American Nurseryman*, published by the American Association of Nurserymen, runs advertisements for professional gardeners' apprentices. Someone may be looking for a propagation assistant or nurseryman's assistant. You can request single issues of the magazine by calling 800-621-5727. The Apprentice Alliance, 151 Potrero Ave., San Francisco, CA 94103, 415-863-8661, offers apprenticeships in gardening.

Alice held an informal apprenticeship as a garden helper and now has a successful garden maintenance business. She says being a gardener is a "tough row to hoe" but she is glad she is doing it. She got started at age 3 working for friends and relatives. Sometimes she was paid and sometimes she volunteered. Then, for 15 years, she worked as a lab technician doing animal science research. She left her job and started work as a day laborer, helping a local judge and his gardener to do yard clean-ups and doing day work for local contractors. The judge's wife knew people who needed help and who became her first clients. She got somebody to teach her pruning, and learned on her own about insects and the use of chemicals. Her clients were generally seniors and second home owners. Her work is seasonal and she generally works alone. She recommends that you be in good physical health; there is a lot of twisting, reaching and bending.

Path #5: Landscape maintenance

This is a specialized form of gardening. As a helper, you can learn about the care of lawns and shrubs. Getting experience in such a company is good training for starting a business or for sitting for the city, state or federal examinations for turf managers. Landscape maintenance and turfgrass maintenance businesses can be started with a relatively small amount of money.

Path #6: Internship

The American Association of Botanical Gardens and Arboreta, 786 Church Rd., Wayne, PA 19082, 610-688-1120, has an extensive list of college-level botany internship programs.

Path #7: Master Gardener program

For experienced gardeners, the local extension service of a state university may provide part-time training for gardeners who are experienced, want more training and are willing to teach gardening in their communities (see county listings under Cooperative Extension Division, in your phone book). "Master Gardeners" is a nationwide program. Land-grant colleges in 33 states offer training; in exchange the students do volunteer teaching work with local sponsors. No formal training is required for entrance. The training lasts about three months and costs $100. It covers landscaping, basic botany, and pest management. This certified "Master Gardener" credential could be helpful in gaining employment or in getting clients for a gardening service.

Path #8: Formal training

Community colleges offer two-year degrees in horticulture, often in conjunction with local botanical gardens. The two-year degree may not improve your pay very much, but even a few courses in turf management or tree maintenance, for example, will help you find your first job more easily.

Certified professional-level programs are offered at botanical gardens. A high school diploma will be required for entrance. Financial aid is not usually available for these courses, nor are basic biology courses available, but the courses themselves are taught by professionals working in the field.

After high school graduation, you may want to attend Longwood Gardens' Professional Gardener Training Program. This two-year program is offered every other year to 14 individuals who have a high school diploma. Trainees work in all areas of the garden and receive classroom instruction as well. Graduates are sought by botanical gardens, commercial horticultural enterprises and estate gardens. Longwood Gardens also offers an internship program for college students. In both these programs students receive free housing and a stipend. They also have an extensive continuing education program. Contact Dave Foresman, Longwood Gardens, Kennett Square, PA 19348, 215-338-6741. For other programs see MacMillan's *Blue Books, Degrees Offered*. These listings include certificate programs and short-term training.

Job: Landscape Architect

The landscape architect studies a given setting and then determines how man-made elements may be designed to complement the natural setting. Some states license landscape architects after they practice for several years and pass a comprehensive examination. There are both bachelor's and master's degree programs in landscape architecture. You do not have to major in landscape architecture as an undergraduate to enter a master's degree program. In fact, a shortened master's degree program for those coming from a bachelor's degree program in landscape design is not accredited by the American Society of Landscape Architects. The first step is to get your state's requirements. For a list of accredited programs, write to the American Society of Landscape Architects, 4401 Connecticut Ave. NW, Washington, DC 20008, or call 202-686-ASLA.

Job: Farmer

Path #1: Farm apprenticeship

The Maine Organic Farmers and Gardeners Association, P.O. Box 2176, Augusta, ME 04330, 207-622-3118, offers apprenticeships with Maine farmers. This is a good opportunity to learn organic farming and try out farming as a career possibility.

Path #2: College agricultural programs

Agriculture, horticulture and forestry are some of the majors offered at agricultural colleges. A four-year degree from an agricultural program can lead to a career in ornamental horticulture, forestry, farming, agribusiness (large-scale farming which requires farm managers, researchers and developers) and agriculture education. For information about such programs, consult MacMillan's *Blue Books, Degrees Offered.*

The American Society of Agronomy (crop and soil science), 677 South Segoe Rd., Madison, WI 53711, 608-273-8080, offers a booklet, describing agronomy and listing all college programs in the country that offer this specialty.

Anne (*Vocational Biographies*) is an agronomist for the U.S. Department of Agriculture (USDA). She got her degree in agronomy from a state university. She helps farmers and other landowners get the most out of their soil without damaging it. While in college, she spent two summers in the training program of the USDA Soil Conservation Service, learning to survey, designing layouts for irrigation and staking out terraces and waterways. She also plans wetlands protection and manages wildlife and timber areas. Much of the work farmers do is subsidized, so Anne works out legal contracts, plans the work with the farmer and then makes sure it is done properly.

Path #3: Work as a farmer

Many small farms have gone under in the last 20 years. Today farming usually means agribusiness—large-scale farming—with a large investment. However, there are still viable small farming businesses. For example, farms in the New York Hudson Valley raise anemones for the metropolitan market, raise plants for drying, raise sheep for wool, give spinning demonstrations and other tourist events and raise goats to make cheese for the New York City market. There are eight successful vineyards in the Hudson Valley in New York state. None of these enterprises supports a family, but combined with other work makes a livelihood and a rural lifestyle for the owners.

Terry Silber felt that she could not make a living in her climate from farming alone, so she and her husband began selling vegetables to restaurants, making coleslaw from the farm's cabbage and developing a mail-order catalog. They held a spring fair/open house to sell seedlings and crafts, and then started selling to boutiques. They started workshops for community gardeners to promote the farmers' market, and their classes and seminars have become an important part of their income. Now they have a mailing list of 10,000 to whom they send their gift, seedling and workshop catalogs and are finally making a living from their farm. Terry's book, *A Small Farm in Maine,* describes their struggle to find a crop that could be profitably marketed.

With as few as a third of existing farmers expecting their children to carry on the family business, 15 states now have programs to match young people with farm families seeking employees or buyers, says John Baker of Farm On, the linking service, based in Iowa. In another program, established farmers help young farmers by sharing machinery, cattle and contract hogs.

The magazine *Successful Farming* sponsors a yearly conference called Farmers for the Next Century, a national conference for beginning farmers and ranchers in Columbia, Mo. The conference includes hands-on advice for those with limited capital and "mixer" time where older farmers can scout for landless employees who might work into partial ownership. Rotational grazing, alternatives to conventional livestock marketing and crop production tips have also been some of the topics at the conference. For information about the conference, write to Conference Manager, Successful Farming, 2510 River Bye Rd., Adel, IA 50003.

Selling and Managing

These occupations require an entrepreneurial personality. For success in this field you need to value and enjoy selling or influencing, and leading. Support services, bookkeeping and accounting are included because they are part of business.

Managers/Executives
Support Services
Bookkeeping/Accounting
Banking/Finance
Sales/Marketing
Law
Politics/Civil Service

Managers/Executives

Becoming a business manager or executive cannot be approached directly; it must be attained. These are not entry-level jobs. Sometimes companies take what they call "management trainees," but usually these college graduates have technical knowledge from courses and training which they will bring to the job. More often an employer wants M.B.A. graduates as managers, and M.B.A. programs want applicants to have five to seven years of work experience after undergraduate college.

Generally, you need to get experience and become knowledgeable about a specific industry and get training for an occupation or job if you want to be an executive in that industry, but each industry is different. Usually you will need a college degree to advance to management, especially in a large corporation. Successful managers can advance to vice president, president or chief executive officer (CEO) of the company. In small businesses, there are more opportunities in terms of new openings and chances of moving up within the company.

Your experience in a particular industry is worth a great deal on your resume. You will lose valuable time if you move around among industries. After completing your education, which should be occupationally focused, you need to decide in which industry you want to practice your new occupation. More top CEOs come from sales or marketing than from any other fields. If marketing is your goal, do you want to market fashion or pharmaceuticals? Devoting some solid research time to exploring at this point can save you time, effort and money.

Choose industries that interest you from the list below and then read about these fields in this book. After you learn about the preparation for these industries, come back to this section for more information about the managerial side of business. Here is my list of industries:

advertising and public relations (Selling and Managing)
aerospace (Solving Practical Problems, The Sciences)
agriculture (Solving Practical Problems)
automotive (Solving Practical Problems)
aviation (Solving Practical Problems)
banking (Selling and Managing)
broadcasting (Arts and Communications)
chemicals (The Sciences)
computers and electronics (The Sciences,
    Solving Practical Problems)

consumer products (Solving Practical Problems)
energy (Solving Practical Problems)
fashion (Arts and Communications)
film and entertainment (Arts and Communications)
financial services (Selling and Managing)
food and beverage (Solving Practical Problems)
health services and pharmaceuticals (The Sciences)
hospitality (Solving Practical Problems)
insurance (The Sciences, Selling and Managing)
manufacturing (Solving Practical Problems)
paper and forest products (The Sciences)
publishing (Arts and Communications)
real estate and construction (Selling and Managing)
retailing (Selling and Managing)
telecommunications (Solving Practical Problems)
transportation (Solving Practical Problems)
travel (Selling and Managing)
utilities (Solving Practical Problems)

Fortune magazine reports on industries in its annual issue devoted to evaluating businesses. It looks at manufacturing (defense, steel, machinery, auto, chemicals, food); high tech (computers, semiconductors, telecommunications, pharmaceuticals); natural resources (energy, agriculture, forest); services (retail, wholesale, health care, transport, restaurants, utilities and entertainment) and finance (banking, insurance, securities). At some point, be sure to check out your choices in *Fortune.* The annual issue will give you further background and vocabulary, plus current information on industry-wide advances and setbacks which have a bearing on the labor market.

Can you take an entry-level job and begin to get on-the-job training in your industry and move up (even if you want more education later) or will you have to have more education even to enter your industry? One additional step you may wish to take is to look at how *Forbes,* in its annual survey of all industries, discusses and rates the best companies in the industry.

Job: Business manager

Path #1: Entry-level job

Most new job openings are created by small businesses, rather than major corporations, and their openings are often filled from within the company. Workers may do a variety of tasks and, if they desire, they can learn all the aspects of the business. Clarify what skill you are selling to the employer and what you want to be doing (for example, sales, accounting, customer service, word processing, advertising, promotion). Then begin locating businesses in an industry in which you have an interest. Look at the business-to-business yellow pages. Look also at *The College Placement Annual* which lists firms recruiting new employees and industry trade magazines.

For example, Paul started as a courier for Federal Express. You can get a job with Fed Ex if you are 21 years of age, have a clean driving record and a high school diploma. Paul had a degree in business management. After he proved himself, he was promoted to supervisor and then to head supervisor. (Federal Express hires from within; all jobs are posted.) Now he is station operations senior manager.

On the other hand, Jay got a job with a publisher using family contacts and learned production skills for producing directories. Then he took a job with the competition and eventually became head of production. He never finished college although he did take college courses at an art school. His lack of a degree isn't so important because he is in production and his next job will probably be in production as well.

Path #2: Internship

Most internships sponsored by large corporations are reserved for engineering, computer science and accounting students. However, if you have other interests, talk to the person handling internships at your college. Sometimes a college will have connections with local businesses and you'll be able to apply for an internship in your interest area.

According to a *Mademoiselle* article by Jane Walker, Kathy is going to Taiwan as a Fulbright Scholar and then to work as an investment analyst for an investment brokerage firm. Later she plans to enter business school. On her own initiative, she found a university in Mainland China where she could study Chinese as an undergraduate, so that she could use her Chinese language skills as an investment banker. The International Association of Students in Economics and Business (AIESEC) sponsors a foreign business exchange summer program with a small stipend for interns. Write to them at AIESEC, 135 West 50th St., 20th Floor, New York, NY 10020, or call 212-757-3774.

College students can get good business experience by taking positions in student government. For example, Lynne Liakos supervised 1,400 employees as the first female president of Harvard's Student Agencies. She will go to business school after working in marketing. Her decision to get work experience before going to graduate school for business reflects the recent trend among M.B.A. programs to take more mature students with solid employment records.

The International Trade Administration of the Department of Commerce offers college students the opportunity to volunteer in offices around the country for the summer. Trade development, international economic policy, U.S. and foreign commercial service and import administration are some of the tasks. Students of international relations, marketing, economics and business administration may apply. Filing dates are from January 15 through March 15. For more information, contact the Student Volunteer Program, International Trade Administration, United States Department of Commerce, Room 4808, 14th St. & Constitution Ave. NW, Washington, DC 20230, 202-482-3301.

Path #3: Bachelor's degree

In previous decades, the student who graduated from a four-year business school was able to get a job as a trainee in a major corporation, but this isn't true anymore. There is also some indication that M.B.A. programs prefer a less specialized degree. What they really want is an Ivy League undergraduate degree, then three to five years of business experience before you apply. Unless you are becoming an accountant, this degree is not recommended.

Insurance companies, advertising agencies, banks, brokerage houses, food manufacturers and utilities hire some liberal arts graduates for sales positions or as management trainees. Companies express interest in liberal arts majors, but this usually means that the major should be in statistics or science and from an Ivy League liberal arts college.

Generally however, when companies recruit on campus, they want engineers, accountants and computer scientists. For the liberal arts graduate, jobs with major companies are scarce.

Path #4: Graduate degree

The top 20 M.B.A. programs want to see five to seven years of work experience before you apply. The top 20 programs, according to *The Gourman Report* are:

Harvard University	University of Michigan—
University of Pennsylvania	Ann Arbor
Stanford University	Northwestern University
Massachusetts Institute	Carnegie-Mellon University
of Technology	University of Illinois
University of Chicago	Cornell University
Columbia University	New York University
University of California—	Dartmouth College
Los Angeles	University of Pittsburgh
Indiana University	University of Texas
University of California—	Duke University
Berkeley	University of Wisconsin

Both the law degree and the M.B.A. are not the magic ticket they were in the 1980s. It is important to understand that most managers or business administrators need a skill (engineering, marketing, computer science, accounting or finance, for example), on-the-job training and experience as a supervisor to advance to high levels of management. In other words, you don't prepare to be a manager; you prepare in another field and then get management experience on the job.

In a survey by John Kotter, of 115 graduates of Harvard Business School's class of 1974, about 40 percent had been fired or laid off at some point in their career. Very few joined a large firm and moved up; most took the entrepreneurial path, the small business path or supplied or advised large corporations. According to a March 19, 1995 article in *The New York Times*, Kotter says leadership is helping a group develop a sense of where it's going, creating an environment that makes people feel stronger and motivated. Where you should lead depends on business trends; you need to look closely at the M.B.A. programs' placement statistics and the careers of the people in classes before yours.

Path #5: Your own business

For many career-changers, this may be the best option, risky as it is. Of course, your product or service should fill an unmet need, so that it will be valuable to the public. Most advisors suggest that you first get a job in the kind of business you want to start.

Generally, you must invest in your own business to start; loans come after you have proven your business can succeed. Venture capitalists want established and profitable businesses. County, state and federal government can help. For example, one agency, the Small Business Administration, can be found in the blue pages of your phone book. The Senior Core of Retired Executives (SCORE) provides access to retired businesspersons on a one-on-one basis. You can talk out your problems and they will give you honest feedback. It is listed in the phone book as well.

Here is an example of a successful business idea: Richard Jurmain is an unemployed aerospace engineer who developed a doll to give young people a realistic sample of parenthood. The doll is programmed to shriek at random intervals 24 hours a day. Teenagers, as a class assignment, take the lifesized doll home for three days to get an idea of life with a newborn. The only way to get it to stop crying is to feed it by holding a key into its back for 20 minutes— the approximate time to feed a newborn. A microprocessor monitors how long the baby cried before it stopped and if it was handled roughly. He developed the prototype in his garage. Jurmain said that he has orders for 10,000 dolls; each doll costs $220. The doll is called "Baby Think It Over." Call 619-268-2525 for information about ordering.

Buying a franchise may also be considered. In 1990, Ed Stufano, a former sheet metal worker and his wife Stella, owner of a hair salon, bought a Subway sandwich franchise. At the printing of a September 18, 1993 article in *The New York Times*, there were 8,000 Subways with average annual sales of $275,000 to $350,000 each. Ed and Stella signed the contract for the franchise ($10,000), negotiated a lease, started renovations and opened within a year. Their startup costs were $100,000; they have 10 employees, most of whom are part-timers. He works 40 to 60 hours a week and she works about 20. They expect to break even three years after opening. (Breaking even means they are not making a profit, but they are receiving their salaries.) They pay an eight percent royalty fee to Subway but they like the fact that they control their own future.

According to an article by Earl Gottschalk, Jr., in *The New York Times*, the disclosure documents from franchises must be reviewed by a lawyer who is knowledgeable about franchising and, to get a realistic picture, you must talk to other owners. The demand of those looking to buy franchises has driven up the prices. One franchise consultant suggests buying a franchise that produces a 15-percent annual return on your capital within two years, plus a manager's salary.

According to a January 18, 1993 article in *Forbes* magazine, video game fanatic Steve Harris started publishing a video game newsletter at 15, featuring reviews, game-playing tips and high scores, and flew to trade shows and tournaments to sell it for $2 apiece. He dropped out of high school to manage a video arcade and started publishing *Electronic Gaming Monthly*, which an entrepreneur recognized as a good idea and financed the first 165,000 issues ($70,000) in exchange for a contract to distribute anything Harris developed. Now, at 26, Harris has four video game magazines and is earning $2 million a year.

Path #6: Management consulting

This seems to be the haven of the unemployed. It is not for the beginner or the financially strapped. There are many books about consulting (advising business owners). The most successful consultants are selling information they had access to at the old job—information new employers want. Consulting may be an option for the career-changer, depending on your former occupation and industry.

Support Service jobs

Secretary/Administrative Assistant
Purchasing Agent
Personnel/Human Resources Worker
Recruiter

Property Manager
Customer Service Worker
Flight Attendant
Nanny or Butler/Houseman
Delivery Person
Travel Representative

Job: Secretary/Administrative Assistant
Path #1: Word processing
Word processing training is often offered to quick typists for free by temporary agencies. Data entry (usually the inputting of numbers) training is also available for free. Data entry pays about $10 an hour, according to the *Occupational Outlook Handbook,* and is quite monotonous. Training as a typist is available through your public adult education program or through computer software programs.

Path #2: Advanced secretarial work
Secretaries, also called administrative assistants, organize and run projects for corporate executives in addition to handling correspondence. They need to be highly literate, have the right computer software training and the appropriate appearance to fit into a business environment; often they have college degrees. They need to know about data entry systems and electronic administrative aids such as advanced telephone equipment and electronic filing and messaging systems. Legal secretaries need to know data retrieval services and electronic production of legal documents.

If you choose to go to secretarial school, choose your program carefully. (See the placement rates at the end of their catalog.) Both local colleges and private business schools can offer you training. Sometimes the local college will have an adult and continuing division which may offer the right kind of course.

The Certified Professional Secretary examination is given in six parts. You can get college credit for passing each part. Finance, business law, office systems, administration and management are some of the topics included on the examination; you need on-the-job experience to be eligible to take it but it is a way to earn college credit. Many colleges grant credit hours for the CPS rating to those enrolled in degree programs. Request a free copy of *Capstone* magazine, from Professional Secretaries International, P.O. Box 20404, Kansas City, MO 64195-0404, 816-891-6600, a company that sells study materials.

Office managers are usually support people who advance, as the boss recognizes that they may be able to eliminate office chaos. They are sometimes called administrative service managers and can make between $30,000 and $40,000 a year with experience.

Nancy Hanks's career shows what can be learned from a job as a receptionist-typist. Hanks served as the chairperson for the National Endowment for the Arts (NEA) from 1969 to 1977. She started her career as a receptionist for the Office for Defense Mobilization, a civilian agency set up "to run the Korean War" as she put it. Her degree from Duke University was in economics and political science. As a receptionist, she learned the defense establishment and then later worked for the President's Advisory Committee on Government Organization with Milton Eisenhower, Arthur Flemmings and Nelson Rockefeller. She typed and learned about agencies; later, she increased the budget of the NEA from $11 to $114 million in eight years. Hanks proved herself invaluable as a typist. People who were rising took her with them. She got a chance to learn because she was useful to some very smart and powerful people. Her story shows that where you work, in whatever capacity, is often more important than your entry-level job description.

Job: Purchasing Agent

Purchasing is an important job when you are buying parts for a manufacturing outfit or when you are in charge of supplies for a giant bureaucracy. Guaranteeing price, quality and timeliness of delivery is all part of the purchasing agent's job; a background in the business is required for hire. The work is usually learned on the job, perhaps working in production on the line or in quality control, or assisting the purchasing agent. According to Kathy and Ross Petras, the average salary for a purchasing executive is $40,700.

Job: Personnel/Human Resources Worker

In addition to support staff and managers, some personnel or human resource departments have recruiters, trainers, meeting planners (often ex-secretaries or administrative assistants), relocation specialists, benefits specialists and compensation specialists. For example, at one company one manager is in charge of employee training and development, employee relations, safety, health services and wellness programs; and another manager is in charge of employment, affirmative action, compensation, employee assistance and benefits. Both report to the vice-president of personnel. In the not-for-profit sector, especially the state, workers are chosen to train other employees and are called staff development specialists.

If you are interested in personnel management (human resources management), you need work experience in the field to see how your particular industry works. Often people in the personnel field learn the field by starting as a secretary or salesperson. Get experience before you invest in graduate training: you will need office skills to make yourself immediately useful. Personnel management jobs at larger companies require the bachelor's degree at a minimum. Some entry-level titles in very large companies include job analysis, performance appraisal or college recruiting.

You may decide that you need a law degree to succeed in the personnel field. *Personnel Journal,* a trade magazine, offers advice about avoiding lawsuits from employees in areas such as sexual harassment, employment discrimination or family medical leave.

Job: Recruiter

Recruiters for computer specialists, engineers with special backgrounds or executives are called headhunters. They work on commission, either in their own agency or for an agency. Companies use them to find people with particular skills; often recruiters phone into other companies and try to convince workers with special skills to change jobs so the recruiter can fill the work order. The employee can move to a higher paying position and the new employer can get a person with the necessary skills.

Often workers in personnel or personnel agencies go on to become recruiters or open their own agencies. All this is learned on the job and you may not need a college degree to get into a placement agency or personnel agency.

For example, Jean had a background as a bookkeeper. She didn't finish college but she was a very hard worker, and landed a job in an agency that places bookkeepers and accountants. Later she went on to open her own agency.

Job developers and employment counselors work to find jobs for their graduates. For example, Elaine (*Vocational Biographies*) places the graduates of an art institute. Most semesters she has a 100 percent placement rate. She knows the skill levels of her graduates and the needs of employers in the area. This kind of service makes the institute a very desirable choice from the student's perspective.

People who work in placement agencies are working for other employers; they are paid to make good matches but always must keep the needs of the employer and their own commission in mind. These workers have often worked in the same field as they place others and have good contacts with employers and the ability to interview and choose good candidates. There are statewide groups of personnel consultants; the reference section of your library may have a directory. This is a good area for the career-changer with hiring experience to consider, because the employer may request no other credentials. The local temporary employment agencies may place administrative assistants, bookkeepers, accountants, data entry people, home health care aides; if you have had some experience in these occupations, you will have an advantage getting a job at a placement agency. See magazines like *HR Magazine* or *Personnel Journal.*

Job: Property Manager

Property management, also called asset or facilities management, may be a good possibility if you need employment quickly, because you can learn on the job. Golf and country clubs, malls, housing and apartment complexes, manufacturing plants and office buildings all need managers. The job includes, in the case of a shopping center for example, determining the tenant mix, developing tenant retention programs and capital improvements to enhance the property's value.

Job: Customer Service Worker

Felicia does telephone orders on the computer for a manufacturer. She could move up and head her department, then coordinate her department and shipping, then get involved with the catalog and marketing. There is nowhere she couldn't go within the company. She got the job because she had a pleasant manner and some office experience.

Job: Flight Attendant

To get hired you need to meet certain weight and height requirements; attendants are usually trained and then tested. They are trained in food and beverage service and in the handling of medical emergencies and safety-related situations. They have some flexibility in scheduling but work many holidays and weekends and spend many hours in airports, waiting for their next flight. College graduates are preferred but they will also consider you if you have had successful experience in serving the public. Older employees used to be let go after a certain age, but they are now staying on the job.

Job: Nanny or Butler/Houseman

Nanny jobs require you to live in your boss's household and work with children in a situation where there are usually no other adults. According to an April 15, 1993 article in *The New York Times*, nanny jobs pay between $250 and $500 a week with benefits. You need experience to be placed by an agency. The American Council of Nanny Schools, Delta College, University Center, MI 48710, 517-686-9417, has listings of agencies and training programs.

According to an article by Julie Lew in *The New York Times*, a butler may run a home with a staff of two or three; a houseman does more cooking and cleaning. The Ivor Spencer International School for Housemen has a 10-day immersion course which is offered six times a year in Los Angeles and San Francisco, and The Starkey International Institute for Household Management in Denver trains high-level employees. Butlers can make $35,000 a year or more; housemen (sometimes called household managers) earn $20,000 plus room and board and medical benefits. Training could come from cleaning or working in a restaurant.

Job: Delivery Person

There are an estimated 7,500 independently owned delivery routes in the New York metropolitan area, bought and sold by the owners. According to an April 19, 1993 article in *The New York Times*, Lois bought such a route delivering Italian bread for $18,000 five years ago. She had an unrewarding office job, had just gotten a divorce and had to put three children through college. She goes to work at 1 a.m., seven days a week, and has an income of $80,000 a year. She is now trying to sell the route for $110,000 so she can move to Arizona. She is paid on the basis of the number of stops and the amount of sales.

These routes cannot be bought on credit; owners want a large down payment and a personal note. Once you purchase the route, you get a customer list, a protected territory, a truck and the right to pick the goods where they are manufactured. The Route Brokers, based in Great Neck, N.Y., matches buyers and sellers of routes. Ask other route drivers for the names of similar kind of brokers in your area.

Job: Travel Representative

Path #1: Travel agent

It is not recommended that you go to school for this very narrow specialty; you can learn on the job using your clerical skills, computer knowledge and travel knowledge. Your local agent may be willing to train you in exchange for assistance. The travel agency business is changing very dramatically at the present time, because airlines and many large cruise lines, for example, are paying less commission to agents. Consequently, agencies are looking for low-wage workers.

Co-op/joint marketing companies like Hickory Travel Systems in Saddle Brook, N.J., are a major part of the business now. According to a June 26, 1995 article in *Travel Trade*, Hickory predicted they would do $4.7 billion worth of sales in 1995. They offer to travel agents: training, marketing and sales support, networking and volume buying power. They are a leader in corporate travel management but other joint marketing companies provide leisure and cruise suppliers.

Path #2: Tour operator

Educators can work in tourist services. A love for the Hudson River led to tours of the Hudson by a professor who had led tours of the Volga River in Eastern Europe, in partnership with a local real estate agent. His specialty may not be the Hudson or American history, but his teaching experience has given him the ability to talk to a group and make the information lively and entertaining.

Some large tour operators operate their own training schools for tour guides. Travel expert and author of *Jobs in Paradise,* Jeff Maltzman, points out that you need to love working with people almost more than you love seeing new places; you may return again and again to the same places but those on the tour may be demanding in endlessly new ways.

The CLIA Cruise Manual, 500 Fifth Ave., Suite 1407, New York, NY 10011, offers information about 34 major cruise lines. Usually these lines are staffed by non-U.S. employees, although the entertainment and athletic staff may be American.

Call 800-ITN-4-YOU to see a sample copy of *International Travel News*, 520 Calvados Ave., Sacramento, CA 95815. They offer a lot of tour information, a part of the travel business that is expanding. *Eco Traveler* magazine will give you a sense of where the business is heading. It lists many tour operators. Write to Eco Traveler, P.O. Box 469003, Escondido, CA 92046-9850, 800-334-8152, for a sample copy. *Specialty Travel, Tour and Travel News, Tour Trade, Tours!, Travel Agent* and *Travel Weekly* are all magazines that will help you understand this business.

See also *Adventure Careers* by Alex Hiam and Susan Angle (Career Press). This is a guide to exciting jobs, uncommon occupations and extraordinary experiences. See also *Jobs in Paradise* by Jeff Maltzman (Harper Collins). This book lists resorts in exotic places that are hiring.

Bookkeeping/Accounting jobs

Bookkeeper
Accountant
Auditor

Job: Bookkeeper

Path #1: Free short-term training

If you are a high school student you can study bookkeeping in school; as an adult you can go to your city board of education's public adult education program, which will include the computer applications for bookkeeping and beginning typing.

Path #2: Work experience

A volunteer position in a nonprofit organization or summer or part-time work as an assistant bookkeeper might be available to you. You can learn on the job and use the experience to begin a bookkeeping career.

Path #3: Paid internship and courses, associate's degree

In many community colleges, students who are in two-year programs in accounting are placed in paid work internships for credit. Don't get the A.A.S.; this degree contains many courses for which credit will not be given if you decide to go on and get a bachelor's degree in accounting. The A.S. degree in accounting will prepare you for a job as a cost clerk, bookkeeper or tax examiner trainee. Look for an A.S. program articulated with a four-year program in accounting so you won't lose credits if you decide to continue your education. Stanley, who has a very successful accounting firm in Manhattan, worked as a bookkeeper during the day and went to school at night to earn his degree and to prepare for the CPA exam.

Job: Accountant

Path #1: Bachelor's degree

There are two kinds of accountants: corporate management accountants and Certified Public Accountants (CPAs). According to the Institute of Management Accountants and the Financial Executives Institute, companies looking for management accountants and public accountancy firms both require the bachelor's degree in accounting. Of late, corporations are complaining that those with the Bachelor of Business Administration don't get enough training in budgeting, product costing and asset management, and they don't want to hire master's degree accountants because they expect too high a salary. Corporations recommend an internship and less study of personal income taxes and external auditing, which CPAs need.

Path #2: CPA

Most states require the CPA to have a bachelor's degree from an accredited program in accounting before they sit for the state exams. In some states, CPAs also are required to have two years of experience, during which time they are expected to work 12-hour days, before they sit for the exams. You can take a bachelor's degree and then begin your accounting training to take the CPA exams at the graduate level in some states. The number of graduates needed to replace retiring workers is great.

The State Board of Accountancy in your state will explain requirements for the various kinds of accountancy in your state. This board can be contacted through the state agency that licenses professionals. See the blue pages at the end of your telephone directory. Contact the American Association of Certified Public Accountants (AICPA), 1211 Sixth Ave., New York, NY 10036-8775, 212-596-6200, or your state board of accountancy to get your state's requirements for taking the CPA exam.

Job: Auditor

To sit for the tax auditor's exam requires the bachelor's degree in accounting. Working for this tax bureaucracy should be considered if you have political skills. Josef (*Vocational Biographies*) examines returns for corporations. He says he is used to being seen as the "bad guy" and often can defuse the situation with some diplomacy. Previously he worked as a controller for one company and a cost accountant for another. His next step will be to supervise agents.

Banking/Finance jobs

Banker
Broker

Banks are businesses. Bankers describe six major areas in their industry: commercial banking (for businesses), retail banking (for individuals), developing and marketing new services, trust management, personnel administration and operations and systems (organizational tasks, via computer). Brokerage houses are organized along similar lines.

Job: Banker

Path #1: Teller

According to the *Occupational Outlook Handbook*, full-time tellers earn an average of $14,800 annually, but most tellers work part-time. High school graduation is a requirement for employment and your skills will be tested before you are hired. Working as a teller can help you get your foot in the door for other careers in banking, but you will be competing against many other tellers.

Path #2: Banking experience

Banks take many of their new officers or managers from fields other than banking because they have business experience. Some transferring into banking are not college graduates—they have learned on the job instead. The American Banking Institute, an affiliate of the American Bankers Association, is a major trainer of bank employees who want to move ahead.

Path #3: Bachelor's degree

Generally bank trainees are college graduates with majors in finance, economics or business. It may be possible to enter banking with a liberal arts bachelor's degree if you have courses in accounting, economics, finance and business law. Large banks in big cities prefer the M.B.A. and commercial banks require it. Of the banking industry's top management, 80 percent have been recruited from the commercial banking field.

The American Bankers Association suggests that, with a college degree and some courses in economics, finance, and business law, you can consider jobs as trust officer, market researcher, public relations specialist, branch manager, credit analyst, loan officer, accountant, programmer or correspondent banking officer. But remember, many banking positions are filled by people with business experience, so it is recommended that you get some during your college years.

According to an article by Peter Kilborn in *The New York Times*, Nino Toscano, a graduate of the University of Delaware, both went to school and worked full-time at MBNA America, a financial services company. He was an economics major who took many computer courses. He is now a financial analyst at a salary of $40,000 with MBNA.

Path #4: Examiner

The operation of all banks is overseen by state or federal examiners. Examiners of the Federal Deposit Insurance Corporation (FDIC) must have the bachelor's degree with 24 semester hours in accounting, economics, finance or business administration and 12 semester hours in accounting. Or, the applicant must have three years of nonclerical banking experience (either in loans, trust management or auditing). You must apply during the "open period" for application, which occurs for a month in the fall.

Working as a bank examiner is a common route by which to enter banking. It requires a lot of travel, but the applicant can express a preference for a region. The Securities Exchange Commission of the federal government and the states also hire and train examiners.

Contact the FDIC, 550 17th St. NW, Room 829, Washington, DC 20429, 202-393-8400. For more information, write for the pamphlet, "Building Your Future, Banking Is the Answer," from the American Bankers Association, 1120 Connecticut Ave. NW, Washington, DC 20036, or call 202-663-5000.

Job: Broker

Path #1: Commodities clerk

Commodities clerks work in the stock exchange itself, where stocks and bonds are sold. The broker, who handles the selling of stocks and bonds for the customer, makes the transaction and phones it into the exchange to make the trade. If you live in a major city with a stock exchange, the operations areas may hire you if you have done some data entry and understand how to enter transactions.

Many start as runners, taking orders to the pits to be filled. Chris has been a phone clerk, an arbitrage clerk and now works as a futures executioner for Goldman Sachs, a brokerage. He works on the floor of the Chicago Mercantile Exchange, buying and selling for a principal on a commission basis. A futures exchange is a place where buyers and sellers meet to agree on a price for a future date; for example, you promise to buy or sell Swiss francs now, hoping that the price will change in the future and you will profit. Chris works from 5:30 a.m. to 2 p.m. and then exercises to work out the stress from a hectic day on the exchange floor.

Executioners earn from $40,000 to $150,000 a year depending on experience and the amounts of personal and company bonuses. Most of these workers are young and, according to a 1995 article in the *Occupational Outlook Quarterly*, published by the Department of Labor, the number of women is growing.

Path #2: Internship

For college students, internships are available at the major brokerage houses. To land one of these you need to consult a directory of brokerage houses and then write to the companies for which you would like to intern. Talk to your college careers officer for more information.

Path #3: Job in a brokerage house

Because investment brokerage houses use so many clerks, tellers, secretaries and data processors, you should be able to get a job if you have graduated high school and are good with numbers. In these brokerage houses, and increasingly in banks which offer investment services, there are brokers who sell stocks and bonds to customers.

Securities analysts, assisted by researchers and statisticians, study the market and suggest which stocks will perform well. Accountants and clerks who work in the accounting department handle the paperwork to transfer securities, and, in the order department, they transfer the orders to the stock exchange.

A summer job as a clerk or assistant librarian at a brokerage house will allow you to gain experience. A clerk with a keen interest in the market and good sales skills can take the exams to become a registered representative, a necessary credential for all brokers. Clerks can move toward becoming officers in the operations (computerized bookkeeping) division of the company, especially if they have computer training. The yellow pages will help you locate brokerage services in your area; Insurance-Investment and Stock and Bond Brokers are two common listings.

Path #4: Registered representative

Large brokerage firms will hire inexperienced college graduates with degrees in finance, business or economics as trainees. Smaller firms want employees with sales experience, above all else. They will help trainees pass the exams to become brokers and keep them on salary while they prove themselves.

There are many career-changers who become brokers, and many high school graduates who begin as clerks or secretaries and then take the examinations to be registered representatives (brokers). You must be sponsored by a firm to take the examination. Occasionally, the college graduate can get a job as a statistician or research assistant and then move to broker-securities analyst by dint of hard work and strong motivation.

For more information about the examination, write to The National Association of Securities Dealers, 9513 Key West Ave., Rockville, MD 20850, 301-590-6500. You could also request "The Job Seekers Guide," ($1) which gives a general description of the industry, from the Securities Industry Association, 120 Broadway, New York, NY 10271, 212-608-1500.

Path #5: Trader and analyst

Merrill Lynch, Salomon Brothers and Morgan Stanley are investment banks. They sell stocks to individuals, but most of their business is proprietary trading, buying and selling stocks for pension funds and mutual funds. According to an April 16, 1995 article in *The New York Times*, the U.S. trading chief of Salomon Brothers, earned $26 million last year; the customer traders earned $400,000 last year on average.

Linda Runyon is an analyst for Merrill Lynch. She advises institutional investors on wireless communications companies that make cellular phones and satellites. She gets a percentage of each trade her customers make. *Institutional Investor* magazine ranked her as the top analyst in her field. She is a graduate of Harvard and Wharton School of Business and has worked at Morgan Stanley.

Sales/Marketing jobs

Salesperson   Public Relations Representative
Advertiser   Marketer

Job: Salesperson

Path #1: Sales with a high school diploma

Selling requires persistence and consists of explaining how the product will meet the customer's needs. There are manufacturer's sales representatives who sell everything from computers to airplanes, personal sales representatives who sell stocks or insurance, and retail sales persons and wholesale trade sales representatives, who sell a wholesaler's goods to a retail store.

Retail sales. You can enter retail sales with a high school diploma. Chances of promotion may be limited in certain businesses such as large department stores, which prefer to train college graduates. In chain drug stores, for example, the sales clerk can become the store manager and then move into a marketing management position if she or he is very successful.

Insurance sales. Jobs in personal insurance sales do not require a college degree, but you must pass licensing examinations. The agent works for the broker, which represents the insured. In New York state the broker must have prior work experience and the agent must be sponsored by a company to sit for the exams.

The company may hire you and train you, and you can get licensed because you work for them. For a person who can see rejections as a possible sale down the road, be accessible to clients and service the accounts, this is a good field. Most insurance policies carry a small payment to the seller for the length of the policy, so older salespeople do well; they have sold a lot of policies over a lifetime.

Many insurance policies are offered through employers in group plans. If you think you would enjoy selling plans like these, speak with someone in benefits in the personnel department of a local corporation. Find out which insurance companies are approaching them.

Diana got into insurance when she moved to a rural area with very few jobs. She saw an employment ad, filled out an application, passed the test given by the company, was given the books to study for her license, got the license, then was told to sell five policies before she could go to the week-long training. The employer was concerned with her ability to sell because she didn't know anyone in the area. She took the training and worked as an agent out of the office, cold-calling families who just had a baby or families who just had a death. According to the U.S. Department of Labor, the median annual salary of insurance sales workers was $30,100 in 1992. Contact the state licensing bureau for more information on insurance agents in your state.

HMO sales. Account executive jobs in HMOs are often available to the high school graduate with some college education. Debbie was doing day care at home, then went back to community college for some business courses. When she felt her two daughters were old enough, she accepted a job at an HMO and shortly afterward made her first sales presentation.

Real estate sales. For information about requirements to sell real estate, call the agency in your state government that licenses agents; the name of the agency varies by state. In New York state, you must be 18, pass a 45-hour course, be sponsored by a broker and pass an examination. To be a broker, you need a year of experience selling, an additional course and a separate examination. Managing properties, like malls and large office buildings, is really a subfield of real estate management. In large cities, there are firms that manage real estate for owners. They collect rent and see to repairs.

Sales for a manufacturer. As a high school graduate, you may be able to get a job with a wholesaler, and after several years of work experience and training, you may be able to sell wholesale to retail stores or other companies. According to a June 13, 1994 *Fortune* magazine article, the G & F company, a molder of plastic parts, took on an inside sales representative, as opposed to a commissioned outside representative, to deal with one important customer. The rep will do technical troubleshooting and on-site inventory (at the customer's factory).

Radio time sales. Radio time sales representatives often enter these jobs from print (newspaper or magazine) advertising. Carolyn (*Vocational Biographies*) worked for her local newspaper in high school. She worked in classified advertising, legal advertising and accounting. She observed that the people in sales were making more money than the journalists writing for the paper. After high school graduation, she went to work for the paper full-time and took some courses in marketing and basic advertising at night. She worked as the secretary to the advertising sales coordinator, and then was offered a job selling ads for the paper. After two years, she left to join an advertising agency where she coordinated media buying and worked as an account executive, helping clients with their ads. She calls clients to ask for ads, makes cold calls on prospective clients and meets with clients to help them plan.

Auto sales. Auto sales is an area you can enter without a college degree if you have successful selling experience and a professional appearance. Cynthia got her job because an auto company executive saw her operating successfully in another selling job. The field as a whole has a big turnover because many people are unhappy with the financial instability that results from selling on commission.

Path #2: Sales for the college graduate or career-changer

The college graduate with scientific, technical or engineering training can often get a sales job. Technical sales jobs, such as selling computers to businesses, jets to the Saudis or biotechnology to hospitals, are the highest paying. A manufacturer's sales representative for a major manufacturer like Microsoft or Apple requires a computer science or engineering degree. Of the 16 top sales firms in various industries, ranked by the magazine *Sales and Marketing Management,* most are in the industries of chemicals, pharmaceuticals, hotels or forest products.

Major retail stores often sponsor management training programs for college graduates. Fashion or home furnishings buyers in such programs start in sales and then move to section or department manager, then to buyer. Lori (*Vocational Biographies*) started as a sales associate and became sales manager, supervising 15 employees in three departments, then moved to a larger store, supervising 30 employees as a sales manager. By this time she had managed a variety of departments and decided to apply in-house for a buyer's job, which she got. She chooses the sportswear and activewear for her store on buying trips to New York, where she meets with wholesale representatives to negotiate good prices. She chooses the items for sales and places advertisements in the local papers. The pay varies, depending on the store and the region but according to a survey by the College Placement Council, printed in *The New York Times,* college graduates starting in retail store chains like The Gap, Kmart, JCPenney, etc., receive salaries from $20,000 to $25,000.

Path #3: Real estate

Big cities offer two unique opportunities in the real estate field for the college graduate: real estate securitization, which involves the formation of real estate investment trusts, and real estate mortgage-backed securities. Both jobs are in commercial real estate; you get ratings on loans and then market these loans. You need excellent math, quantitative and risk analysis skills and an understanding of the real estate market. You would be employed by an investment establishment. Another possibility might be a job in commercial leasing. Real estate advisory firms have training programs for young people with any major; they hire job seekers with natural marketing abilities.

Job: Advertiser

Path #1: Work experience

Temporary, part-time or summer work as a clerk, secretary or assistant in the traffic department of an advertising agency is a good way to learn the language of the business and to make contacts. People in traffic plan, schedule and coordinate jobs.

Path #2: Internship

Hundreds of agencies take interns. They use internships to find talented future employees. Internships are available in most major cities across the country. The American Advertising Federation sells an internship directory for $15 which lists contact persons at each agency. Their free booklet, "Careers in Advertising," explains the basics of the field. Contact the American Advertising Federation, Education Services, 1101 Vermont Ave. NW, Suite 500, Washington, DC 20005, 800-999-AAF1.

The American Association of Advertising Agencies (AAAA), 666 Third Ave., New York, NY 10017, has a 10-week summer internship program for students between their junior and senior years of college. During the summer of 1994, 44 students were placed in 25 agencies. The four basic departments are account management, media copywriting, and research and art direction. Contact Jacqueline Llewellyn, AAAA, 212-682-2500, ext. 288.

Path #3: Advertising account executive

Companies pay advertising agencies to prepare and place advertisements in the media (newspapers, magazines, displays, radio and television). The account executive manages the client's account by researching the product, then developing a marketing plan and an advertising campaign. The AAAA estimates that there are 200 to 300 account manager training programs a year in advertising agencies for the college graduate who has taken some business courses. Of the top 100 agencies, 31 responded to a survey in 1993 reporting that they hired 310 entry-level workers. One common way to prepare as an account executive is to get experience in the advertising or marketing department of a manufacturer after graduation from college. This is valuable experience for the account executive because agencies specialize; some may handle only pharmaceuticals for example, and want people with a knowledge of that industry. Agencies also look for graduates with the M.B.A. degree. To be a media buyer (you buy advertising space for clients), you need the bachelor's degree with courses in marketing and statistics.

According to the AAAA, majoring in advertising is not a good approach for getting a job as an account executive because agencies don't value these degrees. A liberal arts degree is preferred. Journalism, mass communication and advertising majors find employment as media planners and buyers, not as account executives.

Martha (*Vocational Biographies*) is the director of advertising, publicity and promotion for a television syndication company that produces and distributes television shows and movies. While she was getting her college degree, she interned at a TV studio, then she used the experience gained from the internship to become a production assistant for a TV show about women's issues. Her job consisted of reading magazines for interesting topics, booking guests, and making sure the host was briefed before interviewing all guests. She called a contact who was working a television industry convention, was hired to do public relations for a company and got a job at the convention as a promotion coordinator. Soon she was writing the entire promotional package, photo captions, biographies and synopses of shows being distributed, including *Facts of Life, Silver Spoons* and *Diff'rent Strokes.*

Jay Chiat of Chiat/Day, the creator of the Energizer bunny and the UBU Reebok campaigns, headed "the agency of the decade" in the 1980s, according to an article printed in *The New York Times* on January 15, 1995. His past clients include Nike, Pizza Hut and American Express. He got his start creating ads for trailer homes and fishing rods.

For more information, write to the American Association of Advertising Agencies, 666 Third Ave., New York, NY 10017, 212-682-2500.

Path #4: Copywriter

Copywriting at a retail store or mail order house is good experience if you want to enter the advertising field as a copywriter. From it, you will create the materials to build the portfolio you'll need for your job search.

The bachelor's degree is required for the first job. A combination of liberal arts courses and some courses in marketing, management and journalism would be helpful to you. You will need a portfolio of writing samples. According to the AAAA, agencies want someone who "knows what's in, a self-starter who has more than a slight touch of ego, a liberal arts major who has done selling of some sort, especially of himself or herself." For more information about a career as a copywriter, contact the AAAA address above.

Job: Public Relations Representative

Path #1: Internship

In general, working as an intern during college or an assistant after graduation is the way many are trained in this field, but you must have good word processing skills to enter, so you can be immediately useful. Write to the Public Relations Society of America, 33 Irving Pl., 3rd Floor, New York, NY 10003, 212-995-2230, for information about the field and student chapters of the society. Enclose $3.50 for their career pamphlet, "Careers In Public Relations."

Path #2: Copywriter

Because copywriters are trained to write press releases, they can do technical or ethical copywriting for drug advertisers. (This is called ethical copywriting because you will be writing about drugs and you must be careful to accurately describe the products.) Public relations people can also work for schools, museums and businesses under any of the following job titles: public information, investor relations, public affairs, corporate and employee relations and communications, customer relations and consumer relations.

To be a copywriter or public relations worker, you need a knowledge of the industry or area in which you want to work and good writing and speaking skills. Public relations is a field where personal contacts, the right appearance and a portfolio of published samples play a role in building your career. Media contacts are particularly important; often people in public relations enter the field through jobs in journalism, advertising or marketing.

The Publicity Clubs of New York, Boston, Chicago and Los Angeles are places to meet people in the public relations business who might be able to answer your questions. *O'Dwyer's Directory of Corporate Communications* and *O'Dwyer's Directory of Public Relations Firms* list the public relations staff within corporations by name and position. These reference works are available in your library. Contacting people in an area of interest to you may help you set up the right internship.

Joe Feeks's company handles agricultural accounts. According to an article in the *Kingston Freeman* (New York), he promotes in agriculture, veterinary medicine, animal nutrition and related fields. If a client has an antibiotic for hogs, Joe will interview farmers, take pictures and then send press kits to magazines that cater to hog farmers, so the magazines can write articles on the antibiotic. He represents six different companies and employs part-time writers and a graphic artist. Joe doesn't have an M.B.A., which is valuable in public relations, but he does have a science degree; this kind of dual expertise—in public relations and a field related to the industry being promoted—is very important and highly recommended for success in the field.

Job: Marketer

Salespeople eventually may become marketing managers. The salesperson's knowledge of a product's market is essential for the successful promotion of the product. Personal sales (for example, insurance sales), sales promotion, public relations experience or advertising agency work is the best way to get into marketing. Sales promotion is an area of marketing that includes advertising efforts like contests and special offers. Merchandising and marketing are the chief jobs of most business executives.

Millard (Mickey) Drexler (*Current Biography Yearbook*) was brought into The Gap as president in the early 1980s, making the company the number one apparel retailer and the number two clothing brand in the country. Drexler wanted to be a businessman as a child. He was familiar with the apparel business because his father bought buttons and leather for a coat manufacturer and his uncle had a laundry. Drexler got an undergraduate degree in business and an M.B.A. from Boston University. During the summers he interned at A&S (Abraham & Strauss) in Brooklyn. After graduation, he went back to A&S and rose through the ranks, but was bothered by the bureaucracy.

At that point he was tapped to become president of Ann Taylor. He turned this chain into the place for the mid-level corporate woman to buy a wardrobe. Then he was chosen, as a keen merchandiser, to refigure The Gap. Cheap jeans were replaced with good fabrics and classic designs. He added a greater variety of clothing, cleaned up the interiors and got rid of the numbers crunchers. His corporate culture emphasizes close communication at all levels and innovative print advertising campaigns.

When he enters a store he wants to know how particular items are selling, what is being used to clean the floors, why a sale sign is placed in one place and not another. Learning an industry and having "a sense of style" lead to a successful merchandising career.

One example of a marketing company is Dimark in Langhorne, Pa. It does direct-to-consumer promotions for HMOs. Several Blue Cross-Blue Shields companies and Schering-Plough, a drug company, are some of their clients. Dimark can get out a promotion in 90 days; it designs and mails pamphlets, does telemarketing, makes TV and radio commercials, does ad campaigns and provides databases. In 1994, Dimark was chosen by *Fortune* magazine as an up-and-coming company because of its excellent track record in HMO marketing.

Nonprofit organizations are often looking for marketing directors and development coordinators. For example, the Florida Natural Areas Inventory in Tallahassee wants someone to design and implement all aspects of the fund raising strategy and community relations plan. The employee will prepare plans, motivate and coordinate efforts of volunteers, educate and solicit donors and potential donors, supervise the annual giving program, expand the membership and work to increase public awareness of the organization through the media. The ad for this job, printed in the summer of 1995, reads:

> *"The job includes high level contact with trustees, donors, membership, staff, other organizations and the public. You will be working closely with the state director and other staff in planning, budget preparation and chapter board relations. Qualifications: Prior experience in fund raising, business or public relations. Strong communications and personal skills, both verbal and written. Willingness to travel. Commitment to conservation."*

Utilities are making increasing use of marketers as they deregulate. They must compete for customers. Credit card marketing (selling card services to businesses), public relations and sports marketing are growing fields. College students should get internships in college if they wish to enter the sports field. Besides marketing special events, according the to *Occupational Outlook Quarterly,* sports marketers work for teams, universities and sports management companies. Sports marketing directors work with specialists in advertising, promotions and public relations. They license products, select manufacturers, set the terms of the licenses and may advise businesses on how to promote their product using sports.

According to the American Marketing Association, a marketing job in brand management requires coordinating production, sales, research and development, market research, legal details, purchasing, warehousing, transportation, advertising, sales promotion, package development and finances for a particular brand. The M.B.A. is the desirable credential. For more information, "Careers in Marketing" is available from the American Marketing Association, 250 South Wacker Dr., Suite 200, Chicago, IL 60606, 312-648-0536.

Market researchers usually work for large advertising agencies. They design research on consumer perceptions of brand names, effects of length on TV commercials, premarket forecasting, buying decisions and humor in advertising. See the American Marketing Association's *Journal of Marketing Research.*

Law jobs

Paralegal
Lawyer
Arbitrator/Ombudsperson

According to a January 27, 1989 article in *The New York Times,* law requires a talent for self-promotion, the skills of an advocate, the desire to learn the law and the ability to persuade. Most politicians, at all levels of government, are lawyers. A review of the backgrounds of all members of the House of Representatives and the Senate will prove this point.

Job: Paralegal

Paralegals assist lawyers and are primarily liberal arts graduates. The job may include clerical tasks, like coding or legal research. Temporary work in a clerical or secretarial position in a law office can be used to become familiar with the terms necessary to do paralegal work. There are short-term programs at private vocational schools, and some community colleges have certificate or degree programs to prepare people to be paralegals. Big city firms are more likely to use paralegals; in some regions, lawyers now do their own paralegal work.

Laurie (*Vocational Biographies*) helps the attorneys in her firm prepare for trials by researching facts, related judicial decisions and laws. She handles the indexing and summarizing of transcripts taken before the trial and reviews medical records. She had a two-year legal assistant degree, then went on to get a four-year degree and did a summer internship in a law firm. She got a good reference from the firm after graduation, went door-to-door in her small town with her resume and immediately got several offers.

Job: Lawyer

Path #1: Law apprentice

According to a December 20, 1991 article in *The New York Times*, by Robb London, in seven states (New York, California, Vermont, Washington, Virginia, Alaska and Maine), law clerks who assist attorneys for three to four years are eligible to sit for the bar examination. In Maine and New York, they also must have completed at least one year of law school. In these states, law clerks earn money working and save law school tuition; this is especially good for parents and career-changers.

Each state requires that apprentices spend some time each week in tutorials with the lawyer for whom they are working, take periodic tests and read a curriculum provided by the lawyer. (In the eighteenth and nineteenth centuries, all lawyers were trained in this way.) Michael Watkins, a Seattle lawyer and a former apprentice who oversees the apprentice program administered by the Bar

Examiners of Washington state, likes to point out that two Chief Justices of the Washington State Supreme Court and a former managing partner of one of the Northwest's largest firms were educated as apprentices.

Path #2: Take the bar exam

To find out about the requirements to be a lawyer in your state, call the American Bar Association or the state agency that regulates lawyers. Most states require at least three years of college before law school. The specific requirements for admission to the bar in a particular state may be obtained at the state capital from the clerk of the Supreme Court or the Secretary of Bar Examiners. Write to Information Services, American Bar Association, 750 North Lake Shore Dr., Chicago, IL 60611, 312-988-5000.

Lawyers are having a tough time entering as managers or executives, unless, for example, they are moving from real estate law to real estate investment. The number of people with M.B.A.s on the market are challenging lawyers who want to move into business. On the other hand, corporations will continue to need lawyers and these jobs are among the highest paid in the field.

Lawyers are needed in many areas of the society. For example, Kathryn Fuller (*Current Biography Yearbook*) is a lawyer who is head of the World Wildlife Fund (WWF). In the five years she has been president, she has doubled the membership and increased the income to more than $70 million. To date, WWF has arranged the conversion of $51 million in debt to $45 million for conservation through 14 debt-for-nature swaps in eight countries. (A portion of a developing nation's foreign debt is forgiven in exchange for that country's commitment to set aside funds for conservation projects.)

As an undergraduate, Kathryn was a law firm clerk one summer and an advertising copywriter another summer. She majored in English. After graduation she worked in libraries for a number of years. One of these was in a zoology museum, where she met two ecologists who invited her to spend two months in Africa studying the migration of wildebeests. In Africa, she made the decision to go to law school and specialize in wildlife law. After graduating, she clerked for the chief judge of the U.S. District Court, then went to work for the Department of Justice in Washington. Here she specialized in litigation involving the trade in animals, animal products and plant resources.

Later she became chief of the Wildlife and Marine Resources section. While on maternity leave, she started in a master's degree program in marine, estuary and environmental studies at the University of Maryland. After the birth of a third child, she decided to become a consultant for WWF, later becoming a full-time employee and then president.

Construction projects like the tunnel under the English Channel, the nationalization of oil concessions and increased global trade all require lawyers speaking several languages. Another growing area for lawyers is intellectual property and copyright disputes, especially on the computer and in the media.

Another aspect of law is the prosecution of criminals for the state. Janet Reno (*Current Biography Yearbook*), the first woman to become Attorney General of the United States, majored in chemistry at Cornell and then went to Harvard Law School. In 1960, she was one of 16 women in a class of 500. Despite this record of accomplishment, she had trouble finding a job with the large local firms after graduation. She joined a smaller firm and later teamed up with another lawyer to open Lewis and Reno.

She was appointed staff director of the Judiciary Committee of the Florida House of Representatives in 1971. She helped revise the state constitution, which reorganized the Florida court system. Later she helped revise the criminal code as counsel for the state senate's Criminal Justice Committee. Then she went to work for the state attorney's office in Dade County. Her boss suggested she become prosecutor for the county when he stepped down; she became the first woman to head a county prosecutor's office in Florida and won re-election four times.

Job: Arbitrator/Ombudsperson

Lawyers may move on to serve as arbitrators. According to a June 1992 *Nation's Business* article, arbitrators can settle cases before they go before a jury. Businesspeople, especially, like to work out their differences informally to save legal costs. There are firms that provide mediation like Judicate in Philadelphia, Bates Edwards in

San Francisco and Endispute in Washington, D.C.; most arbitrators for these firms are lawyers or retired judges.

Some mediators are citizens who work in courts and schools after a brief training. Often they work as volunteers. If you are trained as an arbitrator, then work in the courts as a volunteer, you may be able to enter the field, assisting in mediations. The mediation or alternative dispute resolution coordinator within your local court system may handle construction, personal injury, wrongful dismissal, partnership disagreements, commercial contract disputes, real estate and landlord tenant disputes, product liability, stockbrokers and client disputes.

Contact The American Arbitration Association, 140 West 51st St., New York, NY 10020, 212-484-4000. This outfit handled 59,424 arbitrations in 1994.

Ombudspersons serve as advocates working within institutions— for example, mental health advocates or the ombudsman in a local hospital to whom patients can turn if they have a problem with the service they are getting.

Politics / Civil Service jobs

Politician	City Manager/Urban Planner
Civil Servant	State Department/Foreign Service Officer

Job: Politician

Path #1: Internship

The first step is to choose the areas in which you are interested and then arrange an internship or volunteer job. In positions like these, you'll be asked to start off by doing research, making phone calls for fund raisers and calling voters before an election to ask them to vote. If you only want to do "issue work" (around a specific issue), try to find a position in that field.

City departments such as your city council and your city department of planning may have internships or programs available for volunteers. Most state governments have internships in the state assembly, senate or office of the governor.

Congressional representatives operate offices in their districts using volunteers, interns and paid staff. Planners and administrators in government are experts in specific areas, e.g. transportation, municipal finance, architecture or engineering. Decide which city department you want to work for and which tasks you would be willing to do as a volunteer for a legislator. Graduate degrees in public administration or urban planning have proved, in many cases, to be much more useful when combined with government experience.

Path #2: Intern with a lobbying group or with the government

Ralph Nader's Public Interest Research Groups have offices in cities across the country. These groups do research and lobbying on environmental, tax and consumer issues. Write to USPIRG, 215 Pennsylvania Ave. SE, Washington, DC 20003, or call 202-546-9707 for information. Consult the *Encyclopedia of Associations* in the library for the names of other groups working in your particular interest area.

The Washington Center places interns in summer or semester-long jobs in Washington in both nongovernmental institutions like the U.S. Chamber of Commerce, CNN and Amnesty International or in executive agencies like the EPA, Defense Department, Office of Management and Budget, Federal Trade Commission and Department of Education. Interns participate in classes and The Washington Forum, a variety of lectures, Congressional breakfasts, White House briefings, tours, site visits, workshops and information sessions.

Multicultural Education, Leadership for America's Cities and Campaign '96 are other seminar titles. The Washington Center is a very large program; it places 100 or so students a year. One intern, Marlo Alford, says working with the college arm of the Department of Education taught her about awarding, monitoring and writing grants and gave her the opportunity to network with prominent political figures on Capitol Hill.

Write to The Washington Center for Internships and Academic Seminars, 1101 14th St. NW, Suite 500, Washington, DC 20005-5601, or call 800-486-8921 for program information. The center also offers a two-week seminar for college women called Women as Leaders.

If your interest is in politics, journalism, civil service, business or law, the center will have a relevant internship. The Washington Center charges about $2,500 in program fees plus housing; you may be able to get college credit.

The Washington Center helps students apply for existing intern positions, so you could also go directly to the agency—for example, to the State Department—to avoid the fee.

Path #3: Legislative assistant

Terry (*Vocational Biographies*) is a legislative assistant to her state senator. She works in his office in Washington researching issues for bills, attending committee meetings, preparing reports, speaking to the press and organizing fund raising. She has a bachelor's degree and worked as a public relations coordinator for the admissions office at her college. She was assistant news and public affairs director for the radio station, and wrote and produced a weekly news program, directing a staff of 15 reporters and eight daily newscasts. She also did a White House internship in the communications department. After graduation, she worked as a volunteer campaign manager for a state assemblyman, then as assembly secretary for another representative. With this background in state politics, she was able to get a job with the senator and now works as his "political person" (handling campaigns), although she does some "issue work," too. She may go on to be the Legislative Chief of Staff, running the Washington office and overseeing the district offices, or she could move into lobbying, run for office herself or work as a campaign consultant.

Getting a White House Fellowship will help your political career. Many White House fellows go on to be senators; fellows hired are symbols of certain political values as well as outstanding people in their own right. You are paid as a government employee at a rate no higher than $56,567 and work as a special assistant to the President. They are looking for people who are or show promise as national leaders. Write to the President's Commission on White House Fellowships, 72 Jackson Pl. NW, Washington, DC 20503, or call 202-395-4522 for more information.

Path #4: Run for office

Campus student government offers a chance to learn about politics by dealing with various constituencies within the university. This is reported to be excellent experience for those wishing to enter political life as elected representatives. If you are interested in politics, you should seriously consider running for office in your community after college. Many local races result in the election of a newcomer. After some town volunteer positions, county assembly or state assembly service could be your next step.

Nora Bredes decided to run for a Suffolk County, N.Y., legislative seat. She had earned recognition because she had worked successfully to close down a nuclear reactor in her area, and had run for office before. According to an October 15, 1994 article in *Your Money,* the Democratic Party supplied a campaign manager, printing and telephone services and volunteer support. In one weekend, she raised $17,000; the entire campaign cost $31,166, which she raised by holding garage sales and wine and cheese parties. She won a two-year seat in her county legislature, for which she is compensated on a part-time basis.

Ann Richards (*Current Biography Yearbook*), the ex-governor of Texas, is another example. She taught junior high school for a while, got involved in politics through her husband, a Democratic precinct chairman, then worked for civil rights and, in 1975, ran for county commissioner. She won, then moved on to Texas state treasurer and then governor.

Bernie Sanders (*Current Biography Yearbook*) became interested in politics because of his older brother, the chairperson of the Young Democrats at Brooklyn College. Bernie transferred from Brooklyn College to the University of Chicago, where he led sit-ins protesting segregated campus housing. After graduation, he spent time on a kibbutz, then moved to Vermont and worked as a freelance writer, educational filmmaker and briefly as a researcher for the Vermont Tax Department. He started an independent party, and ran for senator and governor, while directing the American People's Historical Society in Burlington.

In 1981, his supporters urged him to run for mayor of Burlington. He was elected after a surprise endorsement from the police. Bernie thus became the only Socialist mayor in the country. He insisted on honest and efficient government. To protect the treasury, he computerized the accounting department, opened city insurance contracts to competitive bidding, squeezed more investment income from idle funds and pension contributions and ended the practice of extending low-interest public loans to political supporters. He established free health clinics for the poor and elderly. He erected low-cost housing and shelters for the homeless, expanded services to youth and created a city day care center. He continued to win re-election until 1989, when he declined a bid for a fifth term, but he ran for governor and later won a House seat.

Job: Civil Servant

Path #1: Take the exams for a city, state or federal job

Government hires people in almost every field. Dates of city job examinations are posted at the Office of Personnel of each city. In major cities, there may be review books for the exams. Dates of county and state job examinations are posted at the state Department of Labor office. For federal jobs, go to your regional Federal Jobs Information Center or consult the reference volume, *U.S. Government Manual,* to see which agencies might hire workers in your interest area. Ask the congressperson who represents the locality to get you an interview with the person in each agency who could hire you, as opposed to personnel, which would be more likely to screen you out. The federal newsletter, "Federal Careers," appears every two weeks. Your local library can get you a copy.

Ideally, your goal will not be to work for the government but to be an occupational therapist or engineer or meteorologist. While you are being trained, government jobs will be discussed or, as you do the job after your training, you will become aware of the possibilities in government employment for your field. The pay is not competitive with private enterprise, although the benefits may be impressive.

Job: City Manager/Urban Planner

City managers are responsible to elected officials and taxpayers. John (*Vocational Biographies*) is a city manager in Texas. During college he interned in the personnel department of his city and was encouraged to consider a career in city management. He got a fellowship in public administration after college and served as summer administrative intern for the state of Kentucky. He got a master's degree in public administration and started as the administrative assistant to the city manager, then moved to assistant city manager, then manager. He is appointed, so he doesn't have tenure. John's strong local ties helped him get his first job in city government.

Planners work with developers to meet city codes and keep building projects within the city's overall plan for development. In small towns, planning is done by a volunteer board, but in larger cities, professional planners work with developers. Jobs as city planners are easiest to find in areas which are growing, such as the South and Southwest.

Urban planners often have a master's degree in urban planning or they enter the field from architecture. However, degrees in planning or public administration should be approached with caution by those not already employed in public administration; often planners and administrators in government are experts in specific areas (e.g., transportation, municipal finance, architecture or engineering). New graduates without connections will have a hard time competing for jobs with these people. Plus, recent downsizing of government at all levels has eliminated many of these jobs.

Job: State Department/Foreign Service Officer

Path #1: Internship

The Bureaus of African Affairs, East Asian and Pacific Affairs, Near Eastern and South Asian Affairs, Inter-American Affairs, the Foreign Service Institute and many other bureaus at the State Department in Washington offer paid and unpaid internships during the school year or the summer. Contact the Intern Coordinator, Department of State, Recruitment Division, P.O. Box 9317, Rosslyn Station, Arlington, VA 22209-0317, 703-235-9373.

The International Trade Administration of the Department of Commerce offers internships in Washington and in offices around the country. Students of international relations, marketing, economics and business administration may apply. Filing dates are from January 15 through March 15. Write to DOC, Room 4808, 14th St. and Constitution Ave. NW, Washington, DC 20230, or call 202-482-3301.

Path #2: Corporate managers abroad

A specific major like business or public health, combined with travel and an in-depth knowledge of a specific geographic area, may be more useful than a major in international relations. Technical skills, an international perspective, training in economics and business, and good language skills—perhaps the most important criterion—are recommended.

Other jobs in the field of international relations or foreign affairs also require an area of expertise like child health or commercial law. To work overseas, you will be sent by an American company that values your expertise in a particular area. In other words, job leads abroad will come from your work in the U.S.

Path #3: Foreign Service officer

The U.S. Foreign Service formulates, implements and coordinates U.S. foreign policy. Careers in foreign service require at least a bachelor's degree.

The competition is fierce. (In demand are Arabic, Chinese, Russian and Korean.) If only speakers of English and Arabic are being considered for a particular job, this narrows the field of competition considerably and forces the employer to be flexible about other job requirements. For information about the Foreign Service, call The Career Hotline, 703-875-7490. The Foreign Service exam will be given again in the fall of 1996. In 1995, the Foreign Service wasn't hiring new general Foreign Service officers (also called consular officers).

However, the following positions were open:

facilities maintenance person	medical officer
information management specialist	medical technologist
information management technical specialist (telephone, radio, computer and digital)	nurse practitioner

Closed positions included:

general services officer	communications electronics officer
foreign service secretary	
financial management officer	narcotics control officer
diplomatic security/special agent	personnel officer
diplomatic courier	psychiatrist
construction engineering officer	security engineering officer

These lists give you a picture of what embassies and consulates require. As a foreign service specialist or a general foreign service officer, you will typically transfer to a new overseas post every two to four years and spend part of your career in Washington, D.C. You will need top security clearance.

According to the June 1995 *Foreign Service Journal,* Deborah Derrick is a foreign service officer working at the U.S. Consulate General in Durban, South Africa. She administers a small loan program to encourage educational and economic development in KwaZulu-Natal. She visits communities where the residents must raise money to build a school for their children.

Paul Burns, also served as a Peace Corps volunteer in Lesotho when he was 28. He taught English and biology to secondary school students. He had 60 to 70 students in his classes, in unheated buildings, but he says he learned a lot, and the students did, too. Now he works for the Peace Corps in Washington.

The Peace Corps is looking for technically trained individuals. According to a July 5, 1995 article by Laura Pedersen in *The New York Times,* only one in 10 applicants gets in. Contact: Peace Corps, Office of Personnel, 1990 K St. NW, Room 7007, Washington, DC 20526, 202-254-5170 or 800-424-8580, ext. 225.

Oxfam, CARE or Amnesty International instead may be able to place you in Africa, India, Pakistan, Sri Lanka or Bangladesh. Pedersen suggests reading the magazine *Transitions Abroad* (call 800-293-0373 for information). Be sure you understand what is involved in getting a work permit in the country in which you want to work.

The U.S. Information Agency (USIA) and U.S. Agency for International Development (USAID) also recruit through the Foreign Service. According to the *Foreign Service Journal,* USAID has spent $6 billion in Somalia, Ethiopia, Eritrea, Djibouti, Kenya, Sudan, Uganda, Rwanda, Burundi and Tanzania in the last 10 years. USAID works with private relief agencies, the host country and other agencies, like the State Department, to coordinate their efforts.

The Meridian Center offers cross-cultural training to visitors to the United States; it has programs in conjunction with USIA. Companies like the South African Business Council, law firms, the U.S. Secret Service and foreign embassies use the Meridian Center. For example, 44 Chinese businessmen will attend a seminar there on doing business in the U.S. The Center offers internships. Write to Meridian International Center, 1630 Crescent Pl., NW, Washington, DC 20009, or call 202-667-6800.

It is very difficult to enter the United Nations, but an internship will help. Our representative's office to the United Nations may be the place to start in understanding how your interests and the work they are doing may overlap. According to Kathy and Ross Petras, entering the World Bank, the International Monetary Fund (IMF) or other agency jobs requires experience and an advanced degree, like an M.B.A or Ph.D. in economics.

Charlene Barshefsky is a senior deputy U.S. trade representative. According to a January 27, 1995 article in *The New York Times*, she negotiates with Asian and Latin-American countries and recently negotiated with the Chinese to end trade sanctions against them in exchange for honoring U.S. intellectual property rights. Barshefsky spent 18 years at Steptoe and Johnson, a Washington law firm specializing in trade.

Many diplomats have law degrees and have taught law before entering public service. For example, Adolph Berle, who taught law at Columbia, was a consultant to the Paris Peace Commission after World War I, then part of Roosevelt's brain trust, then Assistant Secretary of State. Later he represented the U.S. at various major conferences abroad and served as our ambassador to Brazil. Law and diplomacy are closely intertwined.

Mitchell Reiss, an expert on nuclear nonproliferation, received a master's degree from the Fletcher School of Law and Diplomacy, a Ph.D. in international relations from Oxford and a law degree from Columbia. He works at the Institute for Strategic Studies and was a White House fellow. The institute is a foreign policy "think tank"— a private organization that influences governmental policy.

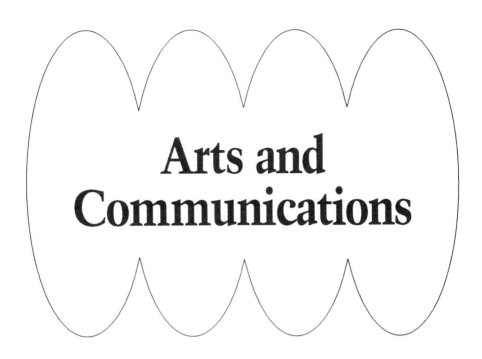

Arts and Communications

For success in this field you need to be creative and willing to take risks. People in these fields tend to veer away from conventionality.

Arts
Entertainment
Video, Film, TV and Cable Programming and Production
Design
Writing
Education/Administration

Arts jobs

Artist   Photographer
Craftsperson   Arts Manager

Fine artists sell to museums and collectors. According to the Bureau of Labor Statistics, even well-known artists rely on sales of their work for only a small part of their income. Many successful New York City painters earn their living by doing carpentry, but connect with other artists to get information about what's happening on the gallery scene. Other recognized painters earn a living teaching at the college level. Craftspersons make beautiful objects for which there is a market. Photographers often do both commercial and arts photography. Arts managers help artists flourish.

Job: Artist

Path #1: Self-support and learning in four related jobs

Work for a framer. Working for a framer will give you some exposure to what artists in the area are doing and provide a place for you to meet other artists in the community, especially if there is not a local art school. With a book on the subject of framing, a framer's T-square and some patience, you can get enough practice to convince an employer to hire you. See the yellow pages for picture framers in your area.

Gallery work/internship. Doing typing and reception in a gallery will give you an idea of what's selling locally and how dealers and gallery owners deal with artists. This can help you when you want to sell your own work. The paid sales assistants generally have college degrees and connections with collectors and museums here and in Europe, perhaps because they have worked in other galleries. Getting a gallery internship through your college or art school will also be a learning experience.

Restoration. Restoration of paintings is one way artists can earn a living to support their own painting. Contact the local museum's Objects Conservation Department to get the names of skilled restorers in your region for training, in which you learn to clean and replace damaged areas on the surface of the painting.

Apprenticeships. Your city or state arts council may be able to help you find an internship or paid apprenticeship with a practicing artist. See the listings in the telephone book's blue pages. If you are offered a position without a salary, you may want to try to get college credit.

Another approach is to write to an artist and follow up with a phone call. The letter should give evidence of an interest in art, specify how many hours you would like to work, the sort of tasks you would like to do and how you got the artist's name. This is a very valuable way to find a role model as well.

Path #2: Find a dealer or gallery to represent you

Getting an agreement from a dealer or gallery owner to represent you and show your work is the way many younger artists have started. This means making an appointment with the dealer to visit you in your studio. Or you can visit a large city after making appointments, and walk around with your work.

According to *Who's Who in America,* Mary Frank, a noted sculptor, studied with Max Bechman in 1950 and Hans Hoffman in 1951, but never got a degree. By the late 1950s, she was showing her work and teaching, and in 1970 she began teaching at Queens College, where she got a tenured position. In the 1960s, she had received a number of prestigious awards, which not only supported her financially but also helped her get tenure later. Mary Frank is now 62, still teaching and working.

Path #3: Get into a slide registry

There may be an open slide registry for artists in your state. For example, The Drawing Center in New York City maintains such a file for unaffiliated artists in New York state. Your state's art council may be able to help you locate a similar service. Buyers of art look at this registry and approach the gallery or artist if interested.

Path #4: Bachelor's or master's degree

Biographies of living American artists show that a majority have earned a Bachelor of Fine Arts (B.F.A.) rather than the Bachelor of Arts, a liberal arts degree. It is possible to get an M.F.A., Master of Fine Arts, after completing a liberal arts degree, however, many artists add the M.F.A. to their B.F.A. If you want to teach painting as your means of support as an artist, you must get both degrees.

Succeeding as an artist means earning recognition rather than money. One of the skills the successful artist needs is an instinct for self-promotion. Artists spend a considerable amount of time applying for grants, selling their work to galleries and applying for entrance to artist-run cooperative galleries and residencies.

Cindy Sherman (*Current Biography Yearbook*) enrolled at SUNY Buffalo to study art. A photography course encouraged her to abandon painting, and her first series of photographs show her gradual transformation. Robert Longo, a friend from Buffalo, showed Sherman's work to the curator of a gallery in Buffalo and her photographs were included in a survey show. After college, she got a $3,000 award from the National Endowment for the Arts (NEA) and moved to New York City. She worked as a receptionist for Artist's Space, whose director opened a gallery called Metro Pictures, where Sherman's work is still shown.

Jenny Holzer (*Current Biography Yearbook*) graduated from Ohio University with a B.F.A. Then she went to Rhode Island School of Design where she was an abstract painter, incorporating writing into her paintings. She won a fellowship to study contemporary art for a year at the Whitney Museum where she continued her textual works and anonymous art for public display. This honor opened up alternative exhibition spaces and her career took off.

Path #6: Get a grant

Your state arts council is also an important resource; they will send you a newsletter with grant deadlines and also share information about local and regional resources. See the blue pages in your phone book. The Information Office of the National Endowment for the Arts, Nancy Hanks Center, 1110 Pennsylvania Ave. NW, Washington DC 20506, 202-682-5566, is another source of support for the artist. The NEA currently gives out 11,000 fellowships to individual artists in many fields: dance, design arts, folk arts, international, literature, media arts, music, opera-musical theater, theater, visual arts. The steps toward a large grant like this are small competitions and regional shows.

Residencies or artists' colonies that allow the artist to work without worrying about room and board are also competitive, but Bob, an artist who had sold to a few galleries, had been steadily painting for years. He applied and got in to one of the most famous colonies on the third try. Some small foundations offer residencies to beginners. Ask your reference librarian for help in finding a directory that lists these for your region.

Job: Craftsperson

Path #1: Apprenticeship

Creating useful and aesthetic objects in ceramics, wood, glass, fiber, cloth or metal is the craftsperson's job. To succeed, you need an understanding of what is salable.

In this path you can learn technical skills, the business end of a craft specialty and see a successful craftsperson in action. Approach someone whose work you find appealing and ask him or her to consider taking you on as a helper. A craft fair is one place where you can see a broad spectrum of work. The American Crafts Council, 72 Spring St., New York, NY 10012-4019, 212-274-0630, will allow you to look at the visual material they have on file for 2,500 craftspersons. To use the registry, you can pay a $5 daily fee or a $40 membership fee which includes a subscription to *American Craft,* which lists events and other valuable information. The Apprentice Alliance, 151 Potrero Ave., San Francisco, CA 94103, 415-863-8661, offers apprenticeships in all craft specialties, including glass, jewelry, fiber art and ceramics.

Path #2: Summer assistantship program

Peters Valley, a regional crafts studio, takes assistants from ages 18 to 70. Assistants work 35 hours a week assisting the resident craftspersons in the six studios: blacksmithing and metals, ceramics, fibers, fine metals, photography and woodworking.

For a $175 to $275 fee, assistants stay five to eight days and get studio space, housing, lunches, weekend dinners and a free workshop. Workshops are generally three to five days long. The program will help you arrange college credit. Contact Peters Valley, 19 Kuhn Rd., Layton, NJ 07851, 201-948-5200.

Path #3: Workshop training

Workshops in various craft techniques are offered by skilled craftspersons in your region. You can get a list of magazines for your specialty—for example glass, clay, fiber, enamel, metal/jewelry, paper/book arts and wood—from the American Crafts Council (see Path #1). The council also has lists of schools and workshops as well as funding sources. *The American Artist,* a magazine, covers workshops in its annual March issue devoted to instruction.

Path #4: Bachelor's degree

Design schools and art schools have degree programs for the artist who wishes to specialize, for example, in furniture design or ceramics. The B.F.A. is usually offered. Degree programs should be supplemented with apprentice training or work experience in a crafts business. See MacMillan's *Blue Books, Degrees Awarded* for school programs in design.

Path #5: Your own business

The crafts business is one in which you are judged by your portfolio, not by your educational background or training. Success in the business means refining technical skills to get a particular result and having a strong sense of style.

Craftspersons have lives that are structured around their businesses; many of them travel to craft fairs on the weekends. A part-time job can allow you the time and some money to build your business. The American Crafts Council (see Path #1), offers information about markets. Send them a stamped self-addressed envelope. The Small Business Administration offers books on the crafts business. Consult the blue pages of the telephone directory to find the district office.

Sally was dissatisfied with her career as an art therapist and decided to become a jeweler when she met a man who had the technical skills she needed for success in business. They married and have been selling their work at craft fairs, in major department stores and through catalogs and photographs for almost 30 years. Jewelry doesn't require a large production area so they do it at home. They have never made a lot of money, but neither of them wants to work for anybody else. They have gotten some support from family and enough good feedback to keep going through good times and bad. They have to produce several new lines a year to keep customers happy, so there is a constant pressure to keep designing and investing in the next fall or spring line. One is choosing a certain lifestyle when one chooses self-employment in crafts. Understanding the trade-offs is important.

Romancing the Woods is a company that manufactures rustic twig furniture and gazebos (small pavilions). It began when a retired advertising executive had the local carpenter build him a gazebo. They went into business together with almost no upfront capital, did $60,000 worth of business the first year through a catalog that they mailed across the country and, a year later, they quadrupled their income. They employ five full-time and two part-time workers. Direct mail catalogs of garden items for those with discretionary income are currently doing well.

Job: Photographer

The major areas in this field are industrial photography, scientific photography, biological photography, arts photography, commercial photography, fashion photography, portrait photography and photojournalism.

Path #1: Work in a camera store

If you are interested in the technical aspects of photography, you can learn a lot about cameras by working in a large camera store. Camera stores in larger cities offer courses for their customers, who may be professional photographers or motion picture camerapersons.

Path #2: Assistantship

Photographers who work in studios, like portrait or commercial photographers, hire assistants. If you can demonstrate an interest in photography, an ability to do some processing and printing and an ability to handle routine tasks like answering the telephone, you can get a job as an assistant. Some assistants freelance, working for a daily rate when the photographer needs them or working as location scouts for large commercial studios.

A local community college may offer a one-year certificate program in photography to prepare assistants, but you can learn from experience. Stylists design and set up shots for photographers. Often they work for a magazine. Sometimes these people are graphic designers and sometimes they have come to the field by way of magazine editorial work or photography.

Path #3: Find your market

Photographing tourists, selling pictures of animals, taking informal pictures of friends, working for a department store photographing children—these are ways of narrowing the market for your photographs. There are numerous photography magazines that have ideas for the amateur photographer who wants to sell pictures.

Path #4: Training after high school

Some art schools offer a major in photography. The programs may give you some technical background, but generally, the best training is available at an institute of technology. These institutes

The Career Atlas

offer two- and four-year degree programs. Liberal arts programs in photography must be supplemented by more technical courses.

Write to Eastman Kodak Company, 343 State St., Rochester, NY 14650, or call 716-724-2783 for booklet T-17, $4.95, which lists programs in still photography.

Path #5: Your own studio

According to Alistair Finley, professional photographer, the establishment of a studio requires a considerable capital investment (in the range of $50,000 to $70,000), and you will need six or so years of experience before starting your own business. Working as an assistant in a studio is good preparation for having your own photography business.

Path #6: Corporate photographer

Corporate photographers take pictures for annual reports and work freelance. Tony (*Vocational Biographies*) does annual reports for companies, brochures, displays, photojournalism and art photography. For annual reports, he tries to capture all aspects of the company for the shareholders and customers. In the Army, he was assigned "designer and painter." Afterward, he worked as a reporter and photographer, learning after he started the job. He dislikes promoting himself but it is his responsibility to secure his next assignment.

For scientific or biological photography, you will need specialized technical training in photography and college-level science training. Scientific, biological and industrial photographers often enter the field, after their dual training, by working for industry in a large manufacturing company's photo department or research laboratory.

Path #7: Photojournalist

News photography often can be learned on the job. According to photojournalism expert, Irwin Lassiter, in a May 7, 1995 article in *The New York Times,* the University of Missouri at Columbia, Syracuse University and Western Kentucky University have reputable photojournalism departments. Write to Mr. Lassiter at Eastman Kodak (see Path #4), for a list of schools offering Eastman Kodak scholarships for photography training.

Annie Leibovitz (*Current Biography Yearbook*) went to the San Francisco Art Institute to be a painting instructor, but a night course in photography caused her to change her focus. She visited Japan and, during her junior year, she lived on a kibbutz and worked on an archaeological dig. Upon her return, a *San Francisco Chronicle* reporter encouraged her to show these pictures, and one of Allen Ginsberg smoking a marijuana cigarette, to *Rolling Stone* magazine. *Rolling Stone* put her on a retainer while she was in college and, after graduation, sent her to New York City to photograph John Lennon. From 1973 to 1983 Leibovitz was *Rolling Stone's* chief photographer. Later assignments included shooting The Rolling Stones on tour and working for *Vanity Fair.*

Jobs: Arts Manager

Arts management—the administration of galleries, theatres, nonprofit artists' organizations and foundations—is a field that has grown over the last few years. Managers or administrators handle budgets, raise funds, do publicity and oversee the production of publications. Very often management is a second career for the dancer or actor, for example. This field requires good communications skills, credentials, a fashionable appearance and experience in the arts. A person with a good record of raising money for nonprofit organizations and arts organizations in particular will be able to find a development job in an arts organization. Fund raising can be done as a volunteer, so this is an opportunity you can create for yourself.

Path #1: Volunteer in a museum

Museums usually need volunteers because the educational division may offer tours and classes, the public relations and publications departments may need assistants and even the restoration department may allow volunteers to do routine tasks. Volunteering is an excellent way to learn about museum work and talk with professionals in the field. Beth (*Vocational Biographies*), who had a bachelor's degree in history, started working as a volunteer at her local museum. She designed a local history exhibit depicting her town in the pioneer era of the 1880s, got artifacts from people in the community and trained volunteers to tell about the exhibit. Still a volunteer, she conducted research that helped the county historical society obtain national historical markers for two structures; one of these structures became The Heritage Farmstead and Beth became the executive director.

Path #2: Internship in a museum

Almost all museums offer unpaid internships to college students. In fact, there are many more intern positions for college students than there are job openings for employees in museums. As an intern, you might register additions to collections, do conservation work and public relations. The Smithsonian museum complex offers internships for undergraduates in all areas. Sometimes these carry a stipend. Contact the Office of Fellowships and Grants, Smithsonian Institution, L'Infant Plaza, Suite 3300, Washington, DC 20560, 202-357-1300.

The Metropolitan Museum of Art, Division of Educational Services, sponsors 14 work-study paid internships for college juniors and seniors interested in museum careers. Interns work on departmental projects (curatorial, administrative or educational), give gallery talks and work at the Visitor Information Center. You should have a strong background in art history. The Cloisters, the Met's medieval division, takes eight interns (first- and second-year college students). The deadline is February 3. Write to: Coordinator, Summer Internship Program, Department of Public Education, The Metropolitan Museum of Art, 5th Ave. at 82nd St., New York, NY 10028, or call 212-879-5500.

An internship can clarify for you the skills you will need for an arts management career, versus a career as a curator, for example. Art/SEARCH, the employment service bulletin of the Theatre Communications Group, Inc., 355 Lexington Ave., New York, NY 10017, 212-697-5230, lists administrative and production positions, internships and apprenticeships.

Path #3: On-the-job training in a museum

The registrar of a museum, who keeps track of each piece in the collection, may hire you as an assistant if you are computer-literate, have a strong interest in the museum and have had some experience, perhaps as a volunteer. Working in the registrar's office is a good way to learn about the collection. Curators and conservators also hire assistants.

Large auction houses and antique stores are like museums in terms of the merchandise and expertise of the employees. You can learn a lot about antiques and the business of selling them by working for an antique shop. See the yellow pages in your telephone directory for local shops.

Graphic artists are sometimes needed for the growing education and publications departments of large museums. Marketing students may be hired by the publicity, advertising or public relations departments of large museums, and some museums need mechanics and carpenters.

Path #4: Advanced degree

Museum curators have doctorates in art history, with emphasis in particular specialties. Arts educators who work in museums may have advanced degrees in arts education. They develop educational programs, work with public schools, conduct tours, prepare graphics and write grant applications. Their jobs overlap with museum science professionals, so you may have to compete with curators who have degrees in specialties like fine arts or archaeology, or museum science and museum studies training.

Path #5: Museum studies

Executive directors of museums have a good fund raising record and perhaps an M.A. in art history, museum studies or business administration. For example, the Center for Contemporary Arts in Santa Fe, N.M., provides programming in visual, performance and cinema arts, and operates a teen cultural center. The executive director supervises a staff of 35, and is responsible for development, grants, programs and budget. According to ads in *Aviso* (see page 205) the salary ranges from $35,000 to $85,000 for this position.

Theme park design is a flamboyant first cousin to museum and exhibit design; cities look to their science museums to attract tourists to blighted urban areas, thus the interest in strong customer appeal. According to a July 5, 1995 article in *The New York Times,* the New Jersey State Aquarium at Camden was recently redone by BRC Imagination Arts, a theme park design company based in California. They installed exhibits of macaws and Caribbean fish and hired mariachi bands and roaming groups of South American dancers. The lobby is dominated by a seven-foot-high replica of the jaws of a 50-foot shark. Another exhibit is a 12-foot shark statue, every inch of which is interactive. The children can move the fin, inventory the stomach or lift flaps on the tail that answer questions.

Write to the Center for Museum Studies, Smithsonian Institution, 900 Jefferson Dr., SW, A.N.I., Room 2235, MRC 427, Washington, DC 20560, 202-357-1300, to arrange an internship in a museum or for workshops for museum professionals.

For information on museum science training and a list of placement resources, contact The American Association of Museums, 1225 I St. NW, Suite 200, Washington, DC 20005, 202-289-1818. The association publishes *Aviso,* a monthly newsletter with a listing of job opportunities around the country. A subscription is $30 a year for nonmembers. This organization also offers *The Official Museum Directory,* listing museum personnel all over the country. A large library may have this volume.

Path #6: Arts management

Linda (*Vocational Biographies*) is the cultural affairs director for the city of Charleston, S.C. She raises money for the arts in Charleston and decides who will receive the money. You will be better prepared for a career in arts management if you have taken some business courses, and perhaps have a certificate in arts management, but the most important criterion is leadership experience in the arts.

Entertainment jobs

Model   Dancer
Actor   Musician
Theatre Designer

Job: Model

Path #1: Agency work

In some of the major cities where there are fashion industries and advertising agencies, like New York and Los Angeles, there are agencies that find work for models. These agencies require a modeling resume and photographs. Before making an investment in photos, call the agency to get their requirements; the agency may have specific instructions. *Ross Reports Television,* Television Index, Inc., 40-29 27th St., Long Island City, NY 11101, 718-937-3990, has lists of talent agencies and casting directors. Send $5.60 for a single copy.

Some models are discovered by scouts, but for every 1,000 people who walk into an agency, perhaps 10 or 20 will model. Elite, Ford and IMG are large agencies in New York City. According to an article by N.R. Kleinfeld in *The New York Times,* models can make $2,000 a day. If you were to get a contract with a makeup company or be on the cover of *Vogue,* it would happen in the first couple of years, when you are a "fresh" face.

Path #2: TV commercials, voice-overs and walk-ons

To be cast for a television commercial, you must register with an agency that provides talent for advertising agencies that make commercials. To be a walk-on for a soap opera, for example, a casting director for a particular show must choose you. For lists of these agencies and names of casting directors, consult *Ross Reports Television.* To register with agencies and casting directors, you will need guidance before making such a big investment. In the beginning, use postcards to follow up on picture and resume instead of phone calls. You must be able to be reached by the agency during the day so you can learn of possible engagements.

Job: Actor
Path #1: Put on a play

Sometimes theatre faculty of local colleges welcome an opportunity to get involved with a community group. Those who really want to act, as opposed to those who want to be stars, make opportunities for themselves to get experience. Acting experience can be had if you are willing to locate a theatre space in the community. Often churches have halls that are available to local groups. Community centers and auditoriums may have space available. Local businesses may be willing to make a contribution if the program gives them a credit. Most of Hollywood's discoveries are in their teens so it is very important to clarify your interest early.

Path #2: Audition

The audition experience itself is useful and offers a chance to exchange information with other beginners. Many of those auditioning will have only high school play experience. Regional theatres are good places to try out and can offer you opportunities. For names and addresses of these regional theatres, consult *The Theatre Directory,* published by Theatre Communications Group, Publications Department, 355 Lexington Ave., New York, NY 10017, 212-697-5230. Cost is $6.45. Your library may have a copy. Actors' Equity has 202 auditions in New York City in March, the height of the casting season, when summer stock directors come to the city. These auditions are for members only (see Path #4).

Path #3: Internship or apprenticeship

There are many opportunities for high school students to work as apprentices and college students to work as interns in nonprofit professional theatre. Interns clean the stage, work in ticket offices and play walk-on roles. Most roles for principals, in summer stock at least, are filled through the director's connections among professional actors but interning is a good way to get a sample of the theatre. It is especially valuable in learning the technical, business and administrative aspects, although there are some opportunities for actors. See Path #2 for the address of the Theatre Communications Group, which publishes Art/SEARCH, a bulletin with listings of internships and apprenticeships in regional theatres in the technical theatre area (scene shop, painting, properties and costume shop). A subscription costs $45.

Path #4: Getting into the union

If you have been hired and have signed a contract, you are eligible for union membership. Many union shows reserve a certain number of places for nonunion actors and all shows cast nonunion members after they have seen union members. There are 36,000 members of the Actors' Equity Association and 7,000 eligible performers who have participated in the Membership Candidate Program.

The Membership Candidate Program allows nonprofessional actors and actresses and stage managers to credit their work at certain Equity theatres toward membership in the Association. The program is operating in Equity Dinner Theatre, League of Resident Theatres (LORT), Resident Dramatic Stock, Non-Resident Dramatic Stock and Resident Indoor Musical Stock Theatres, as well as some other regional theatres. For a list of all the theatres, write to: Actors' Equity Association, 165 West 46th St., New York, NY 10036, or call 212-869-8530.

When you sign an Equity contract, you are eligible to join Actors' Equity from the date of signing. You are also eligible if you are a member of any of the following unions: AFTRA, SAG, AGMA, AGVA, HAU, IAU, SEG or APATE. Actors are eligible for the Screen Actors Guild (SAG), for example, if they have been employed in speaking roles by theatre companies that are SAG members, if they have been members of an affiliated performers' union for at least a year or if they have worked as SAG-covered extras players for a minimum of three work days.

Casting directors for films have their own union which they may enter after two years of screen credits; often they work as freelancers or can be on staff at a studio, network or production company. In New York City, the International Alliance of Theatrical Stage Employees and Moving Picture Machine Operators of United States and Canada (IATSE), 1515 Broadway, Suite 601, New York, NY 10036, 212-730-1770, is a good resource for information.

Path #5: The agent

Agents are informed of auditions and send people who have a real chance of getting the part. Agents make their living, of course, by taking a percentage of actors' earnings after they get them jobs. Spending a lot of time pursuing an agent may not be advisable because beginners often get nonpaying parts. The union for actors, Actors' Equity, has a list of franchised agents. These agents have demonstrated to the union that they are legitimate. They interview both union and nonunion members. Contact Actors' Equity for their list.

Path #6: The showcase

Showcase productions are theatre productions where Actors' Equity allows the producer to give the cast minimal pay in exchange for an interest in the production. Showcases allow new plays to be seen and new actors and actresses to be introduced to the public and to agents. You learn about these casting calls for showcases through your connections and through the union.

Path #7: Bachelor's degree

Entrance to colleges with acting programs is very competitive and based on auditions. The aspiring actor or actress should measure his or her talents against others in this national talent pool, even if you decide to get a liberal arts degree rather than a degree in acting. There may be a regional audition schedule for entrance and help with auditions for students at graduation. These auditions are attended by casting directors, agents and theatre personnel from around the country.

Some of these conservatory programs admit students after two years of college. There are others that only take students with the bachelor's degree. Most offer the Bachelor of Fine Arts in Acting. Competing for entrance to these programs will give you an idea of the extent of your talent. Meryl Streep, to cite one example, went to Yale Drama School.

Job: Theatre Designer

Technical theatre includes the technical, design and business side of theatre production. Stage designers, theatre technicians, stage managers, set designers and theatre administrators are included in this section. Many people who work behind the scenes in the theatre start learning their jobs as volunteers and get the jobs through friends or internship programs.

Path #1: Internship

An internship in summer stock or regional theatre is a good way to learn about the technical aspects of play production and stage design. It can include hanging lights, building scenery, stage managing, acquiring free props, writing letters to arts funding agencies and foundations, working on the budget, writing press releases and designing advertisements for the local paper.

Set designers may be trained in interior design and theatre design. But sometimes designers can begin work as apprentice carpenters and then get work in a studio that builds sets for the theatre or for the movies. See Video, Film, TV and Cable Programming and Production for the names and addresses of unions that may be able to help you locate workplaces in the region.

Art/SEARCH lists hundreds of internships in production and administration. A subscription is $45 a year. Write to Theatre Communications Group, Publications Department, 355 Lexington Ave., New York, NY 10017, or call 212-697-5230.

The New Jersey Shakespeare Festival, Route 24, Madison, NJ 07940, 201-377-5330, offers 80 internships for preprofessional actors, designers, technicians and theatre administrators. Send them a picture and a resume in exchange for application material.

The Costume Collection, c/o Theater Development Fund, 1501 Broadway, Suite 2110, New York, NY 10036, 212-221-0885, offers two to eight paid internships to assist staff in costume rental; students are offered classroom work in costume design and construction.

Performing Arts Resources, 270 Lafayette St., Suite 809, New York, NY 10012, 212-966-8658, is an organization that may be able to help you, as well.

Path #2: Bachelor's or master's degree

Getting a bachelor's or a master's degree in theatre design will give you formal training in set, costume and lighting design. Conservatory programs offer some of the best training in technical and design areas. There are few paid positions for the graduate, so students should get the broadest training they can in order to meet the requirements for a broad range of jobs. Fashion design may include training in costume design for the theatre.

Job: Dancer

Some liberal arts colleges in major cities offer a bachelor's degree for students who want to continue with professional-level dance training and study the liberal arts and sciences at the same time. Often professional dancers are high-school age and attend performing arts high schools, in New York City, for example.

Path #1: Audition

Professional-level training, starting before and continuing through high school, is the only path for the professional dancer. As Ellen Jacobs points out in *Dancing: A Guide for the Dancer You Can Be* (Addison-Wesley), it's a short career at best and you must have a lot of determination. Even established dancers and choreographers take odd jobs now and then. Many professional dancers return to college after their careers wind down to prepare for a college teaching career in dance. Other second careers for dancers include dance administration and management, criticism, history of dance, dance notation and dance therapy. See The American Dance Guild's newsletter, which lists auditions: The American Dance Guild, 31 West 21st St., 3rd Floor, New York, NY 10010, 212-627-3790.

Path #2: Dance therapy

Dance or movement therapy is the psychotherapeutic use of movement that furthers the emotional and physical integration of the individual. Therapists work in psychiatric hospitals, developmental centers, correctional facilities and rehabilitation facilities. Creative and expressive therapists face a competitive market because these specialists are only employed by large hospitals and rehabilitation facilities. To become a registered dance therapist you need a master's degree in dance therapy. For information contact the American Dance Therapy Association, Suite 108, 2000 Century Plaza, Columbia, MD 21044, 410-997-4040. (For information about arts therapy, write to the American Art Therapy Association, 1202 Allanson Rd., Mundelein, IL 60060, or call 708-949-6064.)

Expressive or creative therapies include art, dance, music and drama. Hahnemann Medical School in Philadelphia has a Creative Arts in Therapy master's degree program. For work with children, expressive therapy is critical. Some people trained in these modalities are in charge of the rehabilitation services at large hospitals. A directory of local hospitals and rehabilitation facilities may be available in the reference section of your library.

Job: Musician

Future performers in solo concert, orchestras and operas are usually studying very seriously by their early teens and go to music schools after high school. In the popular music field, the competition to play or sing for a living is equally as intense as it is in the classical field.

Path #1: Live it out

Career counselors in music advise that the clients live out, rather than repress, the desire to be a musician. Playing in different locations and with various musicians will allow you to make contacts. You should try to join a band or organize your own band. When the group is ready, photographs, a press kit, flyers, a resume and demo tape or video can be prepared. This kind of self-promotion is an important part of success in the business. Organizations that book bands, catering establishments, local restaurants and clubs with live music, folk festivals and the local Department of Recreation should be contacts.

Clint Black (*Current Biography Yearbook*) is a country singer and songwriter who writes all of his songs and coproduces his albums. He started playing the harmonica at 13 and taught himself to play the guitar from songbooks. His brother had a band and when Clint was 15 he started singing harmony and playing bass guitar. Clint dropped out of high school to be a singer. He took a day job as an iron worker, and when the band broke up he struck out on his own on the Houston nightclub circuit. He believes songwriting can be a craft. As he said in one interview, "You don't have to be drunk and left by your lover to write a song about it." At the age of 25 and after six years on the circuit, he signed with a well-known band and the RCA label. The Nashville Network and Country Music Television established Clint on the country music scene and helped him create a market for his first album.

David Geffen (*Current Biography Yearbook*), who may soon be Hollywood's first billionaire, started as a record producer. His mother had a corset shop in the house and Geffen watched her do business, learning about negotiating and integrity. He always wanted to be a businessman. After failing out of several colleges, he went to work in the mail room of the William Morris Agency in New York City. He was promoted to signing rock groups to contracts, and then to junior agent. In 1968 he became an executive vice-president at Creative Management, representing Crosby, Stills, Nash and Young, and Peter, Paul and Mary. He sold the music publishing company he co-owned for $4.5 million, and he set up his own music management company, Asylum. Later, he sold Asylum to Warner Communications, stayed on as president and built Asylum/Electra. Then he had his own label, Geffen Records, which made tens of millions of dollars a year in the early 1980s. Movie production came later.

The Recording Industry Career Handbook, available from The NARAS Foundation, 3402 Pico Blvd., Santa Monica, CA 90405, guides young people who are interested in making records with some good advice and a real picture of the industry.

Path #2: Songwriter working for producer

Composers of classical music usually teach in colleges and popular songwriters usually do other things as well to support themselves. A stint doing any type of work, including sweeping floors, for a producer of background music or demonstration records will allow you to get inside the business, which is something songwriters need for contacts.

Record producers are concentrated in New York, Los Angeles, Nashville and Toronto. An alternative is for the songwriter to connect with a group that is going places and write songs for them. Songwriters should not use melody or lyric-writing services, nor should they send unsolicited lead sheets or demonstration records through the mail because their material may be stolen.

For career seminars in music, contact your local branch of the National Academy of Recording Arts and Sciences. Ask them for a contact person at the branch in your area: National Academy of Recording Arts and Sciences (NARAS), 4444 Riverside Dr., Suite 202, Burbank, CA 91505, 818-843-8233.

The Songwriter's Guild will send you information on contracts, licensing and copyright to protect your songs. Their address is 1500 Harbour Blvd., Weehawken, NJ 07087-6732.

American Federation of Musicians (AFM), 1501 Broadway, Suite 600, New York, NY 10036, 212-869-1330, ext. 211, has 450 chapters across the country, with a membership of 190,000. Contact them for the closest local or consult the white pages in the telephone directory.

Robert Gerardi's book, *Opportunities in Music Careers* (VGM Career Horizons), may be helpful. Kenny Rogers and Len Epand's *Making It in Music* (Harper and Row) describes, in detail, the business and promotion side of a group's success.

Path #3: Film composer

Highly paid composers of music for films can make $175,000 a year. The lower salaries usually involve a package deal in which the composer must pay the musicians with his or her own money. On average, a composer earns a few thousand dollars per film. There is no union for composers. Most belong to either the American Society for Composers, Authors and Publishers (ASCAP), 7920 Sunset Blvd., Suite 300, Hollywood, CA 90046, 213-883-1000, or Broadcast Music, Inc. (BMI), 8730 Sunset Blvd., 3rd Floor, Los Angeles, CA 90069, 310-659-9109. These two organizations collect royalties for composers when their songs are played.

The International Alliance of Theatrical Stage Employees and Moving Picture Machine Operators of United States and Canada, 1515 Broadway, Suite 601, New York, NY 10036, 212-730-1770, may be able to help you. ASCAP is not a union; it handles performance rights.

Video, Film, TV and Cable jobs

Cameraperson	Film Editor
TV Production or	Movie Director
Program Assistant	Screenwriter
Film Production Assistant	Producer
Special Effects/Film Designer	

Television may not expand much more, but other parts of this field (film, video and cable) are exploding. This is a field like photography and writing, in which the quality of the work and the personal contacts, rather than school credentials, are what count. Film, TV networks, cable networks, the telephone and the computer have all become part of something called global communications, linked together by satellite or coaxial, digital or fiber cable. For example, Time-Warner, a cable television company, and U.S. West, a telephone company, have become partners in the building of an advanced digital system. Executives move between industries, from film to TV to cable.

Almost any job in the field is a good bet because the whole field will require enormous amounts of film and video products. You need to decide whether you want to shoot the movie, direct it, produce it or write the screenplay. Doing your own show on public access will give you a good understanding of all the jobs in this field. Call the headquarters of the local cable company. Ask for information about training sessions or workshops offered for members of the public who wish to participate in public access. Public access programming is required by law and is part of the franchise agreement that the cable company signs. You can volunteer to work on a show or produce your own. The cable company will send you information about requirements and facilities.

Job: Cameraperson

Path #1: Formal training

Many cinematographers (they shoot the movie) have master's degrees in cinematography but many others got more technical training in photography at a post-high school institute and started as still photographers. Some filmmakers graduated from four-year college degree programs in film. Others began as assistant camerapersons through personal contacts and good samples. There are film programs offered at art schools and at universities with film departments. Take a look at MacMillan's *Blue Books, Degrees Offered*. For a list of institutions granting specific degrees with a major emphasis in motion picture photography, write to Eastman Kodak Company, 343 State St., Rochester, NY 14650, 716-724-2783.

According to the cinematographer's union, the salary scale begins at $420 for an eight-hour day but renowned cinematographers can make $15,000 per week. Cinematographers may belong to the American Society of Cinematographers, P.O. Box 2230, Hollywood, CA 90078, 213-969-4333, which has 300 members.

Path #2: Getting experience in corporate video production

With a high school diploma or through a college internship, you can seek a job as an assistant in the film department of a corporation. This department may be called the film department, the public relations department or the audio-visual department. You need to find out who makes videos for training, public relations or commercials.

A knowledge of video production gained in such a job may allow you to enter cable television production or the broader field of public relations and advertising, depending on your interest. Experience with in-house corporate production could also prepare you as a video recording engineer in television. A videotape engineer needs more technical training.

Bob (*Vocational Biographies*) is a senior camera operator for Allstate's home office. He studied one year at each of five colleges and finally decided he wasn't getting enough out of college television departments. These programs, however, did allow him to land a job at a small video production company, which gave him some valuable work experience. Then he decided to take a job with a film production company, doing odd jobs. Later he became a freelancer on commercial and industrial projects, starting as a grip (unloading equipment), then as a gaffer (electrician's helper), then as an assistant cameraman.

When he began at Allstate, he worked for a while as a still photographer and then became the program camera operator for a weekly video magazine. Now he works with the producer, the director and the client, someone from Allstate's sales or underwriting department, for example. Bob could make more money shooting news for television but the pace isn't for him.

Gwen (*Vocational Biographies*), the media projects manager for a major union, began her media career by auditioning for a position as a talk show host at a local TV network. She got the job and went on to produce shows, then moved to WETA, an educational channel where she specialized in teleconferences. Now she produces a video newsletter, arranges teleconferences in as many as 50 cities at once and advises union officials in their relations with the press and other media.

For more information, see *Educational Industrial Television,* a publication which will help you understand this field and give you some company names. *Videography* and *American Film Magazine* may also be helpful.

Job: Television Production or Program Assistant

Entry-level jobs at the cable networks like Discovery or USA include mail room worker, production assistant, programming assistant or dubber's assistant. These job titles are found at public television stations, but cable networks may be more accessible.

Barry Diller started in the mail room of the William Morris Agency. According to a March 1, 1993 article in *Time*, Diller bought one of the earliest examples of interactive television, QVC. This home shopping channel did $1 billion in business in 1995. Viewers use their telephones to buy merchandise, and operators and computers handle the order, right through to delivery.

Another young man, Steve Seng, does post-production editing of commercials and television shows for Atlantic Video. According to the *Occupational Outlook Quarterly,* he started as a dubber's assistant. In a production company, this would have been an intern's job but in post-production, internships are rare. After being ans assistant, Steve became a dubber. Also called sound mixers or rerecording mixers, dubbers produce soundtracks. In 1995, a dubber with no experience might make $17,000 and have to work the graveyard shift, but working at night has its advantages. You can learn more about the equipment because you may be alone and you can work at your own pace. After a year, the next job for Steve was assistant editor, and after another six months, editor.

Entry-level jobs also include production or program assistant, or production secretary/researcher. In production or programming you generally need a four-year degree and secretarial skills, at least at the TV networks.

One exception is Barry Diller, who, according to the February 1993 issue of *The New Yorker*, dropped out of college and got a job with one of the biggest talent agencies in Hollywood, the William Morris Agency. Shortly afterwards, Diller landed a job at ABC-TV as a programming assistant. Later, as head of programming, he began *Movie of the Week,* the first network series of made-for-TV movies. Along the way, he showed both his creativity and his brilliant negotiating skills. At 32, Diller became chairman of Paramount Pictures, then head of the Fox television network. When he left Fox, he was able to buy enough stock in QVC to become chairman. His career shows the close relationship that has developed between film, television and cable. It also shows the role of determination: "The single most determined guy I ever saw," recalls ABC founder Leonard Goldenson. "He'd just as soon run through a door as open it."

It is important to understand how small many local TV stations are. When Diller ran the Fox network, he had a $500-million-a-year business with only 218 employees. He did no national news and only gave the affiliates 12 hours of prime-time programming a week, so he could manage with a small staff. Diller was good at keeping costs down and profits way up.

According to *Current Biography Yearbook*, in Brandon Stoddard's first job in advertising as a television programming assistant, he conducted studies to determine who the audience was for particular shows. He also presented campaign ideas and advised advertisers on which shows to sponsor.

At his next job, with Grey Advertising, he moved from program operations supervisor, to director of daytime programming, to vice president in charge of radio and television programming. In 1970, he accepted a job as director of daytime programming for ABC. Four years later, he was named network vice president of motion pictures for television and went on to do a number of award-winning mini-series, including *Roots*.

Many work their way up in television by starting at local television stations. Hilda (*Vocational Biographies*) went to Syracuse University and majored in writing for broadcast. She spent a year working at a community college's audiovisual program, scheduling audio-visual equipment and conducting video tapings. Then she got a job as an associate producer for a children's television show at a Syracuse station. She saw an ad in an alumni placement newsletter for a children's TV producer—and got the job. Hilda gets help from a cameraperson and director who orchestrates the taping of shows. She and the videographer do the editing. The next step for Hilda would be to produce for a network or a cable station, like HBO.

Russ (*Vocational Biographies*) began working for an educational and public access channel with a college degree and some experience with a video cassette recorder. As a favor to a friend, he wired up a closed-circuit TV system to tape a meeting of the local bar association and also interviewed witnesses for the court. Another friend at the local cable channel called Russ to videotape a session of the city council on an emergency basis and two weeks later offered him a job as a production assistant.

Sometimes career-changers can enter programming through sales. In a small studio, the manager or owner of the station may do all the programming, but sometimes, you can get a job in programming using your public relations or sales skills. TV media salespeople often have backgrounds in print advertising or radio. For example, one head of sales for a TV station in New York state was in charge of advertising for a group of local weekly publications. Her job now is to sell ad time to advertising agencies or to businesses. Sometimes a station will hire someone with a public relations background to be director of community affairs.

None of the unions in this field will find you a job—you must first find the job, then join the union. However, you should pay the union local a visit after locating the right chapter for your interest and talk to someone about the sorts of places that might be hiring. Most locals don't have formal apprentice training.

There are two competing unions in the field: The International Alliance of Theatrical Stage Employees and Moving Picture Operators (IATSE) and the National Association of Broadcast Employees and Technicians (NABET). IATSE will send you a list of their union locals across the country. Many locals employ camerapersons, grips, sound and lighting technicians, editors, television studio employees, etc. Each group has its own union, but all are part of the Alliance. Both these unions offer classes. For example, in New York City, a two-year class on set painting for apprentices is available, sponsored by IATSE, 1515 Broadway, Suite 601, New York, NY 10036, 212-730-1770, or (West Coast Office) 14724 Ventura Blvd., Penthouse Suite, Sherman Oaks, CA 91403, 818-905-8999. The Alliance will help you locate the right union and the right local.

NABET is a single union with many local chapters. However, both unions have members in many of the same crafts. Contact: NABET, 1 East Wacker Dr., Suite 2210, Chicago, IL 60601, 312-755-1212.

Job: Film Production Assistant

Film production companies produce films for television or make commercials, documentaries, public relations, industrial, sales, educational training and medical films. Samples of films you have made will help you get a job in one of these companies. Once in the door you can learn a lot, so take nearly any job offered. The contacts and training will help you.

According to a February 11, 1993 article in *The New York Times,* after graduating from Princeton, Richard Brody began working in television commercials as a production assistant—"coiling cables, stocking the juice machine and pouring acid on pizza to give it that homey, bubbly look." He worked as a production assistant on a few feature films, then became assistant to a TV commercial director who was making a documentary. Brody got the interviews on video for the documentary and directed a good deal of another film for the same director. Now Richard is finishing his first feature, *Liability Crisis,* after a three-year struggle to raise money and shoot the film. A producer friend raised the money for the movie, which they are entering in film competitions. If it wins, it will be a big break for them, but for now he works part-time as a word processor to supplement his family's income.

To find film production companies in cities across the country, see *Quigley Publishing Company Directory,* 159 West 53rd St., New York, NY 10019, 212-247-3100. This lists companies, government film bureaus, film distributors, film processing labs, cutting rooms, editing services, television broadcasting companies, cable operators and TV stations as well as guilds, unions and even biographies of people in the industry. (Quigley also publishes a *Motion Picture Almanac*).

See also the useful directory *Backstage TV, Film and Tape Syndication Directory,* Backstage Productions, 330 West 42nd St., New York, NY 10036, 212-947-0020.

See also *The Shoot Directory,* 1515 Broadway, New York, NY 10036, 212-764-7300. It costs $62 and lists advertising agencies, production companies, post-production/editing/video production labs, visual effects/animation/computer graphics companies, interactive multimedia companies, music and sound companies.

Job: Special Effects/Film Designer

Special effects personnel are usually hired for films through a contract with the effects company for which they work. A script is offered, the company places a bid and an agreement is reached.

Production designers work closely with the director, creating models and plans from which the director works. Kim Bailey, who writes a column for IATSE's newsletter, explains that model-making is now done on the computer and sets are starting to be produced in the same way. The shows *Babylon 5* and *Seaquest DSV* used computer-generated background sets. Union minimum for art directors or production designers is about $2,000 for five days of work. You are eligible to enter the union after 30 days of work with a union company.

Job: Film Editor

According to the Motion Picture and Videotape Editors, a member union of IATSE, apprentice film editors receive $703 per week. Some professional editors receive between $6,000 and $8,000 a week. Sound editors belong to the same chapter and earn the same starting salaries as apprentices.

Job: Movie Director

"Making the Low Budget Feature Film in New York: It Can Be Done" is the topic of an all-day seminar sponsored by New York Women in Film. Linda Gottlieb, whose film *Dirty Dancing* was a hit, spoke at the seminar. The senior vice president for production at Cinecom, Leon Falk, says that if you develop a project in the $4 to $8 million range, there are many potential buyers. *Chutzpah*—a Yiddish word for nerve—is an important attribute needed by independent filmmakers for success.

Eric Schaeffer and Donal War, two young men who majored in theatre and "did time," as they put it, in low-level production jobs in Hollywood, made *My Life's in Turnaround,* which opened at the 1993 San Francisco Film Festival. "Turnaround" is the euphemism in Hollywood for a screenplay that has been shelved. According to a June 12, 1994 article in *The New York Times*, they made their film for $160,000. While driving a cab in New York City, Eric met several well-known actresses who agreed to be in the film.

According to an article by Bernard Weinraub in *The New York Times*, Curtis Hanson, director of *The River Wild,* dropped out of high school to write movies. He got a job as a film critic for the local college newspaper and then created and edited *Cinema,* a film magazine for which he interviewed his favorite directors, editors and film composers. He wrote screenplays and directed suspense and action films, gaining public attention with *The Hand That Rocks the Cradle*.

Fellows of the American Film Institute may enter with or without an undergraduate degree. They offer the M.F.A. and certificate programs in cinematography, directing, editing, producing, production design and screenwriting. For example, would-be directors take courses in directing the actor, cycle project analysis, narrative workshop, short screenplay development, approaches to film, seminars and production in the information age. The second year stresses the skills needed to get apprenticeships and other entry-level work. Tuition is $13,000 a year; however, you can attend their professional training division on a course-by-course basis. Contact the American Film Institute, 2021 North Western Ave., Los Angeles, CA 90027, 213-856-7690. This institute has some very successful alumni and faculty.

The Directing Workshop for Women at the American Film Institute is for women writers, editors and executives. One successful graduate, Randa Haines, directed the film *Children of a Lesser God*. The free workshop can get you a calling card—the film you direct in the workshop. There is a $50 application fee (address above).

The Director's Guild offers a formal training program for would-be assistant directors, for individuals with four-year degrees or three years of experience. Applicants must take an all-day written test and an oral exam. Only one percent pass. Write to Assistant Director's Training Program, Directors Guild of America, 14144 Ventura Blvd., Sherman Oaks, CA 91423, or call 213-289-2000.

Organizations for filmmakers provide a chance to talk to or correspond with other filmmakers. For example: The Association of Independent Video and Filmmakers, 625 Broadway, 9th Floor, New York, NY 10012, 212-473-3400, may provide a way to meet others in the noncommercial field.

Women Make Movies is a New York group that offers services to women filmmakers: 462 Broadway, 5th Floor, New York, NY 10013, 212-925-0606. This group distributes films made by women, and offers showcase opportunities, internships, workshops, seminars, networking, skills exchange, a newsletter and a film archive. This organization may be able to connect you with filmmakers in your region.

For internships, apprenticeships and information about other unions and job placement services, write to The American Film Institute, Education Services, The John F. Kennedy Center for the Performing Arts, Washington, DC 20566. Send $3 for "Factfile #2, Careers in Film and Television."

See also Mel London's books *Getting Into Film* and *Getting Into Video* (Ballantine), in which he discusses a variety of jobs. There are also texts by various authors that teach television and film production. The local textbook store may have them. It is recommended that you use the books as a supplement to experience.

Job: Screenwriter

If you are trying to sell a screenplay to the studios, you need an agent. Steven Starr, a packaging agent for the William Morris Agency, says that young writers and directors outside of Hollywood have a shot at selling their project to Hollywood studios because their work has not previously been rejected.

Steven Bochco (*Current Biography Yearbook*) went to Carnegie Tech in Pittsburgh and got a B.F.A. in theatre. His father got him a summer job at Universal Studios. He then was hired as an assistant to the head of the story department at Universal. He got involved with writing *Ironside* and became the story editor for *Columbo*. Later, NBC head Fred Silverman approached him to develop *Hill Street Blues*.

One screenwriter, Diane English (*Current Biography Yearbook*), was raised in Buffalo. Her father was an alcoholic, resulting in a turbulent childhood; her mother was a homemaker and nightclub singer. In her opinion, comedy material is acquired from an unhappy childhood. Encouraged by a professor who recognized her writing talent, she went to New York City and took a job assisting a theatre publicist. Then she took a job as a secretary at WNET, the New York City public television station, where she was promoted to associate director of the Television Laboratory, WNET's experimental unit. She rewrote the script for a film adaptation of Ursala Le Guin's *The Lathe of Heaven*. The movie earned her a nomination for a Writers Guild Award. She embarked on a career as a freelance screenwriter, and got a TV column in *Vogue*. English had written nine scripts, three of which were produced, when CBS chose her to create *Foley Square,* a comedy about a young district attorney. Then she was executive producer on *My Sister Sam,* and in 1988 she convinced Warner Brothers and CBS to produce her *Murphy Brown* series.

According to *Current Biography Yearbook*, Roseanne's first comedy routines were developed from cutting remarks she made to men who made passes at her. In 1981, at a Denver comedy club, she stood up and did a comic rebuttal to the sexist jokes of the men who had preceded her. In conversing with her family she came up with her concept of "funny womanness," drawing on the female predicament, to produce material and later, the image of herself as a "domestic goddess" instead of a housewife. In 1985 she auditioned for the Comedy Club in Los Angeles, in 1986 she got an HBO special and by 1988, *Roseanne* debuted on television. The head writer on her show makes $2.5 million a year.

Job: Producer

Dawn Steel's book *They Can Kill You...But They Can't Eat You: Lessons from the Front,* describes the rise of one woman in Hollywood in the 1980s. Steel was head of Columbia Pictures and is now an independent producer. She got her job at Paramount from a job in marketing at *Penthouse.*

According to a December 1, 1989 article in *The New York Times*, Geraldine Laybourne, who developed the children's television channel Nickelodeon, taught in a prep school and studied education. In 1971, she teamed up with her husband, who was an animator, to produce shows for children. One of their first clients was Nickelodeon. Laybourne joined the network as a program manager in the early 1980s and by 1989 she was the president of MTV network, which included MTV, Nickelodeon, Nick at Nite and VH1. She used her understanding of education, her husband's skills and contacts and her own experience with her children to produce her first shows.

According to the November 14, 1993 edition of *The New York Times*, Lucie Salhany, head of Fox Broadcasting, dropped out of college at the age of 19 and started working as a secretary at a television station. By 24, she was running the station, and five years later, she moved to a larger station to become program manager. Four years later she became vice president for TV and cable programming at Taft Broadcasting. After a few years, Paramount made her president of its domestic television group. Under her leadership, Paramount became the leader in developing and distributing shows for first-run syndication. Then she moved to Fox after six years as chairwoman of the production and syndication arm, Twentieth Century TV. Now she reports to Rupert Murdoch.

Interactive video (using the remote control to play chess on the television screen, for example) may open up possibilities for teachers to act as producers of educational shows. Teachers who have developed computer instruction will have an edge, but expertise in adult topics, and in teaching adults, will be needed for success as well.

Design jobs

Printer   Architect
Graphic Designer/Illustrator   Interior Designer
Industrial Designer   Fashion Designer

Job: Printer

Path #1: Informal or formal apprenticeship

The days of hot metal (type) on a letter press are long gone. Now presses are controlled by computer and print from a photographic plate. This is created from "the mechanical" (the original art and text) which may also be on computer.

The local branch of the printer's union in the region may offer an apprenticeship or on-the-job training with a contract. At the end of the contract, the apprentice or helper becomes a journeyman printer. This process takes at least three years. No high school diploma is required.

The union may refer helpers to jobs. In some areas of the country, assistants earn $450 to $550 a week. According to the Department of Labor, in 1995, average wages were around $13 an hour for commercial printers. Commercial printing is one area of manufacturing that is expected to grow in the United States. You may choose to find a job yourself as a helper in a nonunion shop. Success as an apprentice-helper may lead to becoming an assistant.

Prep person, estimator and desktop publisher are more advanced positions below management.

Much printing is done abroad but a great deal of corporate work, for example, is produced in the United States. Acme is a big printer in Wilmington, Mass. They print annual reports for corporations and other high-quality work for ad agencies, businesses and foundations including Coca-Cola, Lexus, Reebok and Polaroid.

Acme Digital Labs reconfigures printed materials for interactive CD-ROM. Compared with image data requirements for four-color pictures, motion picture on a CD-ROM uses a lot of megabytes. The ads for production workers generally call for people with experience on a four-color press, with prepress experience on the Macintosh, a knowledge of Scitex systems (filmmaking) or someone with film-stripping experience. The Hennegan Company, George Rice and Sons, and the Graphic Arts Center are other major printers.

Path #2: Private vocational schools

Completing a six-month course in printing at a vocational school may help you get a helper's job if the school is connected with local employers. Another possibility is to get a certificate in desktop and electronic publishing in a year or less; the whole industry is now computer-based. One Worldwide Electronic Publishing Network, a printing alliance, 703-385-2900 or 800-888-9376, will send you information about this growing area.

Path #3: Associate's degree

An associate's degree in printing, which also can be called graphic arts or advertising technology (including desktop publishing and electronic publishing), may be offered by your local community college. A two-year degree will offer enough training for you to work in a print shop or to handle print production in an advertising agency or publishing house. With more experience, you could become a buyer of printing and binding services, collecting estimates from printers for the corporate department doing the project.

Managers usually have college degrees and may start as estimators or salespeople. Rosemary Kelly was an estimator at one firm, moved to another where she was in charge of estimating and customer service, and was recently made president. Her company is one of 16 commercial printing firms owned by a larger firm.

....

Job: Graphic Designer/Illustrator

This is also called commercial art. The illustrator produces art for the editorial (magazine and newspaper features), advertising and book markets. Graphic designers are trained in textile or surface design, layout design, package design, the technical aspects of printing and production, medical, fashion and technical illustration, cartooning and animation. Computer-generated special effects are a Hollywood specialty.

Path #1: Internship

Magazine production experience or graphic design office experience would be very valuable for the design student. You can arrange an internship through your art school.

Path #2: Desktop publishing

Many graphic designers now do typesetting and design on their computers. Here is a classified advertisement which ran in *The New York Times* on January 13, 1995,

"Well-known financial services firm seeks a SR. MAC Operator for its 12 a.m.-8 a.m. shift for formatting financial texts and creating business graphics and presentations, including slides, transparencies, charts. Must have thorough working knowledge of PageMaker, Freehand, MS Word/Excel, Persuasion, Quark and Photoshop and knowledge of laser printers, slide imagers and scanners."

Doing this kind of desktop publishing work for a corporation as a freelancer may be very lucrative, although graphic designers may want to do more creative work. The corporation will appreciate that you can put in visuals and set type at once. The software helps you design the book or presentation right on the computer.

Path #3: Associate's degree

Commercial art is one of the fields in which you are hired on the basis of your portfolio, as opposed to a resume and personal interview. Two-year programs in graphic design, illustration or graphics technology teach excellent technical skills.

Generally, graduates from two- and four-year programs work in a design or advertising studio before freelancing. Getting ahead in this field depends on your creativity and initiative. For example, art director Simms Taback says: "The junior paste-up people are expected to be designing ads in their spare time and showing their work to art directors. This self-promotion is encouraged and it's how you get promoted. Those who fail to understand this won't make it."

Path #4: Small design studio on-the-job training

Take any job offered in a small design studio, publishing company art department, advertising agency, department store and public relations company.

Employers will want to see how you use the computer to do mechanicals, paste-ups, color work, etc. Entry-level positions will require you to show a strong portfolio, but taking courses in production and design will help in preparing. The Graphic Artists Guild suggests that your portfolio should include at least 10 to 12 pieces of work in a consistent style; these should be examples of the kind of work you want to do. If your work samples have been printed, this is a plus. To get work published, do pieces for nonprofit organizations or magazines that are just starting up. Established graphic artists (freelance illustrators, art directors and graphic designers) spend a good deal of time reviewing portfolios, both for their own students and friends. They can suggest what kinds of work should be added to your portfolio to help you get a job.

Path #5: Bachelor's degree

Most art schools offer a major in graphic arts; liberal arts colleges don't offer training appropriate for the commercial artist. Choose the art school over the liberal arts college and make sure you get the necessary technical training so you can handle the complete job, not just the design or illustration.

Typically, art school students study the history of art and graphic design, design for communications, film and photography, typography, graphics production, package design, trademark systems, publications and exhibit design and advertising. The Graphic Artists Guild's publication, *Pricing and Ethical Guidelines,* offers a detailed overview of the field. The Guild itself offers work study jobs to art students, has local chapters around the country and may be able to assist you in finding an internship. Contact The Graphic Artists Guild, 11 West 20th St., New York, NY 10011, 212-777-7353.

Job: Industrial Designer

Industrial design—the design of mass-produced items like cars, televisions or tea kettles—requires a four- or five-year degree in industrial design. Many engineering courses are included in this program. Entrance to school and the job market for graduates are both very competitive. Engineering may be an alternative path or you may choose the broader field of graphic design.

Job: Architect

Architects require some of the same abilities as those of engineers. Drafting experience or training is not good preparation. You gain admittance to school based on a portfolio, which you should think of as a design problem. You are not expected to excel in mathematics or drawing. In most states, to qualify for the licensing exam as an architect, a person must have a Bachelor of Architecture degree (usually five years) and three years of practical experience working under a licensed architect. Architecture programs include courses in engineering, design, graphics and urban planning. According to The American Institute of Architects, most salaries for experienced architects are between $35,400 to $54,600. The average compensation for partners and principals in firms is $58,500. For more information about architecture, write to The American Institute of Architects, 1735 New York Ave. NW, Washington, DC 20006, 800-365-2724.

Job: Interior Designer

If you like to solve decorating problems and have good business sense, you might want to consider interior design. To be a self-employed designer of residential interiors requires the ability to make contact with people who can afford decorators. Interior design for business is the more accessible field because the corporate market is larger.

Path #1: Retail sales

Customers need help with rug choice, fabrics, mixing and matching historic periods, etc. You might start by volunteering your services. A friend or nonprofit group in the community may welcome the free services of a decorator. You should take photos of your work before and after and concentrate on the small items your client will have to buy, like shades, lighting fixtures, floor treatments, etc. Others may see the work and offer further opportunities.

Antique stores, furniture stores, department stores and textile, paint and wallpaper stores all hire salespeople. In many communities, they may hire beginners. You will learn about merchandising working with clients. If you find that you are able to engage clients in consultation, ask the boss to make you an in-house decorator.

Path #2: Assist the designer

If you know interior designers, you may be able to get a job as an assistant; this experience will help in planning your training, if you decide to attend school. Unfortunately, jobs as assistants are sometimes difficult to land for the graduate of a four-year program.

Path #3: Associate's degree, certificate or diploma program

Two-year certificate or associate's degree programs are available to the high school graduate. Schools in interior design offer three-year programs, but they do not award degrees. They may, however, have an agreement with a college that will award the bachelor's degree to the interior design student with one more year of study.

Path #4: Bachelor's degree

With the bachelor's degree in interior design, you can enter a design firm for one to three years of apprentice training. Design studios, retail stores, architectural firms, institutions and corporations all employ graduates as assistants. The apprenticeship period will include a good deal of routine work including typing, cataloging samples and learning about sources for materials. Some designers recommend a non-art school bachelor's degree and then a master's degree in design. They believe this gives you a broader background before you specialize in design. Specialized courses in principles of design, history of art, architecture and interiors, drawing or drafting, visual presentation techniques, space planning, residential and contract design, interior materials and systems, product design and construction and business practices and principles are the courses included in the undergraduate curriculum.

After getting a fine arts degree, Linda started with a department store chain where she got extensive training in custom draperies and window treatments. Then she was in charge of carpets and draperies for another store, then opened her own design studio. She works out of her home, driving from customer to customer, designing room layouts, showing samples and visiting workrooms where furniture or draperies are being made to order. She motivates herself well and makes sure her mark-up is enough to make her a profit.

For more information on careers in interior design, contact the American Society of Interior Designers, 608 Massachusetts Ave. NE, Washington, DC 20002, 202-546-3480. For a list of accredited interior design programs, write to the accrediting agency: Foundation for Interior Design Education Research, 60 Monroe Center NW, Grand Rapids, MI 49503-2920, or call 616-458-0400.

See the magazine *Facilities Design and Management* for information about firms that do mostly corporate business.

Job: Fashion Designer

An interest in fashion, a talent for making patterns and sample clothing, the ability to work under pressure and the ability to modify an idea to cut costs are all essential for the successful designer. Designers routinely travel abroad because production work in the clothing industry is frequently done overseas. Fluency in the language needed in the particular branch of the business can make a difference in entering production in this field.

Path #1: On-the-job training

Learning the production end of the fashion business by getting a job in a workroom, where clothes are produced, is a useful experience. Apprentices are often chosen from those employed in the production workroom, as sewers, spreaders or cutters. Because clothing manufacturers often don't produce their clothing themselves, a knowledge of production and design training can lead to a job in a production company, especially if you have computerized manufacturing experience.

Path #2: Apprenticeship

If you have an "in"—a friend or relative in the garment industry—you may be able to arrange an apprenticeship as a copyist or adapter. After the manufacturer buys permission to reproduce the garment, the copyist or adapter takes a one-of-a-kind designer garment and makes a pattern so the same piece of clothing may be mass-produced. To work as a copyist or adapter takes considerable sewing skill. For apprenticeships in fashion design, write to the Apprentice Alliance, 151 Potrero Ave., San Francisco, CA 94103, or call 415-863-8661.

Path #3: Sell your own line

According to an article by Bernadine Morris in *The New York Times*, Kathryn Conover financed her way through a liberal arts college program by collecting designer clothes from thrift shops, restyling them and selling them. She started her fashion career by making 40 samples of children's clothing and taking them to New York in a suitcase. She returned home with orders from Bonwit Teller, Bloomingdale's, Lord and Taylor and Saks Fifth Avenue. Three years later she made her first women's collection.

Path #4: Certificate in ladies' tailoring

The local community college may offer a short-term certificate program in ladies' tailoring. One summer session of four nights a week may be enough to learn hand and machine skills, construction processes, assembly procedures, fabric cutting and a basic knowledge of fabrics. A high school diploma may not be required.

Path #5: Associate's or bachelor's degree

Most schools that train the fashion designer award both the associate's and bachelor's degrees. A thorough grounding in pattern making, draping and clothing construction is essential for success as a designer. Programs also include courses in textiles, fashion illustration, production and marketing. After graduation from a two- or four-year program, the fashion design graduate usually begins work as an assistant to a designer and later becomes a junior designer or designer trainee.

Norma Kamali graduated from Fashion Institute of Technology (FIT) in New York City with a two-year degree. She started as a fashion illustrator, traveled to London in search of a job and, while abroad, collected antique clothing. When she returned, she opened a boutique and began her own very successful company.

David Chu, president and CEO of Nautica, a major manufacturer of upscale clothing, has a degree from FIT in fashion design. He traveled to the Orient to do business for his family for a year before accepting a position working as a designer for Catalina Sportswear. Three years later he started Nautica.

According to *Current Biography Yearbook*, Donna Karan's mother was a showroom model and sales representative for a manufacturer of clothing and her father was a custom tailor. She fantasized about being a designer and, at 14, worked in a boutique where she learned the basics of fashion design. Her stepfather sold women's apparel and encouraged her to apply to Parsons School of Design in New York City. Her mother worked for designer Charles Weinberg, who recommended Karan to Parsons. After her second year at school, she approached Ann Klein for a job. After nine months she was fired; she admits she was terrified of failure. She worked for a while with another designer, got her priorities in order and then asked Ann Klein to take her back. Very soon, she became associate designer and went on to win many awards and eventually started her own company.

Fashion and costume design are closely related fields. The Costume Collection, a special project of the Theatre Development Fund in New York City, rents costumes by the week to the nonprofit theatrical community. Each summer the Costume Collection sponsors a five-week internship program for students of design and another program for teachers. Students work for a weekly wage in the Costume Collection and take trips to costume houses, fabric stores, museums and wig shops and design their own costume projects. The teachers' program is three-and-a-half weeks long. Teachers work one day a week in the collection and observe the students as they work on their projects. Contact Kenneth M. Yount, Director, Costume Collection, 601 West 26th St., 17th Floor, New York, NY 10001, 212-989-5855.

Writing jobs

Editor
Journalist
Writer

Job: Editor

Path #1: Training in magazine production

A summer job can give you experience in all aspects of magazine production. To get a job you need secretarial graphics production skills (layout, paste up and computer). Consult the New York City telephone directory and the directories of other major cities under Publishers-Periodical for trade publication houses; they produce many magazines under one roof.

Path #2: Internship/on-the-job training in publishing

Publishing houses are receptive to taking interns. Consult the *Literary Market Place* at the local library for names and addresses of publishers, or speak to the internship coordinator at your college. Try contacting the larger houses and academic presses.

Good word processing skills and a knowledge of computers can set you apart from other applicants. A knowledge of film or audiovisual production may be helpful, because this is an expanding field in publishing. Evidence of a love of books can make the difference; work experience in a bookstore, library, book warehouse, paperback book distributor or for the college's publication department will help, and writing book reviews for the local paper is a way to demonstrate an interest. There are no editing majors available at the present time, but college journalism and English majors have a slight edge in getting hired.

Path #3: Internship in magazine editing

Marlene Kahan is the Executive Director of The American Society of Magazine Editors internship program for college students who have completed their junior year. This is a summer program for college students enrolled in a bachelor's degree program of journalism or those have taken journalism courses. Students coming from a liberal arts college must have worked on a campus publication and had a journalism internship. Only one student is accepted from each college or university. Students are placed with stipends at 50 major magazines in New York City. Deadline is December of the year before intended participation. To receive an application, write to The American Society of Magazine Editors, 919 Third Ave., New York, NY 10022, 212-872-3700.

In addition to the program described above, many magazines take interns. For example, Maureen Hunter-Bone, editor-in-chief of juvenile periodicals at the Children's Television Workshop, suggests that young people intern after their junior year or immediately after college. To get an entry-level editorial assistant job after college, you need some collegiate journalism experience or internships, excellent language skills, evidence of writing talent and computer/word processing literacy.

Path #4: Editorial work in publishing

Editors handle reader mail, evaluate manuscripts, check facts, write leads and captions, proofread and edit. Most experts agree that you will have to enter as an assistant to an editor, a secretary, an editorial secretary, a first reader or an editorial trainee. You must have word processing skills, at least a bachelor's degree and to advance, professional-level editing skills. An editing course may be helpful. You begin in the editorial department as an editorial assistant. Another promotion may make you an assistant editor, then editor and senior editor.

For jobs in production and design see graphic designer/illustrator. For jobs in publishing sales and marketing, in which you sell to bookstores, the bachelor's degree is necessary. Texts are usually sold by ex-academics or teachers. For jobs in book marketing, promotion and publicity, you need courses in sales, advertising, public relations and accounting, in addition to some sales experience. Many editorial people in publishing started in sales.

Outside of jobs with book publishers in the major publishing cities—New York, Chicago, Boston and Knoxville—most jobs will be for corporate, professional, religious, business, technical or trade union publications.

The Association of American Publishers has a list of book publishing courses and institutes, such as a proofreading course, in their publication, "Getting Into Book Publishing." You can contact them at 71 Fifth Ave., New York, NY 10003-3004, 212-689-8920.

Path #5: Editorial work in magazines

According to an April 8, 1990 article in *The New York Times*, Robin Wolaner, who started the magazine *Parenting*, learned the business working summers at *Penthouse*, while she went to college. After graduation, she stayed with *Penthouse* as a promotional copy-writer, then went to *Viva,* where she was senior editor. She eventually went to *Mother Jones* as publisher, after learning newsstand sales, direct marketing, forecast sales, subscription economics and financial planning in her prior jobs.

After 15 years in the magazine business, her experience led her to suspect that there were hundreds of thousands of well-educated, upscale, slightly older new parents out there who were potential buyers of a magazine on parenting. She raised $175,000 from 10 investors, including $100,000 to do a direct mail test to see if her targeted market was really interested. They were; she got almost a six percent return rate. Time-Warner was convinced by this evidence to be her partner. Recently they bought her out for between $5 and $10 million; she stayed on as publisher.

Grace Mirabella (*Current Biography Yearbook*) had summer jobs in dress shops during college, and started after graduation in Macy's executive training program. The following year, she joined the merchandising department of *Vogue* where she verified store credits appearing in photo captions. After being promoted to a liaison assignment in the executive editor's office, she left for Florence, Italy, to work for a year on the public relations staff of the designers Simonetta and Fabiani.

Returning to New York City, she became *Vogue's* "shop hound," finding items for a column of the same name. She ascended through the ranks and became editor. Grace was fired because they wanted a new look, and she started her own magazine, *Mirabella,* in 1989.

Job: Journalist

Path #1: Work experience

Newspapers in small towns or suburban areas are good places to look for a first job. When you apply, the editor will want to see what you have written for other papers, including the school newspaper. Submitting book reviews or articles is another way to begin. For on-the-air television and radio journalism jobs, you will need to supply an audition tape (video or audio, depending on the medium of choice).

Path #2: Internship

Internships are essential in this field because they provide valuable experience and companies use them to find talented people. Until recently, this was the way liberal arts students learned the field—there were very few journalism programs at any level. Almost all newspaper, radio and television stations have summer internship programs. Many colleges have their own stations that provide opportunities for students to learn the trade.

The Dow Jones Newspaper Fund, P.O. Box 300, Princeton, NJ 08543-0300, 609-452-2000, sponsors paid summer jobs at newspapers and provides editorial training. The program is open to college juniors, seniors and graduate students. It provides students with a summer's paid editing internship at a daily newspaper or news service. All students receive a free training seminar before beginning their summer of work. Interns who return to school receive $1,000 scholarships. Applications are available September 1 to November 1. Send for their booklet on journalism careers and scholarships. Or you can call 800-DOWFUND to request information.

NBC has a television internship program for students of journalism, accounting, finance and computer science. It requires three full days of work a week. Contact Employee Relations at NBC, 30 Rockefeller Plaza, New York, NY 10112, 212-664-4444. For other possibilities, check radio and television stations. Almost all stations offer internship programs for college students as well as volunteer jobs.

Path #3: Newspaper and broadcast journalism

Almost 85 percent of new hires in journalism have graduate or undergraduate degrees in mass communications or journalism, according to the Dow Jones Newspaper Fund survey. If you major in one of the liberal arts, you should supplement the program with basic journalism courses in reporting, editing, libel law and typography. For broadcast journalism, a degree in liberal arts or journalism rather than in broadcasting or mass communication are the better bets. Communications degrees are recent offerings of the less established schools.

Desk assistants (who distribute material as it comes in over the wire services), production assistants, researchers and production secretaries/researchers are all entry-level titles. Generally, in the larger stations, these positions require the bachelor's degree.

Frank (*Vocational Biographies*) is a journalist. He has an undergraduate degree in journalism from the University of Wisconsin-Madison. He interned at two newspapers during the summers. During the first two years in college he wrote for student publications; during the second two years he wrote for a weekly newspaper and business magazine and occasionally wrote articles for *The Milwaukee Journal-Sentinel*. After college he freelanced, then got an internship with the investigative reporter Jack Anderson. With these credentials he got a job in Maryland as a general assignment reporter, then covered county government for another paper. He started with his current paper on the city desk before moving to his present job as entertainment editor, which he loves. He goes into work at 2:30 p.m. to cover evening events. He makes around $25,000, but could make more working for a paper with a larger circulation.

According to an April 10, 1995 article in the *Daily Freeman* (New York), Jill Abramson, the Washington deputy bureau chief for *The Wall Street Journal*, credits affirmative action for helping women in journalism. She says, "Throughout my career, I've gained because the men in charge have been looking for more qualified women to promote." She helps oversee 40 reporters and editors.

Maggie Rivas is a one-person bureau for the *Dallas Morning News*, covering the U.S.-Mexican border and the Latino community from her base in El Paso, Texas. According to the *Dow Jones Newspaper Fund*, she has visited three continents doing stories, and has been in a hot air balloon, a Mexican jail, at a building collapse, at a meeting between the U.S. and Mexican presidents and in the Hungarian capitol building after hours. This variety of story and the chance to see all these places is what she loves about the job.

Sally Jessy Raphael (*Current Biography Yearbook*) started as a broadcast journalist in Puerto Rico, where her father owned a rum-exporting company. She went on the radio as a reporter, weatherperson, talk show host and newscaster. When she returned to the continent, she tried several jobs until she landed an anchor job for a morning show in Miami. She stayed for five years and then moved to New York City to co-host a morning talk show on WMCA radio with Barry Farber, a popular New York City talk show host. She came to the attention of Maurice Tunick, the producer of Talknet, NBC's syndicated package of radio call-in shows. In 1982, she started to broadcast live for three hours every weeknight from New York City and, in 1983, added a daytime show in St. Louis.

The Pulitzer Prize-winning journalist, Hedrick Smith (*Current Biography Yearbook*), was a correspondent for *The New York Times* for more than 20 years. He graduated from Williams College, got a Fulbright Scholarship to Oxford and then spent three years in the Air Force as an intelligence officer. He began his journalistic career in 1959, covering the civil rights movement and the space program. *The Times* hired him on the advice of David Halberstam, whom Smith had met when Halberstam was working for a paper in Tennessee. Smith was part of the team that interpreted the Pentagon Papers, which *The Times* published.

Joan Lunden (*Current Biography Yearbook*) had traveled a bit, run her own charm school, been to junior college and done some commercials before she was hired as the weatherman's apprentice at KCRA in Sacramento, Calif. Her responsibilities grew, and soon she left to join *Eyewitness News* in New York City as a reporter. A year later she joined *Good Morning, America,* doing reports on new products. After a number of years of hard work, she became co-host.

General printed materials are available from American Women in Radio and Television, 1321 Connecticut Ave. NW, Washington, DC 20036, 202-429-5102. They welcome questions over the telephone if you can show you have done some research.

Job: Writer

Most writers write about what they know well. The science writer for a newspaper usually has studied science in college. The medical writer for the doctor's magazine has a background in medicine or biology. The freelance magazine writer usually specializes in one area—for example, travel, politics or finance. Technical writers often have business, science or engineering degrees or courses in their special areas. Most nonfiction writers are academics writing about their specialties.

According to the February 8, 1995 edition of the *Tallahassee Sentinel*, Bucky McMahon is 39 years old and makes a living from freelance writing assignments for *Outside, GQ* and *Details*. He got started writing a quirky column that ran in the entertainment section of the local newspaper in Tallahassee, Fla. This column was supposed to be purely informational but soon it became a place to investigate "the characters of the night." He developed a following. Then one of his followers sent copies of the column to his editor friends. Bucky got his first assignment because the magazine needed somebody in Florida. Now he is getting regular assignments for around $5,000 an article. If they don't run the article, and sometimes they don't, he gets a partial fee.

Learning about a special area and submitting articles for publication in that area is one way to become a writer. Magazine and book publishers like submissions to be accompanied by samples of other work published. The *Literary Market Place* in the library will list the kinds of material for which magazines and publishers are looking. Literary agents often sell novels, but not fiction for magazines. To write for magazines, you need to submit an idea for a story and samples of other published work. There is a directory of agents' names in the *Literary Market Place*.

Going to school to learn to write fiction probably won't help enough to warrant spending the money, because a strong talent for writing fiction is usually a natural inclination. Many fiction writers are compelled to write, even as teenagers. Often they write the same story over and over, in different forms, but the skeleton of the work remains the same.

Joyce Carol Oates (*Current Biography Yearbook*) has written 50 books including novels, short stories, essays, poetry and plays in approximately 20 years. Her father encouraged her to tell stories, even before she could write. She wrote three novels in high school, entered Syracuse University on a scholarship and, in her senior year, won the *Mademoiselle* magazine college fiction award. She graduated first in her class, went on to get a Ph.D. and has taught creative writing on many campuses around the country.

Education/Administration jobs

Childcare Worker
Audiology/Speech-
    Language Pathology
Elementary/High School Teacher
College Instructor

Adult Educator
Educational/Not-for-
    Profit Administrator
Librarian

Job: Childcare Worker

Day-care centers always need volunteers. Even if you want to be an aide for a summer or a part-time worker, consider attending the local community college, which may offer courses. Day-care center directors may have a master's degree in early childhood. Childcare professionals are working hard to raise the wages of workers as the need for quality childcare continues to grow.

To open your own day-care center, see U.S. Small Business Administration Development's "Quality Childcare Makes Good Business Sense," SBA Publications, P.O. Box 15434, Fort Worth, TX 76119, or contact your local SBA office.

The Council for Early Childhood Professional Recognition, 1341 G St. NW, Suite 400, Washington, DC 20009, 800-424-4310, offers a credentialing program. Day-care workers can merge their experience with training they have received from school districts, agencies, the military or the community college to receive one of four possible Child Development Associate (CDA) credentials: infant/toddler, preschool, family or home visitor. The council also offers bilingual programs in these areas. Day-care workers can also get on-the-job training and the CDA in one year. With added experience, the CDA credential is a qualification for director and teacher in many states. Write to the Council for Early Childhood Professional Recognition about scholarship information and be sure to get your state's requirements for aide, teacher and director positions.

Job: Audiology/Speech-Language Pathology

Two specialists of schools of education are certified audiologist or certified speech language pathologist. Audiologists treat those with hearing disorders. Speech-language pathologists work to help others improve their speech sounds, rhythms and fluency or oral motor problems. Write to American Speech-Language-Hearing Association (ASHA), 10801 Rockville Pike, Rockville, MD 20852 or call 301-897-5700. The median annual salary for speech pathologists and audiologists is $36,000, according to ASHA. Over half of speech pathologists and audiologists work in public schools. Others work in physicians' offices, hospitals and private practices.

Job: Elementary/High School Teacher

Path #1: Volunteer experience

This will help you decide who and what you want to be teaching. Public elementary and secondary schools have programs in which volunteers do tutoring. Paid assistant work in the classrooms may also be available. Prisons and hospitals usually have volunteer tutoring programs.

Path #2: Teach in a private school

Often private schools hire young people right out of college and train them.

Path #3: Teach in a public school

To teach in a public school, you will need the bachelor's degree as well as a certain number of education credits. The number of credits will depend on the state and the need for new teachers. Many states offer alternative ways for people with experience to enter teaching.

Recruiting New Teachers (RNT) is an organization helping new teachers enter the profession. Contact them at 385 Concord Ave., Belmont, MA 02178, 617-489-6000. Their *Careers in Teaching* handbook lists scholarships and information about state requirements. Their Helpline will advise you on what is needed in your state. Call 800-969-TEACH.

Emergency licensure procedures, instituted to recruit teachers during times of acute teacher shortages, exist in most states. These allow you to begin teaching without a master's degree. You need to enroll in an alternative route program in your state to get formal instruction and mentoring. Between 1985 and 1992, 40,000 people were licensed to teach through these alternative programs, according to the National Center for Education Information.

What about majoring in undergraduate education? You can major in a subject area like mathematics or biology as well as in education or you can major in a subject area and take education credits at the same time. In some states this dual focus is required because preparing in education alone has proven to be inadequate. Special financial aid packages, such as forgivable loans, which are dismissed after a certain amount of years of service, or offers to assume outstanding educational loans, are being offered by some states to students majoring in fields where there are critical shortages of teachers—for example, mathematics and science.

The education department of your state will mail you a list of requirements to teach at the elementary and secondary school levels. These materials will help you clarify which license you want, and how to attain it. Average salaries of teachers in the early 1990s varied from $51,278 in Washington, D.C., to $23,000 in South Dakota, according to the National Education Association (NEA). The U.S. average is $34,456, but some teachers with vast experience and advanced degrees are making $80,000 a year in some states.

The Association for School, College and University Staffing, 820 Davis St., Suite 222, Evanston, IL 60201-3451, 708-864-1999, publishes annual studies on the teaching profession nationwide. These studies show that the Northeast holds the largest amount of teachers in the country. Art, physical education, English and social studies are very crowded fields; special education, Spanish and physics are better bets. In some areas, even in the Northeast, inner cities may be recruiting. Talk to a few principals locally to see what their sense is of the market.

Job: College Instructor

You will need a graduate degree to teach at the college level. If you want to teach a liberal arts subject, especially a subject for which there are very few academic or nonacademic jobs, such as English Literature or Sociology, the undergraduate double major may be the answer because of the extremely small number of jobs available. You might study philosophy, for example, and at the same time prepare for employment outside academia by taking courses in a subject that is easier to apply outside the classroom, like economics, statistics or biology. If you decide not to go to graduate school, the transition to employment will be easier. According to a January

24, 1993 article in *The New York Times*, women make up 10 percent of the full professors in the Ivy League, so there is still a very thick glass ceiling in academia.

Henry Louis Gates, Jr., (*Current Biography Yearbook*) is a scholar in the field of Afro-American studies. He is revolutionizing the American educational canon, which he believes ought to include the study of great works produced by non-Western cultures as well as those of Western civilization. On a leave of absence from college, Gates worked as a general anesthetist at a hospital in Tanzania. He was thinking of becoming a doctor, but instead went on to Cambridge University in England and embraced his mission to raise public awareness about the contributions of Black Americans. He became the first African-American to get a Ph.D. from Cambridge. Gates returned to Yale to teach and head Yale's undergraduate program in Afro-American Studies. He is now at Harvard. His most recent book, *Colored People: Letters to My Daughters,* is a memoir.

Job: Adult Educator

Adult education refers to noncollege education for adults. Adult educators work in the public education system, teaching English as a second language, writing skills or typing, to give some popular examples. Vocational courses like bookkeeping, cooking or electrical work may also be offered by the public system. Teachers will be required to have some educational background and experience in the field. Entry-level requirements are spelled out by the personnel department of the board of education, although the requirements differ from city to city. These programs are dependent on taxes and may change from year to year because of cutbacks.

Community colleges offer a variety of nondegree, adult education courses but they require a master's degree to teach the subject area. If there is a great need for a teacher in the subject, they may accept a less extensive educational background, if the applicant is accomplished in his or her field.

Job: Educational/Not-for-Profit Administrator

Education administrators usually enter from teaching and work their way up. Principals in elementary and high schools typically have at least the master's degree in education administration or educational supervision and a teaching certificate. Superintendents of districts may have the Ph.D. In addition, public schools often have administrators at the district, state and federal education offices who direct subject area programs, guidance, career counseling, testing, athletics and professional development. People who fill these positions are ex-classroom teachers or counselors, generally with master's degrees in their areas of specialty. Foundations have similar positions and hire the most reputable people in education.

At the college level, the academic deans (of Law, Medicine, Arts and Sciences, etc.) usually have a Ph.D. in a subject area. College administrators, other than academic deans, usually have bachelor's degrees and are working on advanced degrees. Susan (*Vocational Biographies*), the assistant director for admissions at a small college, started as a part-time counselor and moved up to a more demanding job while earning graduate credits at night. Half of her time is spent preparing publications and the other half in lecturing about the school. Colleges usually have positions available in the registrar's office, admissions, financial aid, development and student affairs. Sometimes these jobs are reserved for surplus teachers.

Donna Shalala (*Current Biography Yearbook*), the current head of the Health and Human Services agency in the Clinton administration, received a B.A. in urban studies from Western College for Women, went into the Peace Corps and spent two years in Iran, teaching social science and serving as the dean of women at the agricultural college of the University of Ahwaz. The Maxwell School of Citizenship and Public Affairs at Syracuse University prepared her to assume the assistant director's job of the urban community development program of the university and to train people for the Peace Corps in Peru. In the summer she taught English in Lebanon and Syria for the U.S. Information Agency.

She got a Ph.D. from the Maxwell School and got a job as an assistant professor of political science. In 1971, she wrote a controversial report for the Citizen's Union of New York City, which established her as an expert on New York City finances. In 1976 she was appointed a director of the Municipal Assistance Corporation, the agency that refinanced the bankrupt city. Then she went to Washington to work for Jimmy Carter's housing agency, then became president of Hunter College, then president of the University of Wisconsin before going to Washington again.

Administrators in nonprofit associations often work their way up, beginning as office workers. For example, an organization for the promotion of chess may be directed by a board and employ an executive director who started as a secretary in the organization. Or the executive director of an association for the protection and advancement of a profession may be chosen because of the way his or her background will enhance the organization. For example, a guild for artists chose an organizer from a union of flight attendants to lead them.

Association Trends, at 7910 Woodmont Ave., Suite 1150, Bethesda, MD 20814-3014, lists some association jobs. Associations are listed in *Gale's Encyclopedia of Associations*. The *Chronicle of Higher Education* often lists administrative jobs in nonprofits.

The National Association for Women in Education (NAWE) provides support for women educators; NAWE members are campus administrators and counselors. The national office is at 1325 18th St. NW, Suite 210, Washington, DC 20036-6511.

Job: Librarian

For a position as a librarian, you will need a master's degree in library science. But even with the degree there are few full-time jobs now for librarians in schools, colleges and public libraries because of budget cutbacks. The 120 or so library programs across the country take students with a variety of undergraduate majors and they are especially interested in students with scientific, technical, engineering or business backgrounds, because these growing fields have job openings for librarians in private companies.

Librarians are also called information professionals and information managers. The American Society for Information Science's booklet "Challenging Careers in Information Science" begins: "Most information professionals have specialized knowledge in a subject area outside the information science field, such as Accounting or Chemistry or Engineering." Many employers require extensive computer training and a master's degree from a graduate program accredited by the American Library Association. Trained librarians may find work in industry or in research centers. Send a stamped, self-addressed envelope to the American Library Association, 50 East

Huron St., Chicago, IL 60611, or call 312-944-6780 for a list of accredited programs.

The American Society for Information Science, 8720 Georgia Ave., Suite 501, Silver Spring, MD 20910, 301-495-0900, has some interesting jobs in their *Jobline* newsletter: information specialist at a chemical company's research center, supervising editor for a company publishing aquatic sciences abstracts, systems librarian for a medical sciences library, several positions at the Institute for Scientific Information, and librarian and information manager at a major geoscience research library. These all require some knowledge in technical areas, a library master's degree, some experience as a librarian or information manager and some computer knowledge.

Special librarians create whole libraries—for example, an AIDS library for a new research center. The librarian of the U.S. Senate; the director of the Time, Inc. library; or the information officer of a major corporation, a university center on addiction and substance abuse or a major music center are all members of The Special Libraries Association. Special librarians provide data to businesses, the sciences, arts and communications.

Bernadette Calley is a special librarian and research librarian at the New York Botanical Garden Library in the Bronx. She is an expert at computerizing card catalogs by pulling together data on books, experts and living plants. The library serves experts, researchers and the staff of the Botanical Garden; it contains 250,000 volumes in 40 languages. For information on a career as a Special Librarian, write to The Special Libraries Association, 1700 18th St. NW, Washington, DC 20009, or call 202-234-4700.

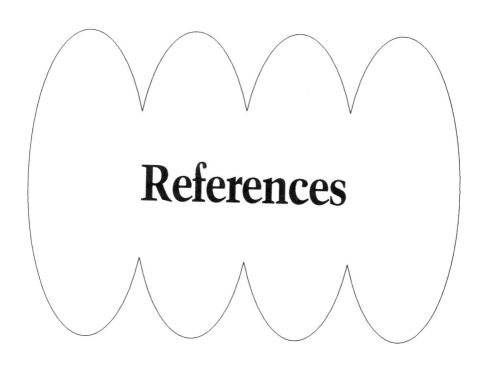

References

Ancker, Jessica, "Budget Cuts in New York State," *Sunday Freeman*, May 9, 1993, p. 12.

Andrews, Edmund, "Both Feet On the Ice and On Wall Street." *The New York Times*, April 16, 1995, p. 15.

Angier, Natalie, "How Biology Affects Behavior and Vice Versa," *The New York Times*, May 30, 1995, p. C1ff.

Auletta, Ken, "Barry Diller's Search for the Future," *The New Yorker*, Feb. 1993, p. 49ff.

Berger, Joseph, "Female Cadets Try to Make Old Attitudes Fade Away," *The New York Times*, Nov. 7, 1994, p. B-1ff.

Bolles, Richard, *What Color Is Your Parachute?*, Ten Speed Press, Berkeley, Calif., 1989, p. 66.

Carmody, Deidre, "Beating Time-Warner at Its Own Game," *The New York Times*, April 8, 1990, p. C-1.

Chambers, Nancy, et al., "25 Hottest Careers," *Working Woman*, July 1995, p. 36.

Collins, Glen, "A Film Maker's Lot: Frustration, Devotion, Rejection and Some Fun," *The New York Times*, Feb. 11, 1993, p. c19ff.

Current Biography Yearbook 1989, H.W. Wilson Co., New York, pp. 37ff, 329ff, 358ff, 549ff.

Current Biography Yearbook 1990, H.W. Wilson Co., New York, pp. 305ff, 353ff, 521ff, 547ff.

Current Biography Yearbook 1991, H.W. Wilson Co., New York, pp. 97ff, 241ff, 267ff, 361ff, 388ff, 399ff, 494, 515ff, 537.

Current Biography Yearbook 1992, H.W. Wilson Co., New York, pp. 13ff, 217, 223ff.

Current Biography Yearbook 1993, H.W. Wilson Co., New York, pp. 167ff, 210ff, 227ff, 413ff, 485ff.

Current Biography Yearbook 1994, H.W. Wilson Co., New York, pp. 52ff, 128ff, 196ff, 418ff, 467ff, 495ff, 513ff, 523ff, 554ff, 581ff.

Current Biography Yearbook 1995, H.W. Wilson Co., New York, p. 21ff.

DePalma, Anthony, "Rare in Ivy League: Women Who Work as Full Professors," *The New York Times,* Jan. 24, 1993, p. 1ff.

Dobrzynski, Judith, "New Secret of Success, Getting Off the Corporate Ladder," *The New York Times,* March 19, 1995, p. 14

Durniak, John, "An Expert Surveys Trends and Schools," *The New York Times,* May 7, 1995, p. C-3.

Fabricant, Florence, "Behind Every Great Chef Is Another Great Chef," *The New York Times,* April 27, 1988, p. C-1ff.

Fatsis. Stefan, "Jay Chiat Sells the Agency of the Decade," Jay Chiat: *The Wall Street Journal,* Jan. 15, 1995, p. 1.

"Focus," *Foreign Service Journal,* June 1995, p. 10.

Gilbert, Lynn and Moore, Gaylen, *Particular Passions,* Potter, New York, 1981, pp. 53-230.

Gabor, Andrea, "The Making of a New-Age Manager," *Working Woman,* Dec. 1994, p. 18ff.

Goleman, Daniel, "75 Years Later, Study Still Tracking Geniuses," *The New York Times,* March 7, 1995, p. C1.

Gottschalk, Earl Jr., "Tax Shop? Gym? Finding a Franchise," *The New York Times,* March 26, 1995, p. 12.

Gourman, Dr. Jack, *The Gourman Report, A Rating of Graduate and Professional Programs,* 6th edition, National Educational Standards, Los Angeles, CA, 1993, p. 27

Holland, John, *Making Vocational Choices,* Prentice-Hall, Inc., Englewood Cliffs, NJ, 1985.

Holt, John, *Teach Your Own,* Dell, New York, 1981, p. 257.

"How They Do It," *The New York Times,* Sept. 18, 1993, p. B3; *Your Money,* Oct. 15, 1994, p. B-3.

Institute for Scientific Information, "Ranking Institutions by Scientific Citations," *The New York Times,* Feb. 12, 1991, p. C9.

Kaufman, Steve, "See You Out of Court," *Nation's Business,* June 1992, p. 58ff.

Kilborn, Peter, "College Seniors Find More Jobs But Modest Pay," *The New York Times,* May 1, 1994, p. A1ff.

Kleinfeld, N.R., "The Face In the Crowd," *The New York Times*, Jan. 3, 1993, p. B1.

Labate, John, *Fortune*, June 13, 1994, p. 121.

Landler, Mark, "China Deal Held Unlikely," *The New York Times* Feb., 3, 1995, p. D15.

Lew, Julie, "Upstairs, Downstairs, A Way to Manage Both," *The New York Times*, April 15, 1993, p. C-10.

London, Robb, "From an Honored Tradition: New Members of the Bar," *The New York Times*, Dec. 20, 1991, p. B-9.

Macdonald, Dan, "This Is One of the Jobs You Dream About," *Tallahassee Sentinel*, Feb. 8, 1995, p. D1ff.

MacFarquhar, Neil, "Camden Aquarium Changes Lines," *The New York Times*, July 5, 1995, p. B-1.

Mall, E & A. Siegel, "Gerry's Kids," *Working Woman,* Nov. 1991, p. 16ff.

Maltzman, Jeff, *Jobs in Paradise*, Harper Collins, New York, 1990, p. 47.

Margolick, David, "An Expert Simpson Witness," *The New York Times*, Dec. 9, 1994, p. B7.

Mariani, Matthew, "Sports Jobs," *Occupational Outlook Quarterly*, Summer 1995, p. 3ff.

Martin, Douglas, "For Those Who Deliver, A Good Take," *The New York Times*, April 19, 1993, p. B-4.

Miller, J.B., "Two New York Neophytes Take a Cue From Pirandello," *The New York Times*, June 12, 1994, p. 20.

Miller, Tom, "Industry News," *Travel Trade*, June 26, 1995, p. 17.

Mitchell, Robert, "Affirmative Action Helps Women," *Daily Freeman*, April 10, 1995, p. 1ff.

Mittelhauser, Mark, "Manufacturing: It's Still the Industrial Age," *Occupational Outlook Quarterly*, Fall 1994, pp. 26-27.

Moreau, Dan, "Good Jobs for Fresh Grads," *Kiplingers*, March, 1995, p. 110ff.

Morell, Virginia, "The Really Secret Life of the Plants," *New York Times Magazine*, Dec. 18, 1994, p. 51ff.

Morris, Bernadine, "A Minneapolis Designer Hits the Big Time," *The New York Times*, April 12, 1983, p. D23.

Nelson, Dean, "Engineer's Ice Plant Helps Power County," *The New York Times*, July 5, 1995, p. D2.

Nemy, Enid, "Trying to Make Money Grow on 26,000 Trees," *The New York Times*, Sept. 30, 1993, p. C-1ff.

"Newspapers Diversity and You," *Dow Jones Newspaper Fund*, 1994-1995, p. 16.

Nieves, Evelyn, "New Jersey Transit Boss Learns to Joust With Legislative Critics," *The New York Times*, May 9, 1992, p. 25ff.

Palmeri, Christopher, "The Player," *Forbes*, Jan. 18, 1993, p. 59ff.

Pedersen, Laura, "Arrivederci Roma, Minding Your Business," *The New York Times*, July 5, 1995, p. D-3.

Petras, Kathy and Ross, *Jobs*, Simon and Schuster, New York, 1993, pp. 108, 127, 163.

Rifkin, Glenn, "For U.S., He's Behind All the America's Cup Hopes," *The New York Times*, Jan. 22, 1995, p. 11.

Rogers, William, *Think, A Biography of the Watsons and IBM*, Stein and Day, New York, 1969, pp. 7-10.

Rubenstein, Caren, "The Nanny Solution, Costly and Complex," *The New York Times*, April 15, 1993, p. C-2.

Schiro, Anne Marie, "Flowers by Appt.," *The New York Times*, June 26, 1987, p. 14.

Shelley, Kristina, "More Job Openings—Even More Entrants," *Occupational Outlook Quarterly*, Summer 1994, p. 4.

Sher, Barbara, *Wishcraft*, Ballantine, New York, 1979, pp. 46, 54.

Sims, Calvin, "Lucie Salhany," *The New York Times*, Nov. 14, 1993, p. 4.

Slade, Margot, "Law Degree Wanes as Passport to Business Job," *The New York Times*, Jan. 27, 1989, p. D-3.

Smith, Kirsten, "Fertile Ground," *Kingston Freeman*, July 15, 1994, p. B1.

Smothers, Ronald, "Atlanta's Police Chief Won More Than a Bet," *The New York Times*, Nov. 30, 1994, p. C1ff.

Stanton, Michael, "Statisticians: Finding Truth In the Numbers," *Occupational Outlook Quarterly*, Summer 1990, p. 36; "Videotape Editor,", Summer 1991, p. 37; "You're a What? Meeting Planner," Summer 1992, p. 27ff.

Tilghman, Shirley, "Science Versus the Female Science Student," *The New York Times*, Jan. 24, 1993, p. A17.

United States Department of Labor, *Occupational Outlook Handbook*, 1994-1995 Edition, VGM Career Horizons, Lincolnwood, IL, pp. 49-51, 139, 369, 237, 257, 292-293.

Vocational Biographies, Vocational Biographies, Inc., Sauk Centre, MN, 1991.P-2-7, P-2-12, P-2-25, P-4-16, P-5-19, P-5-30, P-6-15, Q-1-24, Q-2-6, Q-2-13, Q-3-10, Q-3-21, Q-4-21, Q-6-8, Q-6-11, Q-6-22, Q14, R-3-5, R-4-19, S-3-10, S-3-19, S-5-3, S-5-16, S-5-19, S-6-8, T-7-17, U-7-3, U-7-6, U-7-7, U-7-8.

Wald, Matthew, "Two Scientists Find a Way to Make Cheaper Methanol," *The New York Times*, Jan. 17, 1993, p. A10.

Walker, Jane, "Top Ten College Women," *Mademoiselle*, May 24, 1982.

Webster, Bayard, "A Pair of Skilled Hands," *The New York Times*, Dec. 1982, p. A24

Weinraub, Bernard, "Survival Lesson for the 'River' Director," *The New York Times*, Oct. 4, 1994, p. C-13.

Zoglin, Richard, "An Old Fox Learns New Tricks," *Time*, March 1, 1993, p. 52ff.

Index

6/5/96